LAST CHAMPION
OF YORK

Francis Lovell

Richard III's Truest Friend

LAST CHAMPION OF YORK

Francis Lovell

Richard III's Truest Friend

STEPHEN DAVID

ROBERT HALE

First published in 2019 by
Robert Hale, an imprint of
The Crowood Press Ltd,
Ramsbury, Marlborough
Wiltshire SN8 2HR

www.crowood.com

British Library Cataloguing-in-Publication Data
A catalogue record for this book is available from the
British Library.

ISBN 978 0 7198 2823 2

Typeset by Chapter One Book Production, Knebworth

Printed and bound in India by Parksons Graphics

CONTENTS

TIMELINE

PROLOGUE

IN 1708, WORKMEN LAYING the lining for a new chimney at the old mansion house in Minster Lovell, west Oxfordshire, made a grisly discovery. They had inadvertently opened a large vault that had been sealed for many years and, upon removing the brickwork, were astonished to find inside the room, sitting upon a chair and leaning upon a table, the whole skeleton of a man. The table had been furnished with a book, paper and pens and set aside from the table was a cap and clothing in a decayed state. Upon exposure to the air, the skeleton promptly disintegrated into a pile of dust, which scattered in the draught that wafted into the newly opened vault.

Any educated local of the early eighteenth century would have been familiar with the history of this particular old house and would have immediately deduced that the skeleton could be that of only one man – Francis, Viscount Lovell – and that this man had last been seen alive on 16 June 1487. That the skeleton disintegrated into dust was in some ways a fitting allegory to how elusive Lovell, a previous owner of the house, had been in the latter part of his life. The claim that the body was likely to be his was supported by a letter, dated 9 August 1737, from William Cowper, clerk of the parliament, to Francis Peck, antiquary. Cowper recorded that the skeleton had been found with pen and paper and was richly apparelled, lending credence to the notion that the dead man had been part of the upper echelons of society. Cowper's account was later taken up by John Percival, 1st Earl of Egremont, who, in 1742, fleshed out the story by adding the detail that the skeleton had, in fact, remained whole until exposed to the air.

If we are to believe that the skeleton *was* that of Francis, Viscount Lovell, who was this man whose corpse had evaded discovery for over two hundred years? Lovell had once been extremely important, rising so high in society that he became a close friend of one king and was feared by another. Indeed, he had even created his own king, successfully crowning as 'Edward VI' a boy now better known as Lambert Simnel. Lovell was a man whose unshakeable loyalty to the legacy of his friend, King Richard III, had brought about the battle of Stoke Field, a vicious encounter that resulted in excess of 7,000 deaths over four hours one sunny morning in June 1487. This was the first and most bloody challenge to the new Tudor regime and ultimately proved to be the last battle to be fought during that turbulent period of conflict known as the Wars of the Roses. The challenge was severe. Indeed, at one point, it seemed as if it might topple the new king, Henry VII, and reverse the result of the battle of Bosworth, reducing the Tudors to a brief episode in history. However, it was not to be and, by noon on 16 June 1487, it was Lovell himself, the sole leader of the Yorkist army, who with reluctance turned his horse away from the field of battle and the ongoing slaughter at the Red Gully, and rode into the obscure footnotes of history.

This was not the first time that Lovell had left a battlefield amidst the carnage of defeat. Two years earlier, at Bosworth, he, along with Richard III, had been proclaimed dead by the heralds and the grand pursuivants in their richly embroidered tabards. Notice of his death was clearly premature, for within six months of the battle, Lovell the ghost had re-emerged from sanctuary at Colchester to haunt the new king, Henry VII, and to actively plot his overthrow.

Even so, after Stoke Field there were to be no more comebacks for Lovell, or for any of those who had supported Richard III and sought a Yorkist restoration. Over 4,000 men who had taken to the field in this cause were now dead – roughly half of all those that Lovell and his fellow commanders had led into battle earlier that morning. Those who survived desperately sought to escape Tudor vengeance as they were hunted throughout the length and breadth of England and Wales. The full majesty of the law was brought to bear and the dread parliamentary punishment of attainder (the loss of land, wealth possessions and title) was applied to the rebels whose very blood was now deemed tainted, depriving future generations of rank and status. Those who had been loyal to Richard III's legacy and who had hoped that rebellion would restore their fortunes now found their party broken and themselves facing a very bleak future indeed.

But what of Francis Lovell? What became of him as he despondently rode away from Stoke Field having suffered his second defeat within two years? His family certainly believed well into 1488 that he was alive. Indeed, his wife Anne and her mother, Lady Fitzhugh, sent her husband's close friend, Edward Frank, released in October that year from the Tower of London, to look for Lovell in the north of England, but Frank was to return empty-handed. On 19 June, Lovell was presumably still alive because, on that date, James IV of Scots issued a letter of safe conduct to Lovell and four other named persons, plus their servants, to enter Scotland for one year. It is thought possible that he took up this offer and crossed over the border into Scotland as there is testimony from a 'simple and pure person' given before the Lord Mayor of York in 1491 that he had met Lovell in Scotland. However, no other historical source corroborates this and no other witnesses have been identified. In truth, it is difficult to imagine that, having issued a safe conduct, James IV would not have entertained Lovell openly at his court, yet the records of the Scots court make no mention of Lovell or of any of his party. In the ongoing cold war between England and Scotland, it would have made little sense to possess a trump card in your hand and not allow your opponent to see it. Similarly, one can be sure that, if Lovell had been at liberty in Scotland, he would have made efforts to contact Margaret, Duchess of Burgundy, sister of Edward IV and Richard III, as had a number of his colleagues.

We can, however, be sure of one thing – that, having escaped from the battle of

Stoke Field, Lovell had no thought of giving up the struggle to restore a Ricardian candidate to the throne. After all, Richard's 'true' heir, his nephew, Edward, Earl of Warwick, was alive and there were still some sympathisers who had been unable to declare their hand prior to the battle of Stoke Field. With this in mind, it is quite plausible that Lovell could have retired to his boyhood home of Minster Lovell, close to the river Windrush, to rest and recuperate and wait for the hue and cry to die down. Here in his erstwhile home, now granted to Jasper Tudor, the new king's uncle, Lovell would be hidden in the last place that his enemies would look. It has been argued that this is improbable since Lovell, having been absent for the previous two years, would not have had time to rebuild necessary loyalties and personal attachments in what would have been his family home. This fails to take into account that Lovell (after August 1485, the most wanted man in England) had been able to traverse the country undetected and seemingly at will, a feat he could only have accomplished with a network of dependable support. Likewise, there is nothing to suggest that Jasper Tudor, who had only been present in England (let alone at Minster Lovell) since the summer of 1485, had been able to replace the loyalty that had been owed to the Lovell family for generations with a loyalty to himself. Indeed, the very nature of the mystery of Francis Lovell's final disappearance is evidence of the profound loyalties that he could inspire in others. Despite the blandishments of Henry VII and the offer of a reward, no one ever came forward to betray Lovell's final fate. Thus, the dessicated remains discovered in 1708 could indeed be those of Francis, Viscount Lovell, the last champion of York.

1 THE GHOST

'Lovell our dogge'

FRANCIS LOVELL HAD BEEN a significant presence around Richard III for the previous two years (1483–1485), enjoying high office and the confidence of the king. This was hardly surprising since they had been friends since youth, both having been part of the household of the great Earl of Warwick, known as 'the kingmaker'. They had first made each other's acquaintance about 1465 and almost all sources state that they had been close friends ever since. This relationship was acknowledged by Charles Ross in his seminal biography of Richard III:

> Francis Lovell was Richard's closest friend, a relationship (like that of William Lord Hastings with Edward IV) enshrined in his position as Chamberlain of the royal Household which involved close and regular contact with the king.[1]

This proximity and intimacy with the king was to bring Lovell the only notoriety for which he is remembered. In 1484, a supporter of the then exiled Henry Tudor pinned to the doors of St Paul's cathedral a famous piece of doggerel: 'The Catte, the Ratte and Lovell our dogge rule all England under the Hog'.[2] This infamous barb lampooned Richard III's government by likening his principal ministers to animals: the cat (William Catesby); the rat (Sir Richard Ratcliffe); and the dog (Francis Lovell). The hunting dog was a familiar sight on the badge of Lovell's family, the Talbot, hence the caricature succinctly and effectively encapsulated the sense of moral outrage and opposition that many Londoners felt towards both Richard III, disparagingly referred to as 'the Hog' after his badge of the white boar, and those who had most influence about him, debasing them all to the status of domestic animals.

Unfortunately for Lovell, this very successful piece of anti-Ricardian doggerel endured and has become a shorthand for the way in which he is remembered – with all the attributes of a dog who slavishly follows his master. As a close associate of Richard III, Lovell's memory (such as it is) has been reduced to being a mere adjunct to Richard, standing at the king's shoulder, his best friend throughout his life, yet barely possessing any historical presence himself. The fascination with Richard III, his actions and complex personality, so dominates the historiography of his reign that little attention is given to other members of his court and government who, like Lovell, retain merely a shadowy presence, becoming figures of substance only in the dry legal documents of Henry VII's first parliament in November 1485 where they were declared traitors and attainted. The dread punishment of attainder was something all nobles feared for, apart from the loss of lands, titles and position, a traitor's very blood was deemed tainted, removing any opportunity for their heirs to restore name, honour or title in the future. At the parliament of 1485, Lovell was by far the most prominent supporter of Richard III still alive and at liberty: as such, he was very high on Henry VII's list of condemned traitors.

In fact, prior to that parliament, Lovell had already been declared dead, for, in the immediate aftermath of Bosworth, Henry VII had issued a proclamation in which it was announced that Francis, Viscount Lovell, together with Thomas, Earl of Surrey, and John, Earl of Lincoln, had all been slain. The proclamation read by the heralds was knowingly disingenuous and designed to forestall any further Ricardian resistance by clearly stating that all of the previous king's principal supporters were now dead and thus unavailable as rallying figures. This promulgated the first political lie of the new Tudor dynasty. By inference, it demonstrates the importance the new Tudor regime placed upon the person of Lovell. Rather than regarding him as a mere adjunct to Richard III and of little significance, Henry VII and his advisors recognized him as the most senior Ricardian to have escaped the field at Bosworth and who was now at large and capable of causing trouble in the future. Rather than some ghostly remnant of Richard's reign, Lovell was recognized by Henry VII as the only surviving Ricardian at large with true leadership potential; and so it was to prove as Lovell became the most elusive irritant and effective opponent of the young Tudor dynasty.

Henry VII's official historian, Polydore Vergil, described Lovell as 'an irresolute fellow',[3] a portrayal that was to prove a gross and costly underestimation of Lovell's abilities. For a man declared already dead, Lovell appears to have had an uncanny ability to move undetected around the country at will. Indeed, for an 'irresolute fellow', he demonstrated a remarkable tenacity, moving during 1485/86 from Essex to northern Lancashire and ultimately to Yorkshire, all the while actively fomenting rebellion and plotting treason with his former colleagues in Worcestershire, Breconshire and Yorkshire, culminating in a physical assault on the person of Henry VII at the St George's day feast in York. This was a remarkable sequence of activity for a man already 'dead' and a rude shock to Henry VII, bringing home to him the precariousness of his position on the throne.

With the failure of his first attempt to remove Henry VII, Lovell seemed to vanish once more, yet he never wavered in his opposition to Henry or in his adherence to both the memory of Richard III and his loyalty to what he saw as the House of York's legitimate claim to the throne. To this end he planned the most dangerous conspiracy that the Tudors would face until the Pilgrimage of Grace in 1538. The Lambert Simnel conspiracy still engenders some ridicule as the name appears slightly ridiculous to an England used to more mundane biblical names. The pseudonym was adopted to allow the conspirators to move 'Lambert' around the country without revealing his real identity, while also using a name that would be sufficiently memorable for those involved in the plot to recognize clearly who was being discussed, probably with tongue firmly in cheek. In actuality, there was very little that was remotely amusing for Henry VII, for this conspiracy was an exceptionally dangerous threat to him and the only truly domestic threat he would have to face in his entire reign. As a conspiracy, it was audacious in its inception – the impersonation of a true Yorkist prince, Edward, Earl of Warwick, by a commoner called John ('Lambert Simnel'), whose true identity only came to light after the rebellion had been defeated at the battle of Stoke Field (1487). The conspiracy was meticulous in its planning, and its recruitment and execution demonstrated leadership on a European scale. Despite the fact that the deception almost succeeded, Lovell's reputation was once again overshadowed by memories of his dead co-conspiritors: this time, the young John de la Pole, Earl of Lincoln, and the flamboyant German mercenary, Martin Schwartz. English folk songs would long commemorate the death of Martin 'Swart', and it was said that a weeping willow grew on the spot where a stake had been driven into the dead Lincoln's heart. For Francis Lovell, there is no memorial other than an enduring mystery as he disappeared from historical fact forever.

On 16 June 1487, Lovell rode away from Stoke Field into obscurity, never to be seen alive again. His memory faded – an inevitable result of being on the wrong side of history as the first opponent of Britain's most glamorous royal dynasty. The new regime had at its command all of the new nefarious arts of Renaissance propaganda; these reached their apogee in Holbein's masterful depictions of Henry VIII, who, as 'bluff king Hal', became a figure truly larger than life. The Tudor's divine right to rule was reinforced in public consciousness by the concept of Elizabeth I as 'Gloriana', whilst the Armada portrait of Elizabeth portrays her, not as the Virgin Queen, but as someone at the very apex of victorious regal majesty. These monumental portrayals of the giants of the Tudor dynasty eclipse those, like Lovell, who came before, rendering them almost invisible. However, this is to view history from the wrong end of the telescope. We should not assume that the triumphs of the Tudors were inevitable and inescapable; they were not. Certainly, between 1485 and 1487 the future of the Tudor regime was sometimes precarious, and it was the new king, Henry VII, who was viewed as the usurper by opponents. Francis Lovell was the man who could have changed history and to admire him only for his loyalty is to misrepresent his achievements. Charles Ross wrote of Lovell that 'of his ability we know nothing. Of his loyalty there can be no question, and it persisted after Richard's death.'[4] Yes, Lovell continued to fight for a Ricardian heir to the end, but his loyalty was very much matched by his abilities, which have been overshadowed by more glamorous contemporaries and the subsequent trauma of religious discord. Whether or not the bones found in that Oxfordshire vault that day in 1708 truly were those of Francis Lovell, the time has come to flesh out his reputation, to undertake the task of overturning history's assessment of the man, and to judge him, not only for his loyalty, but also for his actions and achievements.

2 FAMILY, YOUTH AND WARDSHIP

WE DO NOT KNOW the precise date on which Francis Lovell was born, nor indeed do we know much about his formative years. In this respect, Francis Lovell is not unique, as very little of consequence was habitually recorded on the boyhood and youth of most noblemen at this time. Francis Lovell appears, if at all, only as a name in the legal documents that were put in place as a result of his wardships, firstly in the household of the great Earl of Warwick and later in that of the de la Pole family. From these documents we can deduce his lifestyle and whereabouts, but we cannot know how the forces around him moulded the adult Lovell. Consequently, much of Lovell's childhood must of necessity be viewed through the prism of the turbulent lives of others, allowing us only a glimpse of the boy himself.

The Lovell family

Francis Lovell came from a long-established baronial family, which had received individual summons to parliament since 1297. The name 'Lovell' is derived from the nickname *Lupellus* ('wolf-like'), implying characteristics that would have been appreciated far more in the thirteenth century than today. The nickname *Lupellus*, a common soubriquet applied to those with avaricious traits, was supposedly first applied to Robert, Lord of Breheval, who was a retainer of William the Conqueror. The nickname was then shortened into the easier French pronunciation of *Lupel* until finally morphing into the more anglified Lovell.

The first of Francis Lovell's antecedents to be summoned to parliament was John de Lovell, Baron Titchmarsh, in Northamptonshire. John de Lovell married twice and, with his second wife, Joan de Ros, had two sons – John and William Lovell. John, 2nd Baron Lovell, married Maud Burnell, the great-niece of the Bishop of Bath and Wells. Maud brought with her the Burnell estates, which included Acton Burnell, in Shropshire. As followers of Aymer de Valence, Earl of Pembroke, John Lovell served in the Scottish campaigns of Edward I, dying at the disastrous battle of Bannockburn (1314), where his brother William was captured. Aymer de Valence became the guardian of John Lovell's son, another John, who was born in 1314.

John, 3rd Baron Lovell, was never summoned to parliament so technically was not a lord. However, he was a close friend and companion of Edward I, fighting at

Crécy and the siege of Calais. He died in somewhat mysterious circumstances in 1347, and there is some later evidence to suggest that he had been murdered. He was succeeded by his son, John, 4th Baron Lovell, who died young in 1363 and was succeeded in his turn by his brother, also named John, 5th Baron Lovell. This John married Maud Holland, whose dowry doubled the estates of the Lovell family and allowed John to style himself John, Lord Lovell and Lord Holland. The Holland family brought about an indirect link to the Crown as Robert Holland's younger brother had been the husband of Joan the 'Maid of Kent', who later married Edward 'the Black Prince'. John, 5th Baron Lovell, was first summoned to parliament in 1375. He carved a career at court, but in 1388 he was expelled by the enemies of Richard II. John built a new and comfortable castle at Wardour and, unusually, commissioned a book, *The Lovell Lectionary*, fragments of which still survive, allowing us to have one of the earliest biographical pen portraits in the English language. In 1405, he was made a Knight of the Garter. In 1408 he died and was succeeded by his eldest son, John, 6th Baron Lovell, who married Eleanor De La Zouche of Leicestershire. The 6th Baron Lovell died in 1414, leaving as his heir, William, 7th Baron Lovell, who, as a minor, became a ward of Henry Fitzhugh of Ravensworth in North Yorkshire. Lord Fitzhugh arranged for William to marry Alice Deincourt, one of the two co-heiresses of the Deincourt and Grey of Rotherfield baronies. The other co-heiress was Margaret Deincourt, who married the active Lancastrian politician Ralph, Lord Cromwell, who rose to be treasurer under Henry VI. After spending some of his younger years fighting in France, William, unlike his brother-in-law Ralph, preferred a quiet life. William seems to have confined himself to building a magnificent house at Minster Lovell in the English Renaissance style, the precursor of the Elizabethan mansion.

William Lovell's decision to concentrate on his own building projects and to leave to others the world of high politics was perhaps wise. England throughout the 1440s and the 1450s was wrought with noble factionalism and antagonism as the government of the young and ineffectual Henry VI sought to grapple with a series of an insuperable and interconnected problems. Chief amongst these was the legacy of his father Henry V, the victor of Agincourt who had, through his marriage to Catherine of Valois, been recognized as king of France but who had died before being crowned in France. Thus, it was his infant son Henry VI who had been crowned king in Paris in 1429. The coronation of Henry VI should have been the high point of English endeavours in France, but it was, in fact, an attempt to hold back a resurgent French nationalism galvanized by the leadership of the peasant girl, Joan of Arc.

Despite Joan having been captured and burnt at Rouen in 1431, her actions had spurred on France to set in motion an increasingly effective military campaign. The English, now on the defensive, were forced back into Normandy, abandoning, in the face of increased French pressure, Paris and the Île-de-France. A peace conference at Amiens in 1435 had represented the last realistic English opportunity to negotiate from a position of strength. With the death of John, Duke of Bedford, and the Duke of Burgundy switching sides, the English position in Normandy became more and more precarious. English forces were outnumbered and increasingly deprived of adequate resources.

Part of the problem, not understood fully at the time, was the collapse of English revenues from the export of wool and the contraction of agricultural revenues. In a delayed reaction to the effects of the Black Death and the decrease in the population, there had ultimately been a contraction in the whole European economy. The English tax-base, heavily reliant on the export of wool, had collapsed by roughly two-thirds, leaving the English government unable to finance an increasingly unsuccessful and financially crippling war on the continent. Throughout the 1440s, various strategies and commanders were tried in France to little avail and, apart from the presence of the king's cousin Richard, Duke of York, and the Earl of Shrewsbury in France, most members of the English nobility preferred to remain in England rather than take part in a war left to those with a vested interest in France.

After a disastrous campaign in 1442/3, John, Duke of Somerset, was withdrawn from command as was Richard, Duke of York, who then was appointed Lord Lieutenant of Ireland. A policy of peace was adopted with the marriage of Henry VI to Margaret of Anjou, but in 1449 the truce was broken by the English who, now ill equipped and outnumbered, had to face a sequence of overwhelming French campaigns in Normandy. In less than a year, the province, which had been in English hands since 1417, was lost in ignominy; the final English defeat took place at Formigny, and Rouen was surrendered.

To a stunned English populace, brought up on the victories of Edward III and Henry V, defeat was unthinkable unless treachery and treason were involved. The fact that the English position had become increasingly untenable once France, with its greater wealth and population, was united was a truth that interested no one. Neither was the reality that Henry V's victories had left his successor an unrealistic and untenable legacy. Instead, England looked for scapegoats and first in line was the king's chief minister, William de la Pole, who was murdered as he travelled into exile, followed by Edmund Beaufort, brother and successor of John, Duke of Somerset. In the summer of 1450, the south-east of England rose in rebellion under Jack Cade, leader of the commons of Kent, demanding a change in the king's ministers whom the rebels accused of being in the pay of France.

During Cade's rebellion, Richard, Duke of York, returned unbidden from Ireland and accused the king's government publicly of treason and demanded that he should become the king's chief minister. Henry VI, as was his right, resisted and appointed his cousin Edmund, Duke of Somerset, as chief minister, sidelining York. York accused Somerset of complicity in the surrender of Normandy where he had been in command and, as the rivalry between Somerset and York became increasingly bitter, many others felt, like William Lovell, that the best course of action was to abdicate from national politics. This had been achievable for William Lovell, who died in 1455, but it was to be an altogether different proposition for his son, John, Lord Lovell, 8th Baron and father of Francis Lovell, the survivor of Stoke Field.

The rivalry between the Duke of York and the Duke of Somerset reached a crescendo in 1455 at the first battle of St Albans, the start of what we now call 'the Wars of the Roses'. From 1453 to January 1455, Henry VI suffered from a debilitating attack of catatonic schizophrenia that paralysed the Lancastrian government and brought into the office of Protector, the king's cousin, Richard, Duke of York. In January 1455, Henry VI recovered his senses and it was, his contemporaries said, as if he had woken from a dream. Upon his recovery, he questioned the appointment of York and insisted on the return of his cousin, Edmund, Duke of Somerset, as his chief minister and leading councillor. The subsequent exclusion of the Yorkist nobles – the duke of York and the earls of Warwick and Salisbury – from the government of the realm further destabilized English politics. When in May 1455 the king sent out a summons for a parliament to be held at Leicester, the Yorkist lords feared action would be taken against them and diminish their status and that of their families. During the spring of 1455, the Yorkists and their allies began to assemble their retainers and followers to prevent the king holding the proposed parliament. Both sides met at the town of St Albans where the earls of Warwick and Salisbury, with the Duke of York, were able to eliminate their personal enemies, the Duke of Somerset, the Earl of Northumberland and Lord Clifford.

This naked outbreak of factional violence had a significant and unsought impact on the life of John, 8th Lord Lovell,[1] who, through marriage, found his colours firmly nailed to the Lancastrian mast. John had married Joan, the daughter of John, Viscount Beaumont, who was steward to Henry VI's queen, Margaret of Anjou, and a high-ranking councillor. Beaumont was a longstanding servant of the House of Lancaster and had been created the first English viscount on 12 February 1440; he was also a Knight of the Bath and had served as Constable of England between 1445 and 1450 and Great Chamberlain since 8 July 1450. His record of service to the House of Lancaster and his proximity to the queen made him a prominent and committed Lancastrian supporter. His estates in the East Midlands were close to those of his son-in-law, John Lovell, and another councillor colleague, the Duke of Suffolk. His court connections and experience made Beaumont the leading Lancastrian figure in the Thames Valley.

His son-in-law, John Lovell, seems to have wanted to lead a generally uncommitted life at this time, preferring to spend time on his estates, especially at the newly built Minster Lovell in Oxfordshire, nurturing his young family, Francis and his two daughters, Joan and Frideswide. Unfortunately for John Lovell, politics and his close connection with his father-in-law drew him further and further into the Lancastrian camp – so much so that in 1460 he was one of the lords who tried to hold London against the Yorkist forces led by Warwick, Salisbury and Edward, the young Earl of March, and in March 1461 was present on the Lancastrian side at the battle of Towton, victory at which confirmed the Earl of March as King Edward IV. Despite being present at this crushing defeat, John Lovell made his peace with the new Yorkist king and thereafter retired to his estates. Quite possibly, he felt his presence in the Thames Valley was needed by his wife whose father had died in the rout that followed the battle of Northampton (1460). From this point on, John Lovell managed to lead a quiet life, rarely attending court or being found in the company of the new monarch. He died of natural causes in February in 1465, leaving his nine-year-old son, Francis, as his heir.

A ward of the Crown

The death of his father changed Francis Lovell's life forever. Being heir to five baronies, he became an extremely valuable commodity and as a tenant-in-chief of the Crown, his wardship and upbringing were now at the disposal of the king. It is unlikely that Edward IV knew Francis Lovell prior to his father's death. The Lovells shared no kinship or political links with the House of York. It is possible that Edward's father, Richard, Duke of York, may have known Francis' grandfather through shared service in France, but there do not appear to be any residual links between the families, although both possessed estates in Northamptonshire, with the York castle of Fotheringhay and the Lovell barony of Titchmarsh both being centred there.

For Edward IV, the death of the 8th Baron Lovell was a gift horse whose mouth he was not going to examine too closely, representing as it did an extremely valuable source of income that could potentially be in royal hands for the next twelve years – until Francis Lovell reached his majority. The Lovell estate, comprising the five baronies, was the largest estate below comital rank in England, easily being one of the twelve greatest inheritances in the country. Furthermore, the estates were strategically important, concentrated as they were in Oxfordshire, Northamptonshire and Berkshire, dominating the Thames Valley and protecting the western approaches to London and controlling the Thames bridges at Radcot and Abingdon.

Coming within the orbit of the Nevills

Edward IV did not keep the proceeds of the Lovell estates in his hands for very long, for in the autumn of 1465 Richard Nevill, Earl of Warwick, first cousin of the king and the most powerful noble in England, was granted £1,000 per annum from the issues (rental income) of the Lovell estates to 'maintain' the king's brother, Richard, Duke of Gloucester, who was at that time being raised within the earl's household. The young Richard, as a royal duke, would have required financial resources commensurate with his status and prestige and beyond that even of the wealthy Earl of Warwick. Thus, by means of the Lovell grant, Edward was able to ensure that his brother was lavishly maintained as behoved his status whilst transferring the cost of this to somebody else – in this case, the young Francis Lovell. The grant also enabled Warwick to enjoy the reflected glory of bringing up his royal cousin whilst discharging a chivalric obligation to both his king and a kinsman, at no expense to himself. Needless to say, neither the young Francis nor his mother Joan appear to have had any say in the matter.

This fact reflected the reality of feudal law as well as indicating that, with the loss of both his grandfather and his father, the young Francis was shorn of powerful protectors or kinsmen, leaving the Lovells, as Lancastrian loyalists, at the mercy of a Yorkist king with no connection to the family. The death of Beaumont and his subsequent attainder deprived the young Francis of a powerful intercessor at court and, after the death of his father, the only one whose voice would have been likely to be heard. Without his Beaumont kin able to press for wardship, Francis' future was now at the mercy of the king. Whilst Warwick had been granted £1,000 from the issues of the Lovell estate, there was no formal grant of either Lovell's wardship to Warwick, as has been assumed, nor was there any grant giving him control over the estates. Whilst Warwick was entitled to obtain his expenses regarding the raising of the king's brother in his household, he was not given wardship over Francis Lovell or the Lovell estates until the autumn of 1467. Rather, it seems to have been an ad-hoc arrangement with Edward IV responding to a specific problem and addressing the situation by royal warrant rather than by official legal processes and the issue of a crown patent.

For Edward, this had the advantage of solving the problem of his brother's upbringing and education at a suitably prestigious household with no financial burden for him to shoulder. This would certainly appear to be in keeping with what we know about Edward IV's character in his predilection for finding the easiest option and for playing fast and loose legally with vulnerable inheritances. The traditional view is that Edward sought to offer a reward to Warwick commensurate with his status and his achievements on behalf of the new king. Warwick's control of the Lovell estates would expand his influence from the West Midlands into the southern Midlands, from Warwickshire into Oxfordshire, Buckinghamshire and Berkshire. These had been areas into which Warwick had already expanded in 1461–2 when he had been granted the valuable Butler lordships at Newport Pagnell, Great Linford and Little Linford. The acquisition of the Lovell estates would have greatly enhanced his influence in this region and buttressed Warwick's own possessions in these counties. This had been seen as another example of Warwick's venality and his monopolizing of patronage but, rather than look to Warwick for Lovell's preferment, we should look at the actions of Lovell's step-grandmother, Warwick's aunt by marriage, Katherine Nevill, daughter of Ralph, 1st Earl of Westmorland, and Joan Beaufort. In 1430, Katherine had married John, Duke of Norfolk, and was now Dowager Duchess of Norfolk and Viscountess Beaumont. She was one of the most long-lived and powerful women in medieval England, holding vast estates in her own right; she was rich and important enough to act independently and to be able to influence both her nephews, the Earl of Warwick and the young king. It is far more likely that *she* was responsible for the placing of the young and vulnerable Francis in Warwick's household and offering the protection of her kinship network. With the Beaumont lands sequestered, apart from her moiety (or marriage portion), Katherine would have felt responsible for her stepdaughter and her grandchild Francis' well-being.

The main concern of both Katherine Nevill and Francis' mother, Joan, would have been to protect the Lovell estate from partition and despoilment, both of which could easily occur, even under royal wardship. To ensure this, they needed allies to act in their interests and what better allies could there be but one of the most dominant and greatest families in the realm -- Katherine's own family, the Nevills? Very quickly after Warwick obtained the issue of the Lovell estates, a more formal alliance was negotiated. In February 1466, Francis Lovell, then aged eleven, was married to Anne Fitzhugh, daughter of Henry Fitzhugh and Warwick's sister, Alice Nevill. The Fitzhughs were family who had been ennobled in 1321 and were renowned for their military service. Their principal seat was Ravensworth castle in North Yorkshire. Henry Fitzhugh, the 3rd baron, had been a Knight of the Garter under Henry IV and had served as Constable of England at the coronation of Henry V. William Fitzhugh, the 4th baron, had been associated with the Earl of Salisbury in the government of the north during the 1440s and 1450s and it would appear that, at this time, the Fitzhughs came into the orbit of the Nevills of Middleham, to whom they then became committed supporters. Sometime in the early 1450s, Salisbury's daughter Alice married Henry Fitzhugh, 5th baron (1429–72). Their daughter Anne was born, like Francis Lovell, sometime in the mid-1450s, and when the marriage was celebrated in February 1466, it is unlikely that either the bride or the groom had reached puberty and so it is doubtful that the marriage was consummated prior to both reaching the age of fourteen.

The marriage to Anne Fitzhugh was exactly the type of marriage any member of the Lovell family would have negotiated. (Indeed, a previous marriage between the two families had taken place in the fourteenth century.) In this marriage to the Fitzhughs, the Lovells were marrying into a rising baronial house of respectable antiquity, and one with significant connections. Most importantly, the marriage cemented the young Francis Lovell's links with the most powerful family in the country. For Katherine and for Warwick, the match demonstrated the power of Nevill goodwill and the value of the connections at court that the Nevills possessed. For Henry Fitzhugh, who had eleven children to marry off, the match bound him tighter to Warwick, who had demonstrated that he could offer good lordship and was able to discharge his responsibility to his kinsman. Hence, the marriage of Francis Lovell to Anne Fitzhugh represented a significant change in Francis' circumstances. It took him away from his mother's household at Minster Lovell and away from the Thames Valley, into the household of a noble whose name was a byword for magnificence, splendour, generosity and, above all, power.

In the household of 'the Kingmaker'

Richard Nevill, Earl of Warwick, had an income and a status that raised him high above any other in the realm with the exception of the king. From his two earldoms of Warwick and Salisbury, he possessed an income in excess of £7,000 per annum, plus a further income of £8,000 from the great offices of state such as Great Chamberlain of

England, Captain of Calais, Keeper of the Seas, Warden of the Cinque Ports, Warden of the West March and Constable of Dover Castle. This level of income allowed Warwick to retain a large household of over 200 permanent members, with over 150 personnel in attendance at any one time. The outlay on such a large household included the wages payable to such important figures as Lord Fitzhugh, the Deputy Warden of the West March, down to the gardener and janitor at Middleham. A large number of northern gentry were in receipt of fees and wages from Warwick of upward of £10 per annum, paid out of the receipts and rentals of Middleham Castle where a further thirty men were employed as domestic servants.

It is commonly held that Middleham Castle in north Yorshire was Warwick's principal residence and base. Whilst it has been said that it was his favourite residence, it was by no means where he spent most of his time. Warwick's household maintained standing estate committees to oversee the day-to-day running of his affairs at Warwick, Middleham, Cardiff, Carlisle and Calais. His council met frequently at London and the earl often celebrated Christmas at Coventry. Therefore, it is a mistake to assume that either Richard of Gloucester or Francis Lovell would have spent the majority of their time in the north. Warwick's household was peripatetic and after December 1465, when Warwick signed a truce with Scotland, he spent less and less time in the north, which had largely been pacified, leaving its governance in the hands of deputies such as Henry, Lord Fitzhugh, and Sir William Parr.

Warwick's household followed the earl in whatever role his great offices required him to perform. This meant a continual movement between his Yorkshire castles, Warwick and Cardiff, not to mention his residences of Le Herber in London, the Captain's Castle at Calais, and Carlisle. A contemporary account in Bale's Chronicle of London recorded that 'he was named and taken in all places for the most courageous and manliest knight living'.[2] In the same source he was also described as 'Richard the Earl of Warwick of knighthood lodesterre' (i.e., the North Star of knighthood). Warwick, although renowned for his courage, was actually a mediocre military figure: it was in the field of politics that he excelled. Audacious and daring, Warwick was always capable of arousing the passions of the people and engaging popular support for his enterprises. The Burgundian chronicler Chastellain said of Warwick:

> and for certain, among the great men of the world, this man is to be counted one of those, it seems to me, of whom one may write grandly and nobly, so much by reason of their prudence and valour as for their success.[3]

It is important to remember that, since the late 1450s, Warwick, as Captain of Calais, had enjoyed a European reputation, intimately connected with both the French and Burgundian courts. In fact, Warwick had met both Charles VII and Louis XI of France and Philip the Good, Duke of Burgundy, and his son Charles, Count of Charolais. His European reputation had been enhanced by Edward IV's use of Warwick as an ambassador, and on all of these journeys abroad he would have been accompanied by a retinue of not less than two hundred attendants.

Domestically, Warwick, as befitting such a prominent figure, entertained on a stupendous scale. At the apogee of Nevill power, in September 1465, for the enthronement of his brother George as archbishop of York there were two to three thousand guests for celebrations that lasted a whole week. During that time, the guests, who included the great and good of the north of England, prominent Nevill retainers and the mayor of the Calais Staple ate their way through 25,000lb of beef, 24,000lb of mutton and 15,000lb of pork, plus deer, pike, partridge, herons, peacocks, porpoises and seals. This was followed by a dessert course that included custards, tarts and jellies, all washed down by 100 tuns of wine and 300 tuns of ale.[4]

Francis Lovell would have joined Warwick's household at roughly the same time as Edward IV's brother, Richard of Gloucester, either in 1464 or (more likely) 1465. Richard would have probably been two years older than Francis Lovell (Lovell's exact date of birth is unknown) and would have known Warwick significantly longer. Both boys would have been treated the same: in the fifteenth century a boy of noble descent was expected after seven years of age to join a male-dominated household as a clear sign that childhood was over. Here his education would truly begin with training in courtesy, hunting and, eventually, the military arts. Education was deemed to be a 'franchise', the inculcation freely and independently of those qualities deemed appropriate to those who benefited from the combination of good birth and virtue. This was the essence of a noble education, which consisted of *courtesie* (behaving towards others in the correct courtly manner), *largesse* (open-handedness, generosity and magnanimity), *loyaute* (loyalty, which was freely offered to those ranked above and below) and *prowesse* (courage, valour and the performance of feats of arms on the field of battle). These would have been essential requirements for both Richard and Francis, who would be called upon to attend formal banquets as servers and to act in attendance on Warwick on public occasions. Their behaviour and manners had to be impeccable – anything less would reflect badly on the earl's honour.

These elements were the building blocks in the formation of the noble character and provided an essential foundation for moving easily within noble society. In addition to his education, a young noble was expected to undergo training, which started at fourteen as a squire and included the honing of riding skills and learning to master horse and weapons for the hunt. Lovell would have had years of experience of wearing armour to acclimatize his body to it, but at sixteen the serious medieval business of training for war began. Writing in 1455, the Northumbrian soldier John Harding wrote: 'At 14 boys should learn to werray and to wage war, to joust and ride and of castles to assayle.'[5] This was the education required for a boy to enter into the estate of a man.

There is no reason to doubt that between 1465 and 1468, whilst growing from boys into young men, Francis Lovell formed a close and enduring friendship with Richard of Gloucester. This was a friendship that would survive the rising tensions that arose between Warwick and Edward IV. Both boys would have become increasingly aware of Warwick's estrangement from Edward from 1466 onwards when the tensions that began to drive a wedge between the two cousins became more notice-able and the subject of increasing rivalry at court. Indeed, it is hard to believe that these tensions would not have become apparent to the two boys, or that they were unaware of the personal politics involved.

Family politics

It has been suggested that the estrangement between Edward and Warwick arose after Edward's marriage in secret to Elizabeth Woodville in 1464. Contemporary sources state merely that the two fell out over foreign policy issues, specifically over friend-ship with France. Edward was determined to pursue his own policy of alliance with Burgundy, a course of action with which Warwick vehemently disagreed. Warwick also had a justifiable grievance with Edward over the marriage of his two daughters. Edward's queen, Elizabeth Woodville, had a large and impecunious family that were married into the highest noble families in England, snapping up such potential hus-bands as Henry Stafford, Duke of Buckingham, and Lord Maltravers, the heir of the Earl of Arundel. By 1467, the only marriageable candidates of suitable rank and age left for Warwick's two daughters Isabel and Anne to marry were the king's brothers, George, Duke of Clarence, and Richard, Duke of Gloucester.

George was born in Dublin on 21 October 1449, the fifth son of Richard, Duke of York, at that time the richest man in England and Lord Lieutenant of Ireland. George was the third son of the duke to survive to adolescence and grew to be a witness to the political turbulence that wracked England between 1455 and 1471. At a young age he had seen how the extreme turns of fortune's wheel had affected the closest members of his family. Twice his father had become Protector of the realm; twice he had been removed. During Henry VI's periods of mental instabil-ity, Richard, Duke of York, had been victorious in battle only to lose in politics, driven into exile across the Irish Sea, leaving his wife and younger sons, George and Richard, to be humiliated at Ludlow castle, which was sacked by his enemies.

In 1460, the duke had returned in triumph after his party, led by George's first cousin, the Earl of Warwick, had triumphed at the battle of Northampton, at which Lovell's grandfather, Viscount Beaumont, a principal commander, had died beside Warwick's personal enemy, Lord Egremont. George had then witnessed his father try to claim the throne for himself, describing himself as 'the true and legitimate heir of the kingdoms of England and France and of the lordship and land of Ireland'.[6]

Unfortunately for Richard, Duke of York, he did not have long to enjoy the recognition of his claim, which a rather partisan parliament had awarded him in October 1461. Henry VI's queen, the redoubtable Margaret of Anjou, furious that her son Edward had been disinherited, launched a campaign against the Yorkists and defeated and killed Richard, Duke of York, at the battle of Wakefield on 30 December 1460. York's claim to the throne now descended to his eldest son Edward, Earl of March, who, backed by his father's retainers from the Welsh Marches, defeated the Welsh Lancastrians led by Jasper Tudor, Earl of Pembroke, and the Earl of Wiltshire, at the battle of Mortimer's Cross on 12 February 1461. George and his brother Richard were not there to see this remarkable turnaround since their mother Cecily, Duchess of York, had despatched her two younger sons to the care of Philip the Good, Duke of Burgundy, who placed them under his protection at Bruges. George's position changed immeasurably on 4 March when his brother Edward pronounced himself king – a claim he was to make good on the bloodiest battle fought on British soil (with over 20,000 dead), Towton Field. Here, on 29 March 1461, Edward defeated the principal army of the House of Lancaster and firmly established his right to the throne. George returned from Burgundy, no longer merely the third son of the Duke of York, but heir presumptive to the king of England.

On Edward's coronation, George became Duke of Clarence, emphasizing the new dynasty's links with Lionel, Duke of Clarence, Edward III's second son and through whose descent the York family claimed the throne. By 1463 George had been ennobled as 'George Duke of Clarence and lord of Richmond, lieutenant of our most dread Lord king's land of Ireland'. In 1463, although still underage, George became a Knight of the Garter and had vast estates conferred on him, making him one of the richest magnates in England.

Elizabeth Woodville

At this time the agent of Clarence's nemesis was residing in Northamptonshire in the person of a Lancastrian widow named Elizabeth Grey (née Woodville), whose husband John, Lord Grey of Ferrers, had been killed in 1461 at the second battle of St Albans, fighting for Henry VI. Edward IV had become besotted with her and, motivated by 'blind affection and not by the rule of reason', had secretly married Elizabeth in May 1464.

Elizabeth Woodville was not the parvenu of popular legend; nor was she in any sense an appropriate choice for a king to take as his bride, bringing neither wealth nor status to her marriage. The marriage was eventually made public by Edward before the Great Council at Reading on 14 September 1464. The issue was only brought to light because Edward had to make a firm decision as to whether or not to marry the continental princess Bona of Savoy, a marriage alliance for which the Earl of Warwick and Edward's diplomats had been assiduously working for the previous six months. There is no contemporary evidence that Clarence shared or expressed any of the dismissive attitudes towards the Woodvilles prevalent at this time; on the contrary, it was Clarence who escorted Elizabeth into Reading Abbey for her presentation as queen. Regardless of her lack of status, Elizabeth was now Edward's wife and had a proven record of fertility (already having two sons). It could be expected that Clarence's position as heir apparent would soon be over as the new king and queen would obviously hope to have a family of their own very soon. Whilst an addition to the new royal family would have been welcome, Elizabeth Woodville had five brothers and six sisters who now had to be provided for in a manner befitting relatives of the king from scant royal resources. Edward promoted Elizabeth's father to an earldom, making him Earl Rivers and also Lord Treasurer, where it was hoped that he could enrich himself from the profits of office to compensate for the lack of a landed estate. Five of Elizabeth's sisters married peers or the heirs of peers: Margaret married the Earl of Arundel; Eleanor married the heir of the Earl of Kent; Mary married the heir of Lord Herbert; Jaquetta married Lord Strange; Anne married Viscount Bourchier; and Katherine Woodville snapped up the greatest prize of all, marrying Henry Stafford, the young Duke of Buckingham, one of the very greatest and richest landholders in the country. Elizabeth's brothers could also look to preferment from the king, but Edward's resources and available offices were insufficient to effectively endow all of the queen's relatives.

On 26 May 1465, Clarence presided over the coronation of the new queen, who now took her place beside her husband on the throne. The marriage exacerbated tensions that had begun to emerge in the Yorkist polity by 1465–6. Edward had become king as head of a faction of the nobility, the most important part of which in the early 1460s had been the Nevill family, led by the powerful Earl of Warwick and his brothers, John, Lord Montague, and George, Bishop of Exeter. Warwick, Montague and George had been the most consistent supporters of the House of York and their resources and abilities had been crucial in transforming the Yorkist faction from rebels to royalty. This loyalty had been magnificently rewarded in 1461–2, but by 1464–5 strains in the relationship were beginning to show. Edward had come to the throne aged nineteen and, in many respects, was under the wing of his more experienced cousin, Warwick, who was fourteen years older and already carving a European reputation as a naval commander and politician. Edward had apparently been content early in his reign to allow Warwick to oversee large swathes of policy. This began to change as the last embers of Lancastrian resistance were stamped out in Northumberland and along the Scottish border, and Edward began to rely on a coterie of servants of his own choosing, who were totally dependent upon him. These new men – William Herbert, William Hastings and Humphrey Stafford – now began to intrude into areas of royal policy that Warwick had previously regarded as his own. Edward, as king, begged to differ and arguments over foreign policy became symptomatic of rifts between the two men in the royal council. Adding to these tensions was the requirement for patronage and improvement that the queen's family now required; the cornering of the marriage market by the queen's sisters and family was particularly galling for the Earl of Warwick.

Disagreements and tensions

Warwick's disenchantment mirrored that of Clarence who, whilst having a large income and landed endowment, felt himself excluded from any real role and remote from the levers of power that were increasingly in the hands of Edward's friends and

Woodville relatives. Clarence may have felt that the Yorkist party, which had placed his brother on the throne, thus fulfilling their father's ambition, had been sidelined. The York/Nevill party of the late 1450s, which had been based on mutual interest and family ties, was now being superseded by the king's new friends, not only the Woodvilles, but also William Hastings and Humphrey Stafford, who now counted for more in Edward's counsel than the old family relationships built up in the past. In one sense, it could be argued that as Edward matured, it was perhaps inevitable that he would develop an independent policy and move away from Warwick's tutelage. Equally, as king, it was wise for Edward to broaden the base of his support and to offer reconciliation to old Lancastrians and those who had not originally supported him. Yet Edward's treatment of Warwick was, at best, unthinking, and, at worst, a breach of the good lordship that his services on Edward's behalf had given him a right to expect. It also failed to address Warwick's concerns as a father looking out for the best interests of his daughters.

The issue of the marriage of Warwick's daughters brought relations between the earl and king into sharp relief. Given that it was by now extremely unlikely that Warwick would have any more children, Warwick's daughters were the greatest and the most prestigious heiresses of their day as the only offspring of England's premier earl – indeed, England's Caesar. As such, his daughters could have expected to make matches with the very highest in the land, such as the young Henry Stafford, Duke of Buckingham. By 1465, Warwick's eldest daughter Isabel was now fourteen and at an appropriate age for marriage. However, the Woodvilles' sweeping of the marriage board, severely curtailed Warwick's opportunities for a suitable husband for his daughter. As Warwick would have seen it, this reflected poorly on his honour and would have impacted on his good lordship, for if he was unable to obtain an appropriate marriage for his own daughters, what was he likely to achieve for a more distant relative or client?

The two obvious candidates for marriage suitable in terms of rank, prestige and family connections were the king's brothers: George, Duke of Clarence, and Richard, Duke of Gloucester. However, Edward was steadfastly against these matches. The reasons for his opposition today are unclear, but probably revolved around his objection to allowing his overbearing cousin to further increase his influence over his younger brothers. By far the greater problem for Edward was that he had no alternative candidates to offer. As for Warwick, he became resentful of the promotion of Elizabeth Woodville's family and the increasing influence of the king's new favourites, in Edward's councils. He recognized the unpalatable fact that, once he lost power and influence at court it would become increasingly difficult to retrieve the situation. In seeking new ways to retain influence, Warwick looked towards George, Duke of Clarence. Playing on Clarence's disenchantment, Warwick was able to offer him an alternative to his brother's indifference while also be able to free himself from what he saw as an increasingly remote king seemingly intent on alienating those who had been closest to him. Warwick was prepared not just to flatter Clarence, but to dangle before him the opportunities of both marrying his daughter Isabel and uniting with

Warwick to obtain a greater say in the governance of the realm and, using Warwick's power and influence, carve for himself a greater role at his brother's court. Attempts at reconciliation between Edward and Warwick took place throughout the summer of 1468 and into 1469. Ultimately, these attempts collapsed because Warwick could not recognize Edward's standing, not just as his cousin, but as his king. This dissension between Warwick and Edward IV erupted into a renewal of civil war in 1469 when Warwick fomented rebellion in the north. As Edward's favourites, William Herbert, Earl of Pembroke, and Humphrey Stafford, Earl of Devon, raised an army to suppress the northern rebellion, they were met by Warwick's forces at Edgecote in Oxfordshire, where they were both defeated by Warwick and executed without trial. Unsurprisingly, an attempted reconciliation between Edward and Warwick collapsed and Warwick, politically isolated, but now accompanied by Clarence and his daughter Isabel, fled to Calais and then to France.

During the rising tensions over the previous two years between the Earl of Warwick and the king, there is no suggestion that Edward initially wished to remove Richard of Gloucester from Warwick's household. At sixteen, Richard was as yet too young to play an independent role in politics, a situation that would exist until Warwick and Edward's relationship deteriorated beyond repair. During 1467/8, Edward and Warwick clashed more frequently; a by-product of this was the eventual removal of Richard from Warwick's household. With the increasing closeness of Warwick and Clarence, Edward could not risk his other brother also falling under the earl's spell. While tensions arose between Warwick and Edward, there is no suggestion that the relationship between Warwick and Richard was anything other than amicable. However, the friendship of Francis Lovell and Richard would have been severely tested during 1468 when Richard was finally removed from the earl's household on the instructions of the king. This left the friends on different sides of a personal and political divide. As relations between Edward and Warwick deteriorated, it would have become obligatory for Francis, now aged fourteen, to follow his lord into opposition of both his king and his friend. With the collapse of Warwick's rebellion in 1469, Francis and his wife Anne joined her father, Richard, Lord Fitzhugh, at Ravensworth in North Yorkshire. Fitzhugh, acting as Warwick's deputy, had been involved in Robin of Redesdale's rebellion, but after the collapse of Warwick's attempted overthrow of Edward's government and his subsequent departure to France with Isabel and Clarence, Lord Fitzhugh was left to make peace with a resurgent Edward IV.

On 11 July 1469 at Warwick's base at Calais, George, Duke of Clarence, and Isabel Nevill were married by George Nevill, Archbishop of York, in the presence of the bride's mother and father, and the following day Warwick, in their name, issued a manifesto criticizing the king. At this point, Clarence, then aged twenty, broke with his elder brother and began to pursue an individual political course. The manifesto issued by Warwick, Clarence and George Nevill, Archbishop of York, accused the queen and her Woodville kin of enriching themselves at the expense of others. By associating himself with this criticism of the royal family, Clarence, whether through youthful inconstancy or a feeling of being under-used by his elder brother, firmly nailed his colours to the mast, siding with the older Yorkist nobility and those he saw of his blood. Much has been made of the supposed weakness of Clarence's character, apparently coming under the influence of the glamorous and overweening presence of Warwick. Yet it could be argued that here was a prince of the House of York remaining true to those families who had stood with it on the field of battle and shed blood for the cause. Clarence may also have calculated that there would be no place for him at a Woodville-dominated court where he was excluded from those offices to which he felt his birth entitled him, but which were now exercised by the lesser relatives of the queen. Warwick offered through marriage to his daughter Isabel a tangible reward: a great inheritance and a political path to power, backed by the old family coalition.

Clarence's actions in joining with Warwick tipped the scales against Edward IV's government, which now had to recognize that a broad-based support for the manifesto criticizing the Woodvilles existed. Before Edward could mobilize, he was confronted by a series of well-planned and co-ordinated rebellions in different parts of the country. By a sequence of forced marches, Warwick and his retinue were able to eliminate his political opponents. The queen's father, Earl Rivers, and her brother Sir John Woodville were captured by Warwick and executed out of hand. Edward IV, bereft of support, was made captive.

Warwick, along with Clarence, tried to govern through a captive Edward who was the earl's 'guest' at one or other of his strongholds in the north of England. However, this attempt to govern by proxy with a Nevill-dominated council was a failure. Faced with mounting dissension from Lancashire to East Anglia that proved beyond Warwick's resources to deal with, the political initiative reverted to the king and Edward, free once more to act independently, turned the tables on Warwick and Clarence, forcing them to flee before the king's officers in October 1469. Warwick, along with Clarence and his now heavily pregnant wife Isabel, fled first to Calais. Here, Warwick was still the captain; even so, they were denied entry by Warwick's deputy. Under gunfire from the fortress, the seventeen-year-old Isabel went into labour in a small skiff; tragically, the baby was still-born or died soon after birth. Faced with little alternative, Warwick took his small fleet and a number of captured Burgundian merchant ships to the mouth of the Seine to seek political asylum with the French king, Louis XI. The subtle Louis, known as 'the spider' for his web of diplomatic activities, saw an immediate opportunity and invited Warwick to meet him at the capital of Normandy, Rouen.

Warwick 'the Kingmaker' changes sides

In Rouen, at the suggestion of Louis, Warwick was persuaded to consider a political *volte-face* of the first magnitude and to try to regain his position at the centre of English politics with a breathtaking alliance with the exiled Lancastrian queen,

Margaret of Anjou, who Warwick had done so much to undermine during the previous decade. This represented a politically audacious 'U'-turn bordering on rank hypocrisy since Warwick had played such a large role not only in usurping the rule of her husband Henry VI, but also disinheriting her son, Edward of Lancaster. At the cathedral of Angers, the capital of the duchy of Anjou, an extraordinary reconciliation took place between these two irreconcilables. They were now prepared to look past their mutual antipathy and sign a treaty of alliance as a first step to achieving power in England, but only after Margaret had kept Warwick on his knees for two hours before acknowledging him. The alliance was to be sealed by the marriage of their respective children – Edward of Lancaster and Warwick's younger daughter, Anne Nevill. Warwick agreed to help Margaret to recover the throne for her mentally incapacitated husband, Henry VI, in place of Warwick's cousin and now rival, Edward IV. The restoration of Henry would inevitably see Edward of Lancaster restored to his position of Prince of Wales with Warwick's daughter becoming princess of Wales and later queen of England. Whilst this arrangement pleased Warwick, it filled his new son-in-law George, Duke of Clarence, with apprehension and doubt. The Treaty of Angers pushed him further from the throne and the centre of power, as a Yorkist in a new Lancastrian court; it also seriously jeopardized his own position and his estates, which had been carved out of the duchy of Lancaster lands and the estates of those attainted Lancastrian nobles who were sure to accompany Margaret of Anjou and her son on their return to England. The Lancastrian guarantee of Clarence as third in line to the throne after both Henry VI and Edward of Lancaster (and any offspring he and Anne Nevill might have) was so tenuous as to be practically worthless. Neither was Clarence mollified by the prospect of gaining his brother's duchy of York, a reward that would be offset by the loss of the Lancastrian estates he currently enjoyed and would inevitably have to disgorge. During the autumn of 1469, at Angers, Clarence's position was not an enviable one.

In September 1470, Warwick and his adherents led an invasion of England that was successful as Edward IV's support melted away and he was abandoned by large segments of the nobility. With no army except for his closest companions, including his young brother Richard, Duke of Gloucester, Edward was trapped between Warwick's forces advancing from the south and John, Marquis Montague's forces advancing from the north. Edward fled from Bishop's (later, King's) Lynn to his brother-in-law, the Duke of Burgundy, arriving on 2 November 1470. Warwick's complete success opened the door for a return of those stalwart Lancastrian exiles, the dukes of Somerset and Exeter, and for the proposed return of Margaret of Anjou and her son Edward of Lancaster, whose wife, the Lady Anne, was being politely held by her mother-in-law as surety for Warwick's loyalty. Warwick, now master of England, had to accommodate two hostile factions since, although his Nevill retainers were those who had won the realm for his new Lancastrian allies, they were also those who had driven the Lancastrians into exile ten years earlier, and killed and executed their relatives.

A parliament called for November 1470 confirmed the grant of the duchy of

York to George, Duke of Clarence, but it was to be his only gain and he began to feel increasingly like a cuckoo in the Lancastrian nest. Warwick, having burned his Yorkist boats, had no alternative but to continue on his chosen course, while Clarence was increasingly susceptible to offers of reconciliation with both his brothers since his sibling Richard of Gloucester had accompanied Edward into exile in Burgundy. These offers of reconciliation were mediated through their sister Margaret, Duchess of Burgundy, who liked to invoke a family unity between her three remaining brothers.

In accordance with the Treaty of Angers, Warwick's government, in the name of Henry VI, began preparing for war with Burgundy in alliance with Louis XI of France. This spurred Charles, Duke of Burgundy, to offer much needed assistance to his brother-in-law Edward, whom he provided with a small fleet that bore Edward to the mouth of the Humber. Landing on 14 March 1471, Edward merely asserted that he was back to reclaim his father's inheritance. At this time, Clarence was in the West Country recruiting and, by the end of the month, he had amassed a force of 4,000 and had marched into Oxfordshire looking as if to rendezvous at Coventry where his father-in-law Warwick sheltered behind its walls, not daring to offer battle to a now resurgent Edward IV. Warwick had expected Clarence to join him, but instead Clarence veered eastwards and joined forces with his brother Edward. Together, George, Duke of Clarence, Edward IV and their younger brother Richard, Duke of Gloucester, marched on London, which then opened its gates to them. London previously had failed to rally to the shambolic and miserable figure of Henry VI, whom the Archbishop of York, George Nevill, had paraded in a misguided attempt to rally the loyalty of Londoners to the Lancastrian regime. This had backfired, emphasizing the contrast between the young virile Edward and the obviously mentally distracted Henry in his faded and threadbare blue robe.

The House of York re-united

The three Yorkist brothers were reunited and turned to face the following Lancastrian army led by Warwick and Montague. At Barnet on 14 April 1471, Edward IV and most of the peerage of Yorkist England faced his one-time allies and cousins Warwick and Montague, plus their trenchant Lancastrian allies, the Duke of Exeter, and the Earl of Oxford. In a hard-fought encounter that was blighted and complicated by dense fog, the advantage went first to the Lancastrians and then, undermined by the miasma of treachery and suspicion, to Edward and the Yorkists, who won a crushing victory. Amongst those killed were Warwick and Montague; their ally Henry Holland, Duke of Exeter, was captured. The threat from Warwick and the Nevills and the last of the barons was now over.

On the day Barnet was fought, the redoubtable Margaret of Anjou, Henry VI's queen, landed at Weymouth with her son, the seventeen-year-old Edward, the Lancastrian Prince of Wales. She was soon accompanied by the Lancastrian die-hards, the Duke of Somerset and the Earl of Devon. These Lancastrian lords, tapping into deep-rooted local loyalties, soon brought the West Country out in rebellion. Marching through Exeter and Taunton, Margaret moved north towards Bristol, hoping to link with Jasper Tudor's army advancing from South Wales. By a series of forced marches, Margaret managed to stay ahead of Edward IV's pursuing army. Both now began a desperate race towards the strategically positioned bridges over the Severn at Gloucester, but here Margaret found the bridge closed to her by Edward's governor, Sir Richard Beauchamp, who held the castle. Moving on, Margaret marched north, still hoping to avoid a confrontation until the two Lancastrian forces could join up and face Edward as a combined force. Equally, Edward IV was determined to engage her in battle before she joined with the Earl of Pembroke. In this he was successful, trapping Margaret at Tewkesbury on 4 May. In another hard-fought encounter, Edward was once again successful and this time decisively so. Henry VI's son, Edward of Lancaster was slain either in or soon after the battle, as was Lord Wenlock, Warwick's friend and chamberlain. The Duke of Somerset also died and the Earl of Devon and his brother were captured and executed the following day. Margaret of Anjou was captured at Malvern priory. The Lancastrian king Henry VI finally 'died' in the Tower of London soon afterwards, bringing to an end the dynasties of Lancaster and that of Beaufort. The only Lancastrian figure of note to survive the debacle of 1471 was Jasper Tudor who, retreating to west Wales, delayed only to exact vengeance on members of the Vaughan family at Chepstow and to collect his fourteen-year-old nephew Henry Tudor, titular Earl of Richmond, from Raglan castle on his way to the port of Tenby from where he and Henry Tudor embarked for fourteen years of exile in Brittany and France.

It is from the records of subsequent pardons that we know that, during this time, Francis Lovell and his wife were resident in his father-in-law's household in Ravensworth, north Yorkshire. For Lovell, the previous eighteen months would have offered a profound lesson in the precarious nature of high politics and a demonstration of how quickly hubris could turn into despair and dejection.

3 THE BOSOM OF YORK:
THE DE LA POLE CONNECTION

A commodity to be bargained

THE YEAR 1471 WAS a precarious one for Francis Lovell. Now sixteen, he would have been deemed old enough to take his place on the field of arms and, although still very young, he would have been viewed with some suspicion by the returning regime and his loyalty severely questioned. Francis, from Edward IV's perspective, was doubly guilty by association: firstly, as a member of Warwick's household, under his influence and tutelage; secondly, by virtue of his marriage to Anne Fitzhugh, whose father, Lord Fitzhugh, had acted as Warwick's deputy in the north of England since 1464. Lord Fitzhugh had been clearly implicated in treasonous activities in 1469 and had been a dependable supporter of Warwick throughout the Readeption of Henry VI. Francis was to learn early in life the words of Lord Blount: 'be not great about kings for it is dangerous'. Having basked in the companionship of the great of the land, Francis Lovell would soon discover that the wheel of fortune could bring one down as well as raise one up.

It was probably the activities of Francis' father-in-law, Henry, Lord Fitzhugh (whose need was, after all, far greater than that of the youthful Francis), that required a general pardon for his family on 10 September 1471, issued at Westminster:

> General pardon … to Henry Fitzhugh, knight of Fitzhugh and his wife Alice, Francis Lovell, son and heir of John Lovell knight and Anne Lovell, his wife, Richard Nevill, son of George Nevill, knight, Richard Fitzhugh, George Fitzhugh, Edward Fitzhugh, Thomas Fitzhugh, and John Fitzhugh, sons of the same Henry, Elizabeth Fitzhugh daughter of the same Henry, Joan Lovell and Frideswide, sisters of the same Frideswide.[1]

It is interesting to note that even at this early age Francis is given such prominence behind his father-in-law, an already existing peer, and is accorded a higher precedence than Fitzhugh's sons. The government of Edward IV clearly recognized Francis' potential status at an early stage. It is also interesting that the pardon is extended to Francis' two sisters who, like him, were orphaned and now residing with him in the north. It does not need to be said that there is no suggestion whatsoever that the Lovell sisters were in any way implicated in Warwick's activities, but it was as well in the circumstances to look to the future and ensure no further repercussions occurred that could blight their future marriage prospects.

After the crushing of both the Nevills and the Lancastrians and weathering the storm of the previous two years, the government of Edward IV began to impose a new political settlement on the realm. This meant a redistribution of the offices, lands and prerequisites that had been held by the Nevills and a new round of rewards for the supporters of the king. This process began in the spring of 1471 in a way that had direct implications on Francis' patrimony. On 20 April 1471, Humphrey Blount, who had not come out in rebellion with Warwick in 1470, was rewarded with the office of receiver of Lovell's lordship of Acton Burnell in Shropshire and all other substantial Lovell lands in the county. A month later, on 23 May, John Lythyngton was appointed as a receiver for the whole of John, Lord Lovell's estates, the grant stipulating that the estates were now 'in the king's hands by the minority of Francis his son and heir'. An appraisal of the value of the Lovell inheritance was undertaken by an experienced treasury official and a major redistribution of patronage now occurred. Francis Lovell was an important asset and a major element of royal patronage to be conferred as the king saw fit. We can only imagine how the young Francis felt about his treatment as a reward or a commodity to be bargained over for the second time in his young life.

It is difficult to ascertain Francis Lovell's whereabouts between September 1470 and July 1471. We can assume that he was resident with his wife's family at Ravensworth, in North Yorkshire, since Francis and all of the Fitzhughs applied jointly for a pardon at this time. If this was the case, then he would have been a long way from Westminster where the decisions about his fate as a minor and a tenant-in-chief were being made. In fact, a decision was quickly made after the battle of Tewkesbury. On 11 July 1471 at Westminster, it was determined that a:

> grant to the king's brother in law John Duke of Suffolk and the king's sister Elizabeth, his wife of the custody of all lordships, manors, lands and possessions late of John Lovell knight, Lord of Lovell, deceased tenant in chief by knight service during the minority of Francis Lovell his son and Heir[2]

The grant was a reward for the loyalty of the king's brother-in-law, John de la Pole, Duke of Suffolk, and the king's sister Elizabeth, who had stood by Edward throughout. The grant was to be typical of the policies Edward IV came to adopt during his second reign. Gone was the open-handed largesse of the period 1461–5: during his second reign (1471–83), Edward would acquire a reputation as miser, loth to part with estates or cash; also, he would ensure that those who benefited most from royal patronage were his closest family members. The grant of Francis Lovell's wardship exemplifies both. Firstly, at a time when it was rare for women to be jointly allocated rewards or property, this was a joint grant, made to John, Duke of Suffolk, and the king's sister, thus satisfying the need to reward the family. Secondly, the grant emphasizes the land and estates; this is Edward bestowing a reward on a massive scale, the Lovell inheritance being worth between £1,400 and £1,700, with the two manors in Oxfordshire alone having a combined worth of £156 9s 7½d. Lovell is mentioned only after the legality of the land grant has been determined. Since he was already married, Lovell was unable to marry into his guardian's family and so his person was now worth far less than it had been in 1464; such were the realities of fifteenth-century wardship. The grant was a cheap way of Edward conferring a reward that cost him very little whilst serving a political purpose in placing a large inheritance into what amounted to a safe pair of hands. Also, it greatly enhanced the position of the Duke of Suffolk in the Thames Valley as the Lovell estates in Oxford and Buckinghamshire abutted the de la Pole estates centred on their fine manor of Ewelme.

The de la Pole family

Despite their Norman-sounding name, the de la Poles had not come over with the Conqueror. Their origins were, in fact, much more humble – the name being a gentrification of 'of the pool' (the pool in question being that of Hull). The first member of the family to rise to prominence was Michael de la Pole, who began life as a wool merchant in Hull. He became so successful that he was appointed as one of the chief financiers of Edward III's campaigns in France in the 1340s and 1350s. His controversial financial manipulation of the wool trade, England's principal export, earned him the distrust and censure of parliament, but he died peacefully in his bed in June 1366. Before he died, however, he had established his family amongst the landholding upper classes. In lieu of repaying most of the enormous loans Michael had made to the Crown, Edward III had granted him the Ufford estates in East Anglia (principally in Suffolk) when the Earl of Suffolk had died childless. As a wealthy landowner, Michael's son, also called Michael, was able to pursue a military career as a companion to Edward, Prince of Wales, the 'Black Prince', and rose to become an advisor to his son, King Richard II, who made him Earl of Suffolk in 1385. This represented a tremendous leap in status for someone whose father had been born a commoner. Unfortunately, the instability of Richard II's minority proved to be positively poisonous for the younger Michael. In 1388, he and other members of Richard's government and household were impeached and hauled before parliament, accused of treason and corruption. To avoid the charges, Michael de la Pole fled to Paris, where he died in 1389.

He was succeeded by his son, another Michael, who was restored to the earldom in 1398. This Michael focused on expanding his estates in East Anglia, which he did by marrying the Wingfield heiress and generally keeping out of national politics. He did campaign in France with Henry V. However, rather than finding a glorious military career, Michael died, along with many other soldiers, from dysentery at the siege of Harfleur, whereupon the earldom descended to his eldest son, imaginatively called Michael, in September 1415. On 25 October 1415, the new earl formed part of Henry V's 'happy few' at the battle of Agincourt. Unfortunately, this Michael de la Pole and Edward, Duke of York, were the only notable casualties on the English side that day and Michael's younger brother, William, then became Earl of Suffolk, aged just eighteen. In 1417, William returned to France, where he served continuously until 1429, when, at Jargeau, in the Loire Valley, he was captured by Joan of Arc in a battle in which his younger brother was killed. As a high-status prisoner, he was ransomed for the astronomical amount of £20,000 – more than twenty years' income from the family estates. William was released to raise his own ransom, leaving his younger brother Thomas to remain as hostage, only for Thomas to die in captivity in France.

On his return to England, William became a senior member of the young Henry VI's council. Henry, who had come to the throne at nine months old, inflicted on England the longest minority ever, yet the Council of Regency from 1421–35 was remarkably stable despite internal disagreements amongst its senior members. These disagreements, which were sometimes vehement, were principally over the war in France, the legacy of Henry V and the Treaty of Troyes (1420). Under the terms of this treaty, Henry VI had been crowned king of France at Paris in 1429, confirming his father's ambitions, which had been unleashed by the English victory at Agincourt. As the 1430s progressed, English politics was riven by those nobles who wished to trade Henry VI's French crown for peace in an increasingly unwinnable war against an opponent with greater resources and those who saw this policy as a betrayal of Henry V's achievements. In the 1430s, these two factions had been led by Henry Beaufort, Bishop of Winchester, and by Henry's youngest brother, Humphrey, Duke of Gloucester. In 1435, the last chance for a negotiated peace with France had been rejected at Amiens, and English policy had drifted since then.

English policy was not helped by the personality of Henry VI. As the king grew to maturity, it became obvious that he had some unstable traits. He could be excessively pious, wilful, easily led and sometimes quite distracted from the business of government. As he grew, he became more and more convinced of the need for peace and of bringing the war to an end. By 1444, William de la Pole was a senior member of the king's council, which now had to implement the royal policy of peace. As the newly created Marquis of Suffolk, in 1444 William de la Pole was despatched to France to bring back Henry's new French bride, Margaret of Anjou, the fourteen-year-old niece of the French king Charles VII. The bride was initially popular, but that soon changed when the English people became aware of the terms of the marriage contract: not only did the bride arrive with no dowry, which was shocking enough for the times, but to obtain the marriage, the English had also ceded to the French the province of Maine, to the south of Normandy. Both concessions had been traded for a mere five years' truce with the French. These concessions and the entire policy were undoubtedly those of the king, who, against the advice of his ministers and council, was guided by an altruistic notion of Christian piety and determined to proceed despite the reservations of his ministers and his military commanders.

William de la Pole was the minister responsible for carrying out the policy of the king and his council, for which he was elevated to Duke of Suffolk in 1448.

In 1449, while the truce with France was still in force, the government of England decided to put pressure on their wavering ally, the Duke of Brittany, by attacking the Breton town of Fougeres, which belonged to the French Duke of Alençon. The raid was a military success, but the strategy was a disastrous political failure that played into the hands of the French king Charles VII. The breach of the truce was exactly what Charles was waiting for. He launched three armies at Normandy, quickly overrunning the province, which had been hankering for a return to French rule, and defeating the English field army at the battle of Formingy in 1450. England watched in stunned disbelief as the duchy, which had been in English hands for the previous thirty years, was lost in less than one. All of Henry V's conquests had now been lost. The French, who had lost the battles of Crécy, Poitiers, Agincourt and Vernueil, had now emerged victorious from the war. The only explanation for such a disastrous course of events must be treachery. Since the king was beyond reproach, his ministers attracted most of the public opprobrium; they were accused of being in league with the French and thus guilty of treason. In early 1450, the Commons formally charged the king's chief minister, the Duke of Suffolk, with treason and with conspiring to take the crown for his son. Henry VI refused to accept the validity of these charges, but did feel that the Duke of Suffolk should be banished for five years to appease parliament. Having wound up his affairs, the Duke of Suffolk sailed for Burgundy and exile. Off the Kent coast his ship was intercepted by another, the *Nicholas of the Tower*, where a mock treason trial was held, bringing in the inevitable guilty verdict. From here, the duke was taken to a smaller boat where his neck was unceremoniously placed upon the gunwale and his head hacked off with six strokes of a rusty sword; both head and body were then placed upon the beach at Dover.

The de la Pole family suffered a political eclipse after the murder of William de la Pole. His son John succeeded him, but only in the lesser title of Earl of Suffolk. Having witnessed his father's fate, John, Earl of Suffolk, and his redoubtable mother, Alice Chaucer, granddaughter of the poet Geoffrey, eschewed any involvement in politics as it became more and more factionalized and violent during the rest of the 1450s. Aged sixteen, in 1458 the young John was married to Elizabeth, the second daughter of Richard, Duke of York, who after two periods as lord protector had been shunted into the political wilderness by a partisan Lancastrian government headed by Henry VI's queen, Margaret. The marriage carried the odour of political expediency about it, accompanied by a whiff of desperation as both families, now in the political wilderness, sought to make a mutually beneficial alliance through their children. Despite this unpromising start, the marriage does not appear to have been a totally unhappy one, as they produced eleven surviving children.

Any affection Edward IV had for his sister does not appear to have been extended to his brother-in-law. Since 1461, John de la Pole had received scant reward from Edward. This may, in part, have been because he was then only nineteen and had yet to play a prominent role on either the battlefield or in politics. True, he was appointed governor of the honour of Wallingford and restored to the ducal dignity in 1463, but other awards eluded him and those he did receive were paltry in comparison with those showered upon Warwick, Hastings, Herbert and others. John de la Pole, now Duke of Suffolk, did not become a royal councillor, although possibly this may have been his choice, not wanting to make the commitment at this time. He had to wait until 1472 to become a Knight of the Garter, longer than those of a lesser rank and with no claim on royal kinship. It is perhaps true to say that Edward IV bore John de la Pole no ill will, but saw him as someone incapable of undertaking the strains of high office. John, for his part, seems to have been much more interested in expanding his influence in East Anglia and the Thames Valley. The Paston family constantly complained of the pressures he placed upon the local gentry of the region throughout the 1470s, yet Edward, if offering little in the way of support for his brother-in-law's depredations, did little to rein him in, failing to curtail his efforts to reach local pre-eminence.

Creating a power base

It was John de la Pole's ambition to regain his father's influence in the Thames Valley and East Anglia that lay behind the granting of the wardship of Francis Lovell and his estates to the de la Poles. For the king, it rewarded committed supporters and family members by substantially increasing both their income and their local influence with the added bonus of doing it at someone else's expense. From John de la Poles' perspective the governance of the Lovell estates in Oxfordshire, Berkshire and Buckinghamshire bolstered his own power base at Ewelme, which was further augmented by his control of the honour and castle of Wallingford. This made John de la Pole the pre-eminent lord between Oxford and London, where no other magnate could challenge him. It also allowed him to utilize the income brought by the Lovell estates to live and retain a local following at a ducal level. (It had been recognized by John's father William that, whilst the de la Pole income of roughly £1,400 per annum was sufficient to support the dignity of an earl, it was barely half that enjoyed by the dukes of York, Buckingham and Norfolk.) The de la Poles had the highest dignity in the land, but not the resources to match, and so the £1,250 from the Lovell estates were very welcome, indeed.

It also recreated a previous alliance of local power that had existed in the 1450s when, after the murder of John de la Pole's father, William, John de la Pole and his lands had come under care of his father's neighbours and colleagues. The relationship between John, Viscount Beaumont, John, Lord Lovell, and the young John de la Pole had been close, allowing this confederacy of Thames Valley neighbours to control local affairs and government. This pact of the early 1450s had now been recreated, but now, instead of being the junior partner, John de la Pole, Duke of Suffolk, was the senior figure in this confederacy and Francis, Lord Lovell, the junior. The resources of both families could now be used and directed by John de la Pole who, for the foreseeable future, was the dominant figure in the Thames Valley.

John de la Pole, as well as being the king's brother-in-law, belonged to one of England's premier families. Despite their humble origins, by 1471 they were one of only five dukes in England and one of only three dukes in the country that were not of the immediate royal family. At the very apex of the chivalric world, the de la Poles also held more than seventy lordships and manors in twenty-two counties, producing an income of over £1,300 per annum. These lands were concentrated in East Anglia, particularly Suffolk, but with important holdings in Norfolk and Essex, including the key ports of Lowestoft and Gorleston. In Berkshire and Oxfordshire, the de la Poles had inherited the estates of the Chaucer family. Other important concentrations of the de la Pole estates could be found in the East Riding of Yorkshire (modern-day Humberside and Lincolnshire). John de la Pole, Duke of Suffolk, and his wife Elizabeth also had two particularly fine houses at Wingfield and Ewelme, which were built in the new style of a noble home, that is, comfortable and commodious manor houses built for the luxury and comfort of their inhabitants rather than for defence and of which Lovell's family home of Minster Lovell was an early and prime example. At Wingfield, a college was attached for the support and education of poor scholars, whilst at Ewelme the church had penitential cloisters attached. This strong connection of piety and education is one of the less discussed aspects of the nobility during the Wars of the Roses, but was symptomatic of the beginning of an increased interest in theology, literature and the humanities (in this we can see the harbingers of both the Renaissance and the Reformation). It would be tempting to see in this the continuing legacy of John's mother, Alice, a woman so renowned for her learning and her piety that in the early 1440s she had brought up and educated Henry VI's half-brothers – Edmund and Jasper Tudor.

It was typical of the age that whilst the Duke of Suffolk supported such peaceful institutions and sought to both promote lay education whilst safeguarding his immortal soul, we should also be under no illusion that he was also a member of the aristocracy and looked to dominate his own 'countrye'. By the 1470s, the de la Poles emerged as the dominant family within East Anglia, their local rivals from the 1460s (the de Vere family as earls of Oxford and the Mowbray family as dukes of Norfolk) had either quit the field or become emasculated. In the case of John de Vere of Oxford, his loyalty to the House of Lancaster and his personal hostility towards Edward IV had seen him defeated at the battle of Barnet. After launching an abortive attack on St Michael's Mount in Cornwall, John de Vere had been imprisoned in Guisnes castle on the Calais Pale. John Mowbray, Duke of Norfolk, seems to have been a sickly man who was felt to be 'over counselled' by his ducal council; in 1476 he died leaving a very young heiress. The removal of these two great rivals gave John de la Pole supremacy in East Anglia, enabling him to build up a large connection with the local gentry – those who were not part of the de la Pole affinity could be intimidated with relative impunity. The same process of local dominance can be found in other areas of de la Pole influence in Berkshire and Oxfordshire. Here, John de la Pole, from his favoured residence of Ewelme, used his own estates and the royal offices of the honour of Wallingford, together with the Lovell estates, to build up a network of power based on local wealth to influence office-holding and royal patronage. This is exemplified by the complaints of the local Stonor family who, in a similar situation to the Pastons, complained to the king of the infractions of John de la Pole and his henchmen. Alas, their complaints fell on deaf ears.

For the teenage Francis Lovell, the renewal of his family's connection with the de la Poles was crucial because it cemented his links with the inner circle of the Yorkist royal family. John de la Pole's marriage to Elizabeth Plantagenet had made him the brother-in-law of the king. Edward IV had two surviving brothers and three surviving sisters as his immediate family and after 1471 these became increasingly important to him. After the reliance on, and subsequent conflict with, Warwick during the first part of Edward's reign, Edward seems to have been determined not to repeat the same mistakes after 1471. Those, such as William Herbert and Humphrey Stafford, who had been greatly rewarded with confiscated Lancastrian estates had been crushed by Warwick at the battle of Edgecote. Others had died or retired into obscurity.[3] Edward would now retain rewards within his immediate family to the detriment of the broader political nation. Even sons of impeccably loyal Yorkists could no longer be sure of inheriting their father's position as William Herbert, the second Earl, found out to his cost.[4]

Brotherly rivals

Edward's face and patronage now looked upon those with whom he had a direct family connection. Consequently, rewards were extended almost solely towards those whom Edward saw as having a close blood or familial link to himself. No more is this made obvious than in the spring of 1473 when Francis Lovell's friend and erstwhile companion from Warwick's household, Richard, Duke of Gloucester, was encouraged to marry the Earl of Warwick's younger daughter, Anne Nevill. The marriage was a clear demonstration of Edward IV's policy of retaining major political rewards within the royal family. At the battle of Barnet in 1471, the Earl of Warwick, along with his brother, John, Marquis of Montague, had died. Whilst both brothers had died in arms against the king, neither was attainted subsequently as would have been customary for traitors. This enabled George, Duke of Clarence, whose change of side had been crucial in helping Edward IV retain his throne, to make a legal case to inherit the whole of the vast Nevill–Beauchamp inheritance including the two earldoms of Warwick and Salisbury. The claims of Ann Beauchamp, Countess of Warwick and widow of the 'kingmaker', were brushed aside and she was treated as though she were 'legally dead'. Initially, George, Duke of Clarence, claimed all in the right of his wife, the elder daughter, Isabel. This claim was aided by the rumoured disappearance of the younger daughter, Anne Nevill (born in 1455). A contemporary account stated that, to ensure that the inheritance would not be divided between the two sisters, Clarence kidnapped his sister-in-law and hid her in the kitchens of an inn near St Paul's in London. Richard, Duke of Gloucester, found her and whisked her away to sanctuary before marrying her sometime between 12 February and 18 March 1472. The marriage of two first cousins would normally have had to await an appropriate papal dispensation, but while the marriage took place without the blessing of the pope, it did so with the legal connivance of the king.

Richard's marriage caused a further deterioration in the relationship between the three brothers. Clarence felt, with some justification, that he had been forced to part with half of his wife's inheritance and regarded the partition as scarcely legal. He also insisted that the claim of his younger brother had no merit in law, as his sister-in-law, a minor, should have become his ward and due to her age could not legally wed Richard. Thus, Richard's claim to her property and to act on her behalf was also inadmissible. Clarence's sensibilities in this matter were not accorded a high priority by his brother Edward IV, who saw a means by which a politically inflam-matory inheritance could be neutralized and his conspicuously loyal younger brother rewarded at no cost to himself (always an important consideration for Edward), regardless of the somewhat dubious legal chicanery involved or his disparaging treat-ment of Anne, Countess of Warwick.[5] A special Act of Parliament conferred half of the kingmaker's inheritance on Richard, Duke of Gloucester. Francis Lovell now saw at first-hand how both the law and the rights of inheritance could be manipulated in the royal interest under Edward IV, the ultimate arbiter in determining the rightful descent of contentious inheritances.

It is hard to believe that it was a lesson that either he or Richard of Gloucester would forget.

The 'king's Great Enterprise'

As a ward of the Duke of Suffolk with connections to the Yorkist royal family, Francis Lovell would have been aware of the planning for the 'king's Great Enterprise', an invasion of France to renew the Hundred Years' War. From July 1472 preparations were put in place to create a diplomatic front against the French king, Louis XI. In July 1472, the king's brother-in-law, the Earl Rivers, was despatched on an embassy to Francis, Duke of Brittany, to negotiate his support for an English invasion of either Normandy or Gascony. By October 1472, Edward was able to appear before parliament to request assistance in punishing 'the misdeeds and machinations of Louis XI'.[6] He also began negotiations with England's most important ally, the com-bustible Charles the Bold, Duke of Burgundy, who, having twelve great lordships that straddled the border between France and the Holy Roman Empire, was a subject of both the king of France and the Holy Roman Emperor. The 'Grand Duke of the West' was sufficiently rich and powerful to follow an independent policy based solely on Burgundian interests. One of Burgundy's great interests was English wool for without a steady supply of English wool the looms of the Flemish cloth towns of Ghent, Ypres, Bruges and Lille would fall idle, leading to social unrest and a dramatic reduction in the richest source of Charles' revenues. Charles swallowed his personal antipathy towards Edward[7] to maintain the supply of English wool and retain his independence from his cousin and overlord Louis XI, whom he also cordially loathed.

By 1475, preparations were ready. Parliamentary taxation had allowed Edward IV to raise an army of at least 11,450[8] men-at-arms, archers and soldiers, the largest English force sent to France since Henry V's invasion in 1417, which had numbered about 10,000 combatants. The army was transported by shipping that had been hired or pressed from the whole of southern England, including the *Mary Redcliff* of Bristol, the *Margaret Howard* and the *Katherine Rivers*. The king was attended upon by all five dukes (Gloucester, Clarence, Suffolk, Buckingham and Norfolk), three out of the seven earls, and at least twelve barons who were eligible to serve. Very rarely had such a large percentage of the peerage followed their king overseas; all were present as the final muster took place at Portsmouth on 26 May 1475.

We can only speculate whether Francis Lovell was present at the muster, although it seems more than likely that he would have been since, at twenty, he was close to reaching his majority. Certainly, John, Duke of Suffolk was with the army and it is likely that Lovell would have been in his retinue, probably as a squire (a modern-day aide-de-camp). Undoubtedly, Lovell would have been trained for this role from an early age and would more than likely be looking forward to putting into practice all that he had learned at Middleham and Ravensworth. For any young noble, the campaign of 1475 offered the opportunity to establish a martial and chivalric reputation, taking the field against England's traditional enemy. The fact that there is no contemporary record of his presence is not really surprising – indeed, it would have been more remarkable if his guardians had not allowed him this opportunity to further his education in both a military and social setting.

The Duke of Suffolk's retinue was comprised of 130 men at arms and 400 archers. His force was generous in terms of men-at-arms, especially bearing in mind a proclamation of December 1474, which called for an abundant supply of archers and envisaged an army composed of nine-tenths archers. Suffolk's retinue consisting of 25 per cent men-at-arms perhaps reflects his status as a royal duke and the extent of his links with the gentry. It is also worth bearing in mind that a retinue drawn from East Anglia and the Thames Valley would have been drawn from the richest counties in the realm. Suffolk's retinue comprised roughly 6 per cent of Edward IV's army. This, by the best modern estimates, numbered 11,451.[9] Eleven peers raised 516 men-at-arms and 4,080 archers; the largest contingent was led by the Duke of Clarence, who brought 120 men-at-arms and 1,200 archers. The Duke of Suffolk, with much smaller landed resources, was able to match the number of men-at-arms that a royal duke could put into the field and also bring an appreciable number of archers. Suffolk's contingent was the fourth largest, exceeded only by the king's and the dukes of Clarence, Gloucester and Norfolk. The duke himself drew wages of £13.4d per day whilst on campaign.

Edward IV's invasion of France brought the English nobility together in a show of unity that had not been seen for thirty years; twenty-six out of a possible thirty-nine peers accompanied their king across the Channel. It is probable that the twenty-year-old Francis Lovell would have been amongst them, excited by thoughts of travel and chivalry and been aware of the currently fashionable works of classical heroes, such as *The Life of Jason*, soon to be printed by William Caxton.

On 4 July 1475, Edward disembarked at Calais. He had been delayed in London whilst attempting to borrow money from the city's financiers to fund an additional force of archers to reinforce his ally the Duke of Brittany and for his personal expenses. Edward was able to borrow £5,000 from the Medici bank and a further 1,000 marks (£736) from the former agent of the de Medici in London, Gerard Canizani. Lovell cannot realistically have been aware of these private financial dealings but, had he known, he would have been intrigued, if not angered, by this transaction. As of 30 July, Edward IV already owed Gerard Canizani 4,000 marks, for which payment was to be made from the lands of Alice, Lady Grey of Rotherfield, Francis Lovell's grandmother.[10] These estates, which should have descended to him at Easter 1474, were to remain in royal hands until not only the original debt, but any new borrowings by Edward, were fully repaid from these revenues. These financial manoeuvrings fully justified Edward's reputation for parsimony and demonstrated a haphazard legal attitude to the estates of those in his care. It must have been galling to the young Francis on the verge of his majority to find a significant part of his inheritance in the hands of others.

In August 1474, in alliance with the Duke of Burgundy, Edward IV demanded the restoration of Normandy and Gascony from the French king Louis XI. Louis, recognizing the seriousness of Edward's preparations, began to prepare for war. Louis was also aware that Edward and Charles, Duke of Burgundy, were in contact with a number of disaffected French nobles, such as his brother the Duke of Guyenne, who had yet to show their hands. The situation, as Edward saw it, required a joint effort against Louis, which would be in all their interests. However, Charles (called 'the Bold', 'the Terrible' or, more accurately in this instance, 'the Rash') was no longer in northern France when Edward landed at Calais. Since 30 July 1474, Charles had been besieging the insignificant town of Neuss on the Rhine, in the archbishopric of Cologne and had persisted with the siege throughout the winter. The small town stubbornly held out until Charles' financial resources and his army were exhausted. On 13 June 1475, with the town still not taken, Charles left his army and, with a small personal escort, rode to meet his ally Edward. Instead of the armies of the splendid 'grand Duke of the West' arriving in Artois, the sight that greeted Edward was only that of Charles and his personal attendants. Charles, said the contemporary chronicler, Commynes, was ashamed to let Edward see the state of his battered forces and his lack of preparedness for the forthcoming campaign.

This placed Edward in a particularly difficult position. Militarily, he recognized that his 'Great Enterprise' was now seriously compromised by Charles' decision not to participate with the full might of the Burgundian forces. To proceed against the king of France without substantial allies was to invite defeat, but the notion of returning home after two years of intense preparation without offering battle would be personally ignominious and politically very damaging. Equally, having collected so much in taxation from the public purse, the nation expected another Agincourt and would not easily forgive a king who retired without striking a blow. Edward advanced from Calais towards Peronne in the August sunshine, possibly hoping that the promised support from his other allies, the Duke of Brittany and the count of St Pol, would materialize. In this Edward was again to be disappointed: Brittany made no move against Louis XI, while the count of St Pol, breaking a promise to Edward, failed to allow the English access to his town of St Quentin. Even more galling for Edward was the fact that Charles, Duke of Burgundy, his principal ally and brother-in-law, lay in comfort in his nearby town of Peronne, refusing the English army access to any of the Somme towns in his possession or making any move to join Edward. As Edward made a desultory march south, bereft of allies and of ideas, Louis began to raise forces between Edward and his base at Calais and to strongly reinforce those towns ahead of him. On 12 August, Edward received the crushing news that Charles had left Peronne, not to join him but to invade distant Lorraine, leaving Edward in isolation. Almost immediately, realizing his cause was lost, Edward began surreptitious negotiations with Louis.

Louis, delighted to have separated his enemies, responded positively and preliminary negotiations began on 14 August. On 25 August, after the heralds had worked out the details, the English army was provided with large quantities of food, beer and wine (principally pasties and pastries). Soon the town of Amiens was full of inebriated English soldiers who happily drank at the French king's expense and continued to do so for the next three or four days. A few days later, the two kings met on a bridge over the Somme at Picquigny. In his memoirs, the writer and diplomat, Philippe de Commynes, who was an eye-witness to the scene, described it thus:

> The king of England … appeared a truly regal figure. With him was his brother, the Duke of Clarence, the Earl of Northumberland and several lords including his chamberlain lord Hastings.

Commynes goes on to say that Louis opened the conversation with: 'My lord, my cousin, you are very welcome. There's nobody in this world I would want to meet more than you.'

From this point onwards, both kings began to discuss peace and the evacuation of the English army from France. It is interesting to note that Richard of Gloucester was not present and all accounts state that he was not pleased with the notion of a peace settlement. It is perhaps a hollow speculation to wonder if Richard would have discussed his objections with Lovell and whether Lovell shared Gloucester's antipathy towards the king's policy. From Richard's reactions, it is quite clear that he regarded the treaty as a political and military sell-out rather than a diplomatic coup. This attitude would be in line with Richard's tendency to view the world in black and white and act accordingly, ignoring the subtleties, nuances and compromises that his brother brought to kingship. Whether the two young friends discussed the implications of Edward's amity towards the French cannot be known. What we do know is that Louis XI went to great lengths to persuade Richard to adopt a less intransigent position, and invited him to Amiens where Louis presented him with a collection of rich gifts, although Richard did not receive a pension from Louis, unlike Lord Hastings and other members of the nobility.

Edward IV's 'Great Enterprise' ended on 29 August with a treaty of friendship named after Picquigny. According to its key terms, Louis agreed to pay Edward 75,000 crowns to leave France immediately; any differences between the two monarchs were to be settled by four arbiters; and Louis' son, the dauphin Charles, was to marry Edward's daughter, Elizabeth of York, and to provide her with a jointure of 60,000 crowns; Louis was also to pay Edward 50,000 crowns (£10,000 at that time) annually at the city of London. This last clause allowed the English to leave with honour, able to claim that Edward had received tribute from Louis, who had recognized his superior claim to France. Commynes also records that Edward's leading councillors received cash gifts and pensions. These included Lord Howard, Sir Thomas Montgomery, Bishop Rotherham, John Morton, the Marquis of Dorset, Sir John Cheyne and Sir Thomas St Leger. Edward's chamberlain, Lord Hastings, received the large annual pension of £2,000, yet no mention is made of any pension being received by the dukes (Richard) of Gloucester and (John de la Pole) Suffolk. Whilst the majority of Edward's closest advisors appeared quite happy to accept the French king's largesse, it appears that Louis' blandishments were lost on them. (It is frequently said, with little evidence, that John de la Pole was a nonentity, yet a pension was paid to Edward's significantly less important brother-in-law, Sir Thomas St Ledger.)

The treaty signed, the English forces marched back to Calais with many of the rank and file no doubt disgruntled at being denied the opportunities of battle and plunder. This sense of anti-climax must have been felt most by the younger members of the expedition, who had been denied the opportunity to prove their valour and distinguish themselves on the field of battle. Veteran campaigners, such as Hastings, Gloucester and others, who had experienced the grim realities of battle at Tewkesbury and Barnet may have had more ambiguous feelings about the diplomatic ending to this campaign.

Lovell back in England

The experience of travel, being involved in the recruitment, training and deployment, not to mention the logistics and the command of large bodies of men, would have been instructive to the young Francis Lovell. His involvement in the campaign would have now completed his education as a nobleman, requiring as it did an ability to demonstrate military and knightly capability and also *gentilesse* and chivalry, including the elaborate courtesies that formed such a part of French and Burgundian court life. There is little doubt that he was a firm friend of Richard, but he also had strong links with the extended de la Pole family. Nothing is known of his relationship at this time with the future John, Earl of Lincoln, the elder de la Pole child (born 1461/1462), but it is inconceivable that, growing up in the same household, he did not have intimate and close links with him from childhood.

From the 1470s onwards, whilst Francis had been the ward of the Duke and Duchess of Suffolk, his estates had been under their stewardship. During this period, the principal residence of the Duke of Suffolk had been at Ewelme in Oxfordshire, and from here he had established a pre-eminence and connection that covered the whole Thames Valley. The core of the Lovell estates in Oxfordshire, Berkshire and Buckinghamshire had formed a part of that regional dominance and, as such, Lovell's servants, retainers and affinity had remained intact. The duke and duchess' position at court and their occupation of the Honour of Wallingford also ensured that there were no local challenges to their pre-eminence and thus no competition from any other noble family for the local loyalties that previous Lovells had enjoyed.

The Suffolks had been diligent protectors of Francis' lands and estates and, on 6 November 1477, Francis became Lord Lovell, possessor of the largest estate below that of an earl in England, one of the twelve richest peers in England and possessor of a wide inheritance stretching from Oxfordshire to Yorkshire and from Essex to Shropshire. Lovell now received a summons to Parliament indicating that his minority was over and he now had become a man of estate and, as such, able to play a role in the affairs of state.

4 'THE WHIRLING TIMES'

More trouble for the Yorkist brothers

IN NOVEMBER 1477, FRANCIS Lovell became Lord Lovell, Lord Holland, Baron Deincourt and Baron Grey of Rotherfield. These titles, along with their broad acres, bought Lovell a seat in the House of Lords. At this time, this exclusive group comprised two archbishops, eighteen bishops, twenty-four abbots and priors, three dukes, a marquis, seven earls and thirty barons; a grand total of eighty-three of the richest and most powerful of the lords spiritual and temporal.[1] In November 1477, the greatest of these lords had been summoned to attend parliament for the most shocking of reasons – the arrest and accusation of the king's brother, George, Duke of Clarence, on the charge of high treason. Since June 1477, Clarence had been held under arrest at the Tower of London, but had now been summoned to Westminster to answer these charges before his peers on 19 January 1478. This would have been the first political act of Francis' majority – joining with his fellow peers on the benches of St Stephen's chamber to sit in judgement, not only on one of their own, but on one of the greatest peers in the land.

After 1471, Clarence was the greatest peer in the realm; a man whose estates made him the richest of the king's subjects and whose closeness to the king ensured him a role on royal councils. He had been appointed Lord Lieutenant of Ireland and Great Chamberlain of England, as well as a host of other offices. However, after 1472, Edward ensured that the real work was done by trusted deputies and Clarence's role in these offices was essentially a formality. Whilst Clarence may have obtained his brother's forgiveness, Edward never really trusted him. Although Clarence's intervention had been crucial to Edward regaining his throne, Edward still looked askance at his brother and, despite appointing Clarence to high office, Edward ensured that he exercised very little real power. Despite the fact that contemporaries saw Clarence as someone intelligent and talented, he was never really allowed to exercise any independent authority. Edward's latent distrust of his brother was, in the main, justified and could be said to stem from the duke's behaviour during 1469–71.

Even so, Edward's lack of trust in his brother was nothing compared to the queen's hostility. It was said that 'Clarence vented his wrath more conspicuous by his bitter and public denunciation of Elizabeth's obscure family.'[2] In 1469, Clarence and the Earl of Warwick had openly questioned the legality of Edward and Elizabeth's marriage.

This and other slights sharpened the inert sense of social inferiority that lurked behind Elizabeth's regal façade. 'The queen concluded that her offspring by the king would never come to the throne unless the Duke of Clarence was removed; and of this she easily persuaded the king.' Elizabeth's dislike of the Duke of Clarence cloaked a core of real fear for herself, her children and her family. This fear surfaced in a number of ways: John Rouse, the Warwickshire historian, recorded 'a certain prophecy that after E., that is, after Edward IV, G. should reign.'[3] Clearly, Elizabeth Woodville, believing this prophecy, interpreted the 'G' as meaning George, Duke of Clarence, not recognizing that it could just as easily have stood for (Richard of) Gloucester.

Writing later to the Earl of Desmond in Ireland, Richard would lay the blame squarely on the queen's family, and specifically the queen herself, for procuring Clarence's death (in the same way, it is said she had been responsible for the death of Desmond's father in 1467). Whether Elizabeth Woodville plotted or planned for Clarence's death is a moot point. What can be said is that she and her family did little to dissuade her husband Edward IV from taking extreme action against his brother.

Clarence and his wife, Countess Isabel, already had two children, Margaret, Countess of Salisbury who was born at Farleigh Castle on 14 August 1473 and Edward, Earl of Warwick, born at Warwick Castle on 25 February 1475. Clarence's troubles began on 22 December 1476 when his wife died after giving birth to their second son. The Tewkesbury Chronicle attributed Isabel's death at twenty-five to complications arising from childbirth, which seems to be the most likely explanation since the infant died shortly after on 1 January 1477. Clarence, plunged into deep and genuine grief at the loss of both his wife and son, withdrew to Warwick castle. It was from there on 12 April 1477 that, unprovoked, he struck out viciously at his wife's former servants. Her lady-in-waiting, Ankarette Twynho, the daughter of a Wiltshire knight, was dragged from her father's home, brought to Warwick castle and accused of poisoning her mistress.[4] Another servant, John Thursby, was accused of poisoning the little boy, briefly named Richard. Both these unfortunates were brought to Warwick castle where, before a 'packed' jury that had been hand-picked by Clarence, they were convicted and summarily executed.

Worse was to follow for Clarence when, in a separate case, an Oxford astrologer, John Stacey, was accused of sorcery and in his testimony implicated one of Clarence's servants, Thomas Blake. Stacey, alongside Blake, was subsequently accused of using astrology to predict the death of the king and his eldest son. This treasonous act carried the death penalty because it endangered the cornerstone of God's hierarchy by necromancy with its association with witchcraft and the devil. The combination of astrology and necromancy sent a shiver down the collective spine of fifteenth-century society. On 19 May, Burdett, an Oxford cleric and an accomplice of John Stacey, was tried and convicted; the following day, he and Stacey were publicly hanged at Tyburn. Clarence should have had the wit to have left well alone but, in his unbalanced state, he intervened in the most public way possible. Accompanied by Dr William Goddard, a Franciscan friar, Clarence barged into a council meeting two days after the unfortunate conspiritors had been hung. Having read out Burdett and Stacey's declaration of innocence to the assembled councillors, both the duke and the friar then turned and left, leaving behind a somewhat stunned council. Edward IV was at Windsor at the time. When he returned to Westminster, he summoned Clarence to appear before him on 10 June 1477, when he accused Clarence of violating the laws of England and threatening the security of judges and jurors, and promptly imprisoned him in the Tower of London.

On 16 January 1478, Parliament assembled at Westminster with its chief and, indeed, only business being the trial of George, Duke of Clarence, with vague charges against him relating to 'conduct derogatory to the law of the realm and most dangerous to judges and juries throughout the kingdom'.[5]

Our best witness, the Crowland Chronicler, sets the scene, stating that out of fifty-eight peers who were eligible to attend the Parliament, at least thirty-four did (including Francis Lovell), alongside two archbishops and at least ten bishops. We are grateful to the chronicler for this information since that parliamentary roll of attendance is conveniently missing. Of those present:

> not a single person uttered a word against the duke, except the king; not one individual made answer to the king except the duke. Some parties were intro-duced, however, as to whom it was greatly doubted by many, whether they filled the office of accusers or witnesses.

This accords with the usual practice of medieval trials in which the accused had first to undergo the presentation of the Crown's case, for which the accused was allowed no representation or defence. The assembled peers would have been present to testify to the identity of the accused and to agree to the verdict, which would have been reached unanimously. Clarence's situation was even more precarious since the testi-mony of the king was regarded as record by the courts of common law and accepted as unimpeachable truth.

Of those we know to be present, at least six peers were Woodvilles or had Woodville wives and the other senior dukes, Gloucester and Suffolk, were the brother and brother-in-law (respectively) of the king himself. In these circum-stances, Clarence's conviction can be regarded as a foregone conclusion, as the Great Chronicle of London records:

> On the 18th February George, Duke of Clarence and brother to the king, who a certain time before had been held in the Tower as a prisoner, for considerations moving the king, [was] put secretly to death within the said Tower and, as the fame ran, drowned in a barrel of malmsey.[6]

Polydore Vergil hints at some external pressure on Edward when he says:

> but it is very likely the … king Edward right soon repented the deed … He was wont to cry in a rage 'o unfortunate brother, for whose life in this world [no

one] would once make request'; affirming in that manifestly, he was cast away by envy of the nobility.[7]

The method of Clarence's demise and the speculation on whether it was a Woodville-orchestrated plot have detracted from its true significance and its impact, not only on Francis Lovell, but on the whole of the Yorkist political nation.

Clarence's trial and subsequent execution in 1477 was the first act of self-immolation of the Yorkist monarchy of Edward IV, and it reverberated throughout the nobility with tragic consequences in 1483. In the first instance, the arrest and conviction of Clarence came as a bolt out of the blue. In 1477, no threat existed to Edward IV's throne: only two years before, he had led a united nobility in a campaign against France. Admittedly, the campaign had not exactly covered him in glory, but nor had it disgraced him. He had comprehensively defeated all his domestic enemies, who were now either dead on the fields of Barnet or Tewkesbury or seeking accommodation with new political realities. The only intransigents who remained irreconcilable were the earls of Oxford and Pembroke, one of whom was a prisoner in Guisnes castle and the other (along with his teenage nephew, Henry Tudor) a penniless exile in Brittany. Both at this time represented no more than an irritant to Edward IV. By all appearances, Clarence had been politically reconciled to his brother since 1472 and any resentment and antagonism had been kept in check. Indeed, Clarence's actions after the death of his wife and new-born son could be interpreted as an assault on *lese majeste,* but it is hard to see that these actions were anything more than those of a man whose mental state was disturbed by grief. Rather than interpreting Clarence's actions as a political threat, Edward should perhaps have seen them for what they were: the instinctive and irrational acts of a man in despair, looking for someone to blame for his tragic loss. George, Duke of Clarence's personal tragedy was magnified and distorted through the prism of Woodville enmity, with baleful consequences for the polity of England and particularly for the future Edward V.

A more authoritarian regime

The death of Clarence marks the transition of Edward IV from the 'Sonne of York' into a tyrant; from 1477 Edward's rule became more authoritarian and exclusively centred on the immediate royal family to the detriment of his relationships with the wider nobility. Those who had no familial links with the immediate royal family now found themselves increasingly excluded from both royal favour and royal bounty as those closest to the king monopolized both. An early example of this was when William Herbert, 2nd Earl of Pembroke was, upon the death of his wife, Mary Woodville, in November 1478, forced to exchange his father's lands and offices in Wales and his title of Earl of Pembroke for the new title of Earl of Huntingdon and an assortment of estates in Somerset and East Anglia, far from his previous area of influence. It has been said that Herbert was not the man that his father had been as if this justified his being deprived of an inheritance he had enjoyed for the previous seven years.[8] Herbert's lands, offices and estates were now merged with those of the principality of Wales and given over to Edward's heir, Edward, Prince of Wales. This began a pattern of alienation of the higher nobility under Edward IV as the crown increasingly interfered arbitrarily with the laws of inheritance. Henry Stafford, Duke of Buckingham, found himself excluded from the power and responsibilities that his lands, lineage and wealth should have afforded him, including almost all judicial offices apart from his role as a justice of the peace in Staffordshire. In 1476, Anne Mowbray, the heiress of the last Duke of Norfolk, had been married to the king's younger son, Richard, Duke of York (then aged three). However, she died in 1478 while both were still very young. Ignoring the claims of Lord Berkeley and the king's great servant, John, Lord Howard, the Mowbray inheritance remained with the young Richard, Duke of York, instead of descending to the legal heirs. The same disregard for legal niceties prevented the Earl of Westmorland from presenting his claim to the Holland inheritance of the dukes of Exeter, which was now earmarked for the enrichment of the family of the queen's first marriage, the Marquis of Dorset and Sir Richard Grey.[9]

Francis Lovell came of age as these convulsions erupted within the Yorkist monarchy and witnessed directly the origin of internecine strife that was to bedevil English politics for the next decade. The very first parliament in which Francis Lovell sat had been called solely for the purpose of eliminating not only a royal duke, but a close member of the royal family. This represented a new and harsher political climate in which men began to question both the rule of law and the sanctity of the royal house itself. It also called into question previously held loyalties that were now held at a premium. It is no wonder that the Crowland Chronicle came to look back wistfully on the 'triple chord' of the three brothers that had now been so violently ripped apart. Lovell's first public act had been to witness the 'chord' unravel from within as brother brought charges against brother. We must also remember that for Lovell these were not remote figures, but those amongst whom he had grown up since the age of ten or eleven, men whom he knew intimately and with whom he had close bonds. It also brought into sharp relief issues of friendship and loyalty as arbitrary royal decisions polarized the political nation.

Surely these events would have caused Lovell to develop at least an ambivalent attitude towards the queen and her kin? As someone who had been brought up in Warwick's household and, subsequently, the extended Yorkist family, he had little or no link with the Woodvilles, and his loyalties would have been with those members of the royal family who had been his boyhood companions. As an increasingly fractious political situation developed, Lovell, newly come of age, stood not only on the periphery of politics, but also as a witness to the deadly consequences of political miscalculation.

5 A MAN AND HIS ESTATE

A man of wealth and influence

AT THE END OF 1477, Francis Lovell reached his majority and came into his inheritance. Thus, he was able for the first time to enjoy full possession of his lands and income, and was now one of the most important peers in England. With an income of over £1,000 per annum, he was certainly the richest noble in England below the rank of earl. He possessed nearly 140 manors in twenty-two different counties, some of which were the most fertile in England. He was the heir of an old noble house that could count on long traditions of service and local loyalties, which had been built up over generations since the fourteenth century. His estate had been well cared for by the de la Poles during his minority and it had suffered very little degradation. (Certainly, no records exist of the sale of timber and other assets that drew criticism from many heirs when they came of age.) He enjoyed both the support and companionship of the extended Yorkist family and seems to have been equally well regarded by them. Whilst he had not yet begun to sire a family and a male heir yet eluded him, there was little doubt that time was on his side.

He and his wife were able to take their place as the new lord and lady of Minster Lovell and begin to play a role not only in the political life of the county, but also of the nation. It is probable that Francis and his wife took up residence at Minster Lovell in 1478 and that this fine modern mansion, a supreme example of early Renaissance English architecture, would now become his principal home. It is likely that Francis spent some of his teenage years in the vicinity of the Thames Valley under the wardship of the Duke of Suffolk at nearby Ewelme and, if so, he would have been a familiar figure in the area. It was, after all, an area where the Lovells had exercised leadership and authority for the previous eight generations. Indeed, it would have been Lovell's first role to revive that local leadership, which had either been in abeyance or else exercised by others since 1464. His importance as a principal landowner in the Thames Valley was recognized by his first public appointment as an adult on 8 May 1479, when he was appointed the Justice of the Peace for Oxfordshire. This was his sole appointment in such a role at this time, and quite clearly demonstrated his importance in a county in which he exerted considerable influence. As a justice of the peace, he would have sat in judgement on local disputes, dispensed justice in non-capital crimes and summoned and led commissions of Oyer and Terminer to

bring felons to justice and to ensure that justice was locally applied. He was one of
the senior peers for Oxfordshire to sit on the bench of justices and one whose residency in the county meant that he could exercise a large element of judicial power. It
also represented his political coming of age and a recognition that he was sufficiently
well-regarded both locally and nationally to exercise power and responsibility on
behalf of the Crown.

Thus, from 1477 onwards, Francis Lovell was resident in the south of England,
with strong geographical associations with the Thames Valley and East Anglia while
in the orbit of the de la Pole family. Whilst as part of his Deincourt inheritance
he inherited estates in the East Riding of Yorkshire, there is no evidence that he
favoured these estates any more, for instance, than he did his Shropshire estates, for
it was only in Oxfordshire that he began to make a judicial impact. Here his interests
seem to initially be focused, being reappointed to the Oxfordshire bench on 23 May
1480 as Lord Lovell, the highest ranking peer.

The two most vital tasks that any fifteenth-century noble faced was ensuring the
continuation of his noble line and the promotion and consolidation of his family's
local influence. With large estates, a prominent position and the friendship of the
extended royal family, it was incumbent upon Lovell to father an heir as quickly
as possible in order to cement all of these gains. Both he and his wife Anne were
young with no obvious impediments to producing an heir, a task Lovell should have
pursued with robust enthusiasm. Equally, he should, by all the political tenets of the
period have focused on re-establishing his family's pre-eminence in his own locality.
The Lovell interest, particularly in Oxfordshire, Berkshire and Northamptonshire,
should have now been fostered by the presence of an adult head of the family resident
in the area. Bonds of loyalty and allegiance would need to be re-formed and forged
anew, personnel recruited, estate offices filled, clientage established, and rewards
calibrated by the new lord of Minster Lovell and Titchmarsh. After being in the
hands of others since 1464, it was important that these connections be made and
strengthened on a personal level so that the men of the localities could get to know
their lord, and vice versa. In the fifteenth century, loyalty was very much a two-way
street: it was important that Lovell be around to dispense patronage and justice in a
parochial rural society.

These then were the primary responsibilities of a fifteenth-century peer, and
Lovell would need to achieve these by setting up strong links and leadership with the
local gentry and to offer himself as a conduit between the county and the Crown. As
a leading peer, it was important for Lovell to bring local concerns to the attention of
the monarch and to be able to intercede at the heart of the government on behalf of
local interests. What has previously been condemned as 'Bastard feudalism' was, in
reality, a flexible interaction of different and overlapping circles of government. For
a noble to have the cooperation of the local gentry, he had to be effective in bringing
their concerns to the attention of central government and in using his influence at
court to obtain a successful resolution. Equally, for a noble to have standing with the
king, it was essential to translate the royal will into action that would be undertaken

by the local gentry. In this way, the sinews of government extended into every village and hamlet in the country, establishing a viable system of law and order, trust and ensuring the collection of taxation and dues. It was the peer's obligation to foster that trust and loyalty to ensure that the system functioned; it also was fundamental in obtaining men's loyalties in the formulation of a noble retinue and affinity.

It would have been expected that Lovell would be appointed to the bench in those surrounding counties where he had comparable estates, such as Berkshire and Northamptonshire. The importance of this structure and the duty performed by the peer in the body politic of the realm cannot be exaggerated. However, he turned his back on these duties just as his feet were on the first rung of the ladder, choosing instead to answer the call of his friend, Richard of Gloucester, and this perhaps tells us much about the man. His flouting of the obvious and conventional course of action in pursuing 'good lordship' is perhaps especially surprising as he had been estranged from his patrimony for the last fourteen years, living in the households of other nobles, with his livelihood being collected for their benefit, not his, and even his residency being dictated by others. It would have been all too natural then for Lovell to wish to settle down with his young wife on his own property and to enjoy what was his, at last. Instead, he decided to travel four hundred miles north to the turbulent Scottish borders.

Lovell and the campaign in the north of England

Barely three years after gaining his majority and re-establishing his family in its traditional heartland, Lovell once again headed north. The year 1481 marks a new turning point in his career and for the first time we can see the choices that were his to make as an adult and which, ultimately, would influence the rest of his life. In that year, Lovell made a conscious decision to take up arms under the command of his friend, Richard, Duke of Gloucester, and to engage with Gloucester voluntarily as one of his adherents.

It is interesting that Lovell's activities on the border predate the formation of the royal armies by a year and he was clearly not acting on the king's command, for Lovell was fighting on the border with the northern levies of the Duke of Gloucester and the Earl of Northumberland. If Lovell had no real territorial interest in the border (which he did not), nor any obligation to defend it by right of office, it begs the question: what was he doing there?

The clear answer to this is that most elusive of historical evidence – personal friendship for its own sake. In a move that would have fateful consequences, in 1481 Lovell chose to travel the length of the country to stand alongside Richard, Duke of Gloucester, and to take up a command motivated, one would believe, solely by friendship and loyalty. Able to make his own choices, Lovell now made one of the most significant and fateful of his life, deciding that friendship with Gloucester outweighed local duty and obligation.

Since October 1474, relations between England and Scotland had been cordial and the border had been peaceful. Indeed, in 1478 the Scottish king James III, a man of pacific temperament,[1] had offered his sister Margaret as a bride for the recently widowed Anthony, Earl Rivers (whose own wife Elizabeth de Scales had died five years earlier). Edward IV accepted the proposal and the wedding was planned to take place at Nottingham in October 1479. Between December 1478 and the proposed date of the wedding, relations between the two countries were transformed. Responding to the blandishments of the French king, Louis XI,[2] the Scots breathed new life into 'the auld alliance'. James III and his council now began to condone serious breaches of the truce, as border reivers undertook raids and the pillaging of cattle on the English side of the border. If reparations were not made, Edward IV promised to 'make rigorous and cruel war on Scotland'. To back up his threats, on 12 May 1480 Edward appointed his brother, Richard of Gloucester, Lieutenant General over the northern counties, with authority to call out the levies of Cumberland, Northumberland and Westmorland. The Scottish response to this was the burning of Bamburgh, twenty miles inside the English border, by the Earl of Angus, forcing Gloucester and the Earl of Northumberland to mobilize their own retainers in response. In November 1480, Edward resolved at a council meeting to go north and lead the English army at the start of the campaigning season the following year. Come the start of the campaigning season in the spring of 1481, Edward was joined by Earl Rivers, who promised a force of 3,000 men, the Marquis of Dorset, who promised 600 men, and Lord Stanley, who promised 3,000 Lancashire archers.[3] Edward also raised £24,000 by taxation for the campaign. Yet for all of his preparations, Edward, together with Earl Rivers and Lord Hastings, remained at the royal hunting lodge at Woodstock in Oxfordshire, and did not arrive in Nottingham until October that year. This left the defence of the border to the northern magnates, who had been led during the summer by the Duke of Gloucester. In the north, the impact of the Scottish raids, including the destruction of crops and cattle rustling, were magnified by the effects of a bad harvest. Communities in the north commented that Edward preferred the bed to the battlefield and the banqueting table to the tent. For whatever reason, the campaigning season of 1481 was squandered to little or no effect.

Edward's seemingly irresolute response to war with Scotland was perhaps understandable since he needed to keep one eye on continental affairs and the actions of Louis XI while trying to gauge where the true danger lay. This all changed in April 1482 when James III's brother Alexander, Duke of Albany, arrived at Edward's court; Alexander was an habitual plotter and a professional malcontent who has been referred to as 'Clarence in a kilt'. On 11 June 1482, a treaty was drawn up by which Edward promised to promote Alexander's claim to the throne of Scotland and Alexander, in turn, promised to restore to the English the town of Berwick-on-Tweed, which had been ceded to the Scots by Margaret of Anjou in 1460. In a major policy change, on 12 June 1482 Richard of Gloucester's commission as lieutenant general of the borders was renewed and the command of all operations against the Scots now passed into his hands. By 18 June, Richard and Alexander had recruited an army of 20,000 men. The principal commanders of the various additional divisions were the Earl of Northumberland, the Marquis of Dorset, Lord Stanley and Sir Edward Woodville commanding the cavalry and horse. These joined men, including Lovell, who had been on the border with Richard since 1481.

Prior to the start of the campaign, Richard dubbed five knights, all young lords who had long associations with the Nevill affinity and with the defence of the Marches towards Scotland: Scrope of Masham; Lumley; Greystoke; Fitzhugh; and Francis, Lord Lovell. Scrope was an important landholder in Richmondshire and the North Riding of Yorkshire. Greystoke was a Cumberland magnate whose chief residence of Greystoke castle was in the North Riding (now the site of Castle Howard). Likewise, Lumley's lands lay in Durham and the North Riding, as did Fitzhugh's (who was also Francis' brother-in-law). That these young lords should be knighted prior to a campaign against the Scots is unremarkable. All would have known each other and had close links that would have been forged by common upbringing and experiences. Their association with Richard of Gloucester would have been a natural continuation of their families' links with the Nevills going back several generations. Lovell's position was somewhat different: he has often been portrayed as a northerner by association, which would put him naturally at the border with Richard in 1481, but in fact, nothing could be further from the truth.

A romantic notion might suggest that at twenty-five Francis Lovell was overcome by youthful dreams of glory and consumed by a wish to establish his knightly and chivalric credentials on the field of battle. This is unlikely. From the earliest part of his life in Warwick's household, he would have grown up with northerners and borderers who would have had no illusions about the true nature of border warfare. These were men accustomed to the grim realities of raid and counter-raid, and it is hard to see Lovell's father-in-law, Lord Fitzhugh, as anything other than a pragmatic professional and risk-averse soldier. The Scottish border, with its recurrent conflict and bloody reprisals, offered no romance except for the poets who flourished on both sides producing poems or ballads celebrating individuals and events (a supreme example of such literature is the poem *Otterburn Chase*). For those who had to fight, it was dangerous and offered little opportunity to carve a chivalric reputation. Far too often the practicalities of warfare in this bleak area had undone rather than enhanced the reputations of those who sought to command it. Although it could be said that Lovell was not in financial need, neither could the prospect of border warfare be seen to offer anything in the way of plunder or riches. Indeed, two centuries of warfare had left it a forbidding and desolate wasteland, particularly on the Scottish side. In fact, as far as Lovell was concerned, it was likely that the campaign would cost him more than he could ever recoup from the rewards of the campaign.

It is, therefore, improbable that Lovell went north in search of glory or financial gain in the spring of 1481; nor could it have been with any thought of advancement. While it would have been entirely natural for a young man to wish to gain a name for himself and to advance his position in the realm, fighting on the Scottish border was not the way to do it. In 1481, it was already common knowledge that Edward IV was about to lead a campaign against the Scots. If Lovell had been solely seeking advancement and a name for himself, it would have been far easier to have done so under the eye of the king. Lovell himself could have recruited in his own locality and brought his men to join the king's army, especially as the king had to pass through Oxfordshire on his way to Woodstock by September 1481.[4] For Lovell, this would have been a far easier route to prominence: to place himself and his retinue under the command of the king himself or his two senior household commanders, Earl Rivers or Lord Hastings. However, by the time the king was enjoying the thrill of the chase at Woodstock, Lovell was already on the Scottish border.

It is quite possible that the thirst for action common in the young affected Lovell's decision. But it is more likely that he was tempted by the opportunity to undertake a campaign against the traditional enemy, the Scots, under the command of his friend Richard, Duke of Gloucester. Richard's friendship was clearly more important to Lovell than advancement under the eye of the king or the king's more experienced royal commanders. By the autumn of 1481, Lovell had become Francis, Lord Lovell, knight and a commander on the Marches toward Scotland.

Here intermittent warfare took place throughout the autumn of 1481, but Edward's lethargic progress meant that another campaigning season was lost and Edward himself travelled no further north than Nottingham. Although the Marquis of Dorset and Sir Edward Woodville joined them, it was essentially a northern army led by the Earl of Northumberland and Lord Stanley (both acting as Richard's lieutenants) that laid siege to Berwick-upon-Tweed that autumn.[5] After retiring to winter quarters in the spring of 1482, Richard travelled south to the family seat of Fotheringhay castle to meet with Edward IV and the Scottish pretender, Alexander, Duke of Albany. A new treaty of alliance was signed on 3 June, with the English promising to support Alexander's claim to the Scottish throne and he, in turn, making a number of concessions to Edward IV. By July, a force of probably 20,000 men lay encamped outside the town of Berwick-upon-Tweed, which, despairing of relief, opened its gates to the English, who have held it ever since. Although the castle still held out, this was closely guarded by English troops and the rest of the army moved north.

This perilous situation for the Scots was made worse by internal dissension and the factional politics of the Scottish nobility. James III had ruled Scotland since he was a child and was widely unpopular: the nobility resented his promotion of a sequence of 'familiars' from the gentry class, thus excluding nobles from advancement; he was also seen to have 'unkingly' interests, preferring music to warfare and sought a closer alliance with the traditional enemy, England. Pushed against his will by Louis XI of France into conflict against Edward IV, the campaign gave an outlet to aristocratic grievances. As the English advanced northwards through the Merse into Lothian, and as more and more aristocratic estates were burned and despoiled, the patience of the nobility snapped and the Scottish king was seized whilst crossing Lauder Bridge on 22 July. Many of James' 'familiars' and courtiers had crude nooses placed around their necks and were hung from the bridge itself, whilst James was taken back to Edinburgh under close arrest and there imprisoned in his own castle. Unable to face the English army in the field, the Scots forces now abandoned the capital, Edinburgh, in some disarray. In a lesson that should have been remembered by subsequent politicians, politics now contrived to deprive Richard, Duke of Gloucester, and the English of the rewards that their army had won for them. Stepping into the political vacuum left by the retreating Scottish lords, Alexander, Duke of Albany, accepted the commission as lieutenant general of the kingdom, thereby quashing any chance of him becoming an English puppet king (supposedly, the point of the whole campaign). That this had been unexpected can be seen in a letter that Francis Lovell wrote, while actively recruiting and writing on behalf of Edward IV and Richard. On 22 June, Francis wrote to his neighbour, Sir William Stonor of Oxfordshire:

> ... it is said in the country the king proposes to send northwards my Lorde of Gloucestre, and my brother Parr and such other folke of worship as hath any rule in the said north parties, trusting we shall have warr of the Scottes.[6]

Alexander's *volte-face* in abandoning his English allies left the English in a quandary, as a letter from Edward IV to Pope Sixtus IV stated:

> The army which our brother lately led into Scotland, traversing the heart of that kingdom without hinderance arrived at the royal city of Edinburgh and found the king with the other chief lords of the kingdom shut up in a most strongly fortified castle.[7]

Richard could have sacked and burnt Edinburgh to the ground, but this would have been counter-productive and rather pointless as the purpose of the expedition had been to eliminate the threat from the north that an aggressive Scotland represented. James III, against his better judgement, had broken the truce to harass Edward IV's northern frontier and by doing so had diverted English resources away from offering support to the Burgundian rulers, Charles the Bold's daughter Mary and her husband, the Archduke Maximillian. The point of the expedition had been to install a compliant Alexander, who would agree to English demands and pacify the border, and this should be borne in mind when judging the outcome of the expedition of 1482.

Richard needed someone to negotiate with because, despite appearances, he would soon be in a parlous situation as July turned into August and the campaigning season in the north began to shorten. He was 120 miles away from his principal base at Newcastle-upon-Tyne and both food supplies and money were beginning to run short. Military logic dictated that a settlement had to be reached and as much advantage wrung out of the Scots before his resources became so depleted that Richard would be unable to evacuate the city and the kingdom whilst still maintaining discipline and supplying his forces. Taking Alexander at his word, Richard accepted his assurances that he would abide by the terms of the Treaty of Fotheringhay, which was also backed up by guarantees from the citizens of Edinburgh. By 11 August, the English army had returned to Berwick. Crossing the frontier, the army was disbanded save for 1,100 men left to invest the castle of Berwick, which, now having no hope of relief from a non-existent Scottish government, surrendered on 24 August. Despite the perceived successes, the Scottish campaign of 1482 was criticized by government insiders, such as the Crowland Chronicle, which stated:

> Thus, having got as far as Edinburgh with the whole army without meeting resistance, [Richard] let that very wealthy town escape unharmed and returned through Berwick … this trifling gain, or perhaps more accurately loss, for the maintenance of Berwick costs 10,000 marks a year, diminished the resources of the king and kingdom by more than £10,000 at the time. King Edward was grieved at the frivolous expenditure of so much money, although the recapture of Berwick alleviated his grief for a time. This is what the duke accomplished in Scotland during the summer of 1482 …[8]

Here perhaps is the authentic voice of the civil servant looking at the cost of the expedition and what he saw as small tangible rewards. In reality, the threat from the northern border had been eliminated, a friendly English client had been installed north of the border, and one of Scotland's major towns had been recovered for England, making the border much more defensible.

This period is rather overlooked by historians viewing Lovell's life and his subsequent career, content to refer to it as evidence of him as an honorary northerner. Yet it is crucial for understanding what happened later. Lovell was present in the north from at least June 1480 until September 1482 – a period of some twenty-seven months – during which time he was able to gain valuable experience as a military commander and leader of men; he would also have gained some familiarity with the logistics and the requirements of maintaining large bodies of men in the field in a hostile environment. We are unaware of the specifics of his involvement as no record remains detailing the army's various divisions. We can deduce that he must have been a man of considerable abilities to have been made a commissioner of array at the age of twenty-five in an area of which he had had little experience since childhood. For this he must have been able to demonstrate a certain aptitude for command other than just the privileges of birth, plus an ability to provide more than a modicum of leadership, especially in a region where he was a relative stranger and which was notorious for its clannishness. If Lovell did not have the prerequisite military and leadership skills, it would have been difficult for him to have led hard-bitten northerners, inured to border fighting, against their traditional enemy. The evidence points to the fact that not only did Francis do this, but that he was successful in this role. His knighting by Richard of Gloucester is testament to his capabilities – all the more when one considers that others in whose company he was knighted were all northern barons with old Nevill connections. At no point is it suggested that Lovell was viewed as an interloper or as being unworthy of the honour.

Lovell's stint in the north would have provided him with a period of personal development for, between 1477 and 1480, he had come into a man's estate, been appointed a parliamentary peer of the realm, and emerged from the shadow of youth and wardship. Yet it is in the period 1480 to 1482 and whilst on campaign on the northern border that he matured and came of age, putting into practice the martial skills he had learnt as a youth, and acquiring the realities of command and leadership in the field. He would also have learned to foster and maintain loyalty, how to deploy men and how to sustain them during a campaign.

When, after the conclusion of the Scottish campaign, he headed south to his Lovell estates, he could reflect on two and a half years in which he had grown as a man and learned to endure hardships and to experience danger from skirmishes and battle. He would also have gained an insight into the relationships and pitfalls of high politics and had been witness not only to campaign decisions but also to the political convolutions that affected the future course of the relationship between England and Scotland. In the autumn of 1482, Lovell, along with all the peers of the realm, received a personal summons from Edward IV to attend a parliament at Westminster.

Trusted by Edward IV

The parliament of November 1482 was summoned by Edward in direct response to a potentially disastrous rapprochement between his two continental neighbours, France and what remained of the duchy of Burgundy. The two former enemies, Louis XI of France and Archduke Maximillian of Burgundy, had agreed a truce in October 1482, with peace terms finally being agreed on 23 December at the Treaty of Arras. The terms of the treaty solely applied to France and Burgundy and excluded Maximillian's allies, Edward IV and Francis II, Duke of Brittany, who now found themselves ignored by the principal protagonists. This enraged Edward who, according to Commynes, 'thought of nothing else but taking vengeance'. The terms dashed Edward's plans for the cherished marriage of his daughter, Elizabeth of York, to the French dauphin, Charles. It also encompassed the loss of Edward's French pension or tribute, which was no longer paid after September 1482. The treaty also endangered the remaining English continental possession of Calais, which, by the provisions of the treaty, was now surrounded by the French county of Artois, now being Burgundian territory no longer. Parliament was summoned to provide funding for a return to an aggressive foreign policy by Edward towards his continental neighbours. This new belligerence on Edward's part was immediately backed up with a promise to his ally, Francis of Brittany, of 4,000 English archers, who were to serve at England's expense for three months.

Edward's determination to maintain the pressure on France also resulted in the resumption of an aggressive policy against Scotland, doubtless much to the satisfaction of his brother Richard. A new agreement was reached with Alexander, Duke of Albany, to make a bid for the Scottish throne, supported by Richard and the Earl of Northumberland. Northumberland was already on the border charged with the recruitment of 3,000 English archers who were then to be placed under the command of Albany for six weeks at Edward's expense. These proposals were ratified by Parliament in February 1483 and Edward, in an unprecedented act of generosity towards his brother, made over to Richard the counties of Cumberland and Westmorland into a hereditary palatine[9] along with the wardenship of the West March. This involved the surrender of all royal estates in these counties (not a great deal) which, alongside the lordship of Penrith, were to form the core of Richard's newly acquired power in the area. In addition, Parliament gave Richard control over any land that he conquered from the Scots in this and any subsequent campaigns. The creation of the palatinate was an extremely rare occurrence and a remarkable sign of royal confidence and favour. The only previous comparable royal grant had been the creation of the palatinate of Lancaster by Edward III for his son, John of Gaunt, over a century earlier.

The Parliament of 1482/3 was also personally significant for Francis Lovell for, on 6 January 1483, Francis, Lord Lovell, became Francis, Viscount Lovell, only the third man in England to hold that title. The significance of this promotion has been largely overlooked by historians, who have contented themselves with the notion that it was gained inevitably as a result of his friendship with Richard. In fact, Lovell's elevation is almost unique in the second reign of Edward IV, when noble promotion or creation outside the immediate royal family was practically non-existent. Edward had learned from his previous profligacy in distributing titles and lands during his first reign and was now much more circumspect in granting rewards, particularly in the period after 1471. In fact, if Edward had a policy towards the nobility, it tended towards degradation rather than promotion, with George, Duke of Bedford, being stripped of his dignity completely and William Herbert being forced to swap his dignity of Earl of Pembroke for the lesser dignity of Earl of Huntingdon. This seemingly like-for-like swap was, in reality, an acute degradation in both power and status, particularly in Herbert's family home country of Wales. Even trusted servants such as John, Lord Howard, were denied legitimate claims to a share of the duchy of Norfolk and the earldom of Nottingham. It is true that William, Lord Berkeley, had been elevated to the rank of viscount in 1481, but this had, in fact, been a bribe for Berkeley no longer pursuing his claim for a share of the Norfolk inheritance. Only those within the immediate royal family, such as Edward's two sons, had obtained any patent of nobility post-1471. In fact, Edward's only other promotion outside of the royal family had been to appoint to the earldom of Winchester Louis Gruthuyse, the Burgundian governor of Bruges, who had offered Edward refuge in 1470/71. Typically of Edward, this elevation was long on dignity but short on resources as Edward failed to grant Gruthyse any English lands to accompany the title.

The promotion of Francis Lovell was a reward that demonstrated a closeness with the Yorkist royal family and would also suggest that Edward saw in him both capability and loyalty. There is no direct evidence regarding his actions in the Scottish campaign, but he was the only person involved in it to be so conspicuously rewarded. This is all the more remarkable when compared with those who were knighted with him. No such rewards were offered to Greystoke, Lumley, Scrope or Parr. Only Lovell and Richard of Gloucester received any recognition from Edward IV.

It is possible that Lovell's promotion was a deliberate revival of the title held by his grandfather, John, Viscount Beaumont, who had been the very first viscount in England. Killed at the battle of Northampton in 1460, Beaumont's line was attainted, his title had fallen into abeyance, and the Beaumont estates had been vested in William, Lord Hastings. Beaumont's son, also called John, had been pardoned in 1475, yet no attempt was made to restore to him his father's estates and title. So, the resurrection of Beaumont's title as viscount and the awarding of it to his grandson Francis, bypassing the original heir, can be seen as rendering John Beaumont's hopes and expectations of restoration more and more remote.

Lovell's promotion by the king implies not only that Edward trusted him completely, but also that Edward saw him as an important component of the Yorkist establishment. As parliament dispersed, at the end of February 1483, Lovell, now a viscount, could look forward to a future with confidence, his services recognized, his position and rank enhanced and ready to shoulder further responsibilities.

6 THE TURNING POINT

The death of Edward IV

IF FRANCIS LOVELL HAD any plans in the spring of 1483, they probably included a return to the north for the new campaigning season and to take part in the planned attack on Scotland. This had been agreed by Parliament, and Richard, Duke of Gloucester, had already gone north to supervise preparations. Although we have no record of where Lovell was in March 1483, it can be assumed that he was on his estates tending to domestic matters since no contemporary source records his presence either in the north or at court. His attendance to everyday local matters of estate management, the signing off of accounts, participation in the chase and other winter amusements would have come to a sudden halt soon after 9 April 1483.

Sometime during Easter 1483 (28–30 March), Edward IV fell ill. Contemporary sources, such as the Italian chronicler Dominic Mancini, state that the king caught a cold on a fishing trip on the Thames with his courtiers. His condition worsened and was not helped by his excessive physical appetites for 'in food and drink … [Edward] was most immoderate: it was his habit, so I have learnt, to take an emetic for the delight of gorging his stomach once more'.[1] This excess brought on a 'quaterre' fever, which had laid Edward very low by 6 April (when his death was reported prematurely at York); the fever led to an attack of apoplexy (or a stroke). On Tuesday 8 April, Edward attempted to reconcile the rancorous feuds among his courtiers, most notably those between the Marquis of Dorset and Lord Hastings, both of whom had competed for the affections of Edward IV's mistress, Jane Shore. After an illness that lasted ten days, Edward died at Westminster on 9 April, three weeks short of his forty-first birthday. Edward's death at such a young age shocked the political nation, for he had been the dominant figure in English politics since 1461, a strong and vigorous monarch who had demonstrated his capacity to rule in the council chamber and on the battlefield. If not always successful in all his aims, Edward had seen off all his rivals and brought much needed stability to English politics since 1471. As a king, he had enthusiastically undertaken his duty to provide for the succession and had two young sons ready to succeed him. The eldest, also called Edward, was just twelve, having been born on 2 November 1470. Appointed Prince of Wales, he resided at the great Mortimer castle of Ludlow in the Welsh Marches under the watchful eye of the queen's cultured and well-travelled brother

Anthony, Lord Rivers. Too young to rule, Edward was to be helped by his trusted uncle, Richard, Duke of Gloucester, who was appointed Lord Protector in Edward IV's will. With the key players away from London, the king's funeral proceeded as he would have wished. On 18 April, the funeral bier left Westminster Abbey for Windsor via Charing Cross, Syon Abbey and Eltham until it reached Windsor two days later. At Windsor, with much solemnity, the great officers of state broke and threw their white staves of office into the grave as the heralds took off their tabards and did likewise. On being given new coats, the heralds then pronounced the immortality of the monarchy, if not the monarch, and with the cry 'Le Roy est vie, Le Roy est vie', the new reign had begun. Edward IV's funeral was a truly grand affair, conducted with as much panoply and splendour as could have been expected and costing the stupendous amount of £1,496 17s 2d.

Between 23 and 26 April, the significant individuals in the new reign began to head towards London, where a royal council consisting of the queen, the Marquis of Dorset and William, Lord Hastings, remained in place awaiting the new monarch and the putative Lord Protector. The matter of the Lord Protector and his role was a matter of some controversy for whilst Richard, Duke of Gloucester, had been designated Lord Protector of the Realm in the will of Edward IV, this would have little validity after the coronation of the new young king when such a role would be replaced by a new council and, following the precedent of Henry VI sixty years earlier, a council of regency appointed on behalf of the new monarch. This would come into effect on 4 May, the day already designated for the new king's coronation. The new council, formed at royal discretion, would, it was feared, be dominated by the queen's Woodville relatives. The Marquis of Dorset, with an astonishing lack of self-awareness or political sense, crystallized the fears of other members of the council when he was heard to say: 'we are so important that, even without the king's uncle we can make and enforce these decisions.'[2] The hubris of the queen's family was soon to be punctured by events that took place on the great north road at Stony Stratford.

Coup d'etat

The king's uncle, Richard, Duke of Gloucester – so recklessly disregarded by the Marquis of Dorset – was heading south towards London accompanied by his north-ern retinue, whilst the next most powerful noble in the kingdom, Henry Stafford, Duke of Buckingham, (whose whereabouts prior to the end of April are a mystery) moved to meet him. Gloucester and Buckingham both reached Stony Stratford in Northamptonshire on 29 April and from here invited the Earl Rivers, Sir Richard Grey, the king's half-brother, and Thomas Vaughan, who had reached Northampton, to join them at an inn nearby. After a convivial evening in which the new king's party were greeted by 'cheerful and joyous countenance', at dawn on 1 May, Rivers, Grey and Vaughan were arrested and escorted in captivity to Pontefract Castle.[3] Richard and Buckingham then rode to Stony Stratford and there took control of the young king's now leaderless party. On confronting Edward V, they condemned both the officers appointed to his household and the Woodville advisors, whom they blamed for Edward IV's early demise. The young Edward V defended his councillors vigorously, saying that they had been appointed by his father 'in his prudence he had every confidence' and he had seen nothing evil in them and wished to keep them unless they proved to be evil. Also, Edward believed that those appointed for him had the queen, his mother's full support. At this, Buckingham snapped back that 'if he cherished any confidence in her he had better relinquish it'. This was the first recorded intervention by Buckingham and tellingly it was against the queen and her family. It was said that Buckingham loathed her and her kin, having been forced to marry Katherine Woodville, a marriage he believed beneath him. With the arrest and incarceration of the king's household that had overseen his upbringing, Richard's first *coup d'etat* had taken place.

As a justification for his actions, Richard swore to his nephew, the king, that:

> ... [Richard] was only taking precautions to safeguard his own person because he knew for certain that there were men close to the king who had sworn to destroy his honour and his life.[4]

Richard also sent a letter of justification to the council and corporation of London that he had:

> not confined his nephew the king of England, rather he had rescued him and his realm from perdition.[5]

This is the first time that the strident morality and shrill hectoring that was to become such a hallmark of Richard III's reign was to be used; the emphasis of moral degeneracy on the part of the queen and her family and the threat they posed to the peace of the realm were to be recurring themes. The queen and the Marquis of Dorset, on hearing of Richards actions, began to try to raise forces with which to rescue the young king Edward. In this, they hoped to play the legitimist hand and build on the reaction of those in London, who viewed the actions of Richard and Buckingham with shock and horror. However, those members of the political nation who were in London or had recently arrived were unmoved by the queen and Dorset's appeal for support. Whilst not fully condoning the actions of Richard and Buckingham, they saw these as a move against the Woodville family rather than against the young king. Richard, of noble birth, was seen as preferable to the king's Woodville commoner relatives, representing as he did the old blood of England, untainted by the charges of avarice and self-promotion levelled at the queen and her kin. The queen and Dorset's attempts to mobilize support for their family also backfired; their actions simply provided credence to Richard's charges that it was *they* who were plotting against *him*. Abandoned by all, the queen sought sanctuary with her younger son, Richard, Duke of York, at Westminster, whilst Dorset fled. The only Woodville who could now harm Richard and Buckingham was Sir Richard Woodville who, having robbed the treasury, had taken the money to a fleet that now languished rather aimlessly off the east coast and the English Channel. Richard's audacious grab for power had been a complete success: his opponents had been rapidly discredited as self-interested parvenus whose presence around Edward IV had corrupted both the king and the body politic. This justification had been accepted on the whole by the nobility of the realm who, as a body in council, appointed Richard, Duke of Gloucester, as Lord Protector on 8 May 1483.

Richard's assumption of power took the nation by surprise. All sources are consistent in relating this. Also, almost all contemporary sources indicate that his actions at this time were directed against the queen and her Woodville family. If Richard posed any threat to the new king and the succession, this was not discerned, or at least recorded, by anyone at this time. Richard had acted only in concert with the Duke of Buckingham, and so his actions could be interpreted as being not self-interested but the actions of one concerned for the common good of the realm. There is no evidence that Richard brought anyone other than Buckingham into his confidence prior to April 30, and no evidence exists that Richard sought to build up a party of support amongst the nobility prior to his *coup d'etat*. In fact, all the evidence points to him acting as a supremely loyal family member who, having ensured the loyalty of the nobility of the north, moved south with only a conventional retinue that aroused neither fear or suspicion. This had worked to his advantage, lulling Rivers and his party into a false sense of security from which they never awoke. By the time they were aware of Richard's intentions, it was too late and the leadership of the Woodville faction outside London had effectively been decapitated. On 10 May, a new council was constituted in accordance with the precedent that confirmed Richard, Duke of Gloucester, as Lord Protector. The council summoned a parliament for 25 June, and set the date of 22 June for the coronation of Edward V. In the interim, the young king was to be transferred to the royal palace of the Tower of London. He was taken there sometime between 9 and 19 May.

We have no record of Francis Lovell's movements during April and May 1483 and no contemporary source records that he undertook any action in conjunction with Richard. It should be noted that although the original *coup d'etat* at Stony Stratford took place near Lovell's manor of Titchmarsh and in a county where he held a large landed interest, there is no evidence of Lovell's involvement in this. As Richard's friend, he might have been made aware of what Richard was planning at the end of April 1483, and be complicit in Richard's actions. But this is unlikely. Firstly, the timeline is so tight that it would have afforded Richard little, if any, opportunity to gauge the opinion of others – even those of his closest friends – prior to his actions on 30 April. Barely a week had elapsed between Richard's departure from York and the coup itself. Secondly, it would have been counter-productive to have broadened the plot by involving too many others in his plans since this could have diluted the surprise and compromised its security. Thirdly, having determined on the plan, broader-based support would have been irrelevant at this stage; once Richard had ensured the support of Buckingham, the second greatest magnate in the realm, the participation of others would have been irrelevant and unnecessary given that the destruction of the Woodville leadership and the isolation of their adherents who accompanied Edward V from Ludlow had required remarkably few men in the end. Shorn of leadership and direction, they naturally responded to instruction from the king's uncle and their social superiors.

Richard, however, did require support in London after 8 May, now as legitimate Lord Protector. It was after this date that Lovell moves into view. It is probable that he and other members of the nobility would have gathered in London prior to 30 April in preparation for the coronation originally planned for 4 May. On 18 February 1483, Lovell had been reappointed to the commission of peace for Oxfordshire by Edward IV and now, on 14 May that year, this was accompanied by his appointment to the bench of justices for Northamptonshire and the East Riding of Yorkshire. Here we can discern the hand of Richard his friend in appointing a trusted agent to two sensitive areas, particularly Northamptonshire, which was the home county of the Woodvilles and which inevitably harboured many of their followers. With the queen in sanctuary at Westminster and the Marquis of Dorset and Sir Richard Woodville either in hiding or abroad, it was important for Richard to have a reliable friend in the county, to root out suspected treason and respond quickly to quell any sedition that may arise. Similarly in Yorkshire, while Richard's followers dominated in the North and West Ridings, the East Riding had been regarded as the bailiwick of the Earl of Northumberland, so it would do no harm to have a reliable and loyal voice on that bench to counter any threat to Richard's power base. These appointments came to Lovell from an appropriate and duly appointed authority so there could have been few qualms in drawing closer to Richard, Lord Protector.

Lovell's elevation to the bench in these counties formed part of the broadening of support for Richard's regime and its attempts to normalize relations with the household of Edward IV and those members of the nobility as yet uncommitted. Richard, wishing to appear reasonable and conciliatory, accepted the royal council's refusal to allow Earl Rivers and Sir Thomas Grey to be tried for treason as the council saw little evidence of treasonable activities engaged in by them.[6] Following this, Richard and Buckingham, accompanied by Cardinal Bourchier, Archbishop of Canterbury, and Thomas Rotherham, Archbishop of York, offered guarantees for the queen to leave sanctuary at Westminster. Elizabeth (perhaps wisely) refused and was uncompromising in her rejection of both Richard's word and the assurances of the archbishops. Richard's political victory was so complete that during the council meeting of 9 June no one was prepared to speak on behalf of the queen.

Preparations for the coronation and Parliament continued, even without the participation of the queen and her Woodville relatives, and the country at large breathed a collective sigh of relief that the crisis was over. This sense of normality was shattered on the morning of 13 June 1483, when a meeting of the council was called at the Tower, attended by, amongst others, Richard as Lord Protector, Archbishop Rotherham of York, John Morton, Bishop of Ely, Lord Hastings and Lord Stanley. In the middle of the council meeting armed men, led by Richard's henchmen, Thomas Howard, Charles Pilkington and Robert Harrington, entered the chamber and promptly arrested Hastings and the two prelates on the pretext that they had been plotting against Richard. Whether or not a plot existed, Richard was not taking that chance and on 10 and 11 June he had written to his supporters in York and Hull and to Lord Nevill, son of the aged Earl of Westmorland, with news. The corporation of York was informed that Richard required their support:

> Against the queen, her blood, adherents and affinity, which have intended and daily do intend to murder us and our cousin the Duke of Buckingham and the old royal blood of the realm and it is now openly known, by their subtle and damnable was forecasted the same, and also the final destruction and disinheritance of you and other men of honour as well of the north parts as other countries that adhere to us.[7]

This highly charged and partisan report was couched in the same moralistic tone frequently used by Richard and calculated to appeal to regional particularism and northern self-interest. Bringing these requests to the knowledge of Londoners had the double effect of making them aware that a plot had indeed taken place between the queen and Hastings, whilst drawing to their attention that Richard had summoned south his northern multitudes. Both items of news would have had a sobering effect on any fractious Londoners who felt like taking action against Richard, the Lord Protector.

These requests are also revealing as to the extent of Richard's relationships at this time. At a point where the actions he was about to undertake would become irrevocable, Richard can be seen to be soliciting aid from his long-term adherents in the north. The letters to York, Hull and Lord Nevill are no doubt merely a sample of those that have survived from a much larger cache. However, the geographical proximity and regional particularism make it quite clear that Richard had yet to expand his base of trust and support beyond his northern affinity or his alliance with Buckingham. This is confirmed by all contemporaneous accounts speaking of southern awe at another northern invasion – a traditional southern bogeyman. Having disposed of Hastings, Richard had removed the head of Edward IV's household, leaving those whose primary loyalty was to Edward's son and ensuring the lawful succession in as much shock and as leaderless as the Woodvilles. Richard was not long in hammering home his advantage for, on 16 June, he:

> the Protector, being accompanied by the Archbishop of Canterbury, went unto Westminster and there behaved him so gloriously unto the queen with his manifold dissimulated fair promises that neither she nor yet the archbishop had it in them any manner of suspicion or guile. But in good and loving manner, trusting fully it should be for the welfare of the child, delivered up to them the Duke of York....[8]

The queen was persuaded to part with her younger son because it would have been unseemly for the coronation of Edward V to go ahead without the presence of his brother. It has also been argued that she allowed her son to be removed into the custody of the Archbishop of Canterbury (until then a thoroughly blameless man), not into the custody of her avowed enemies, the Duke of Gloucester and the Duke of Buckingham. In truth, the queen had little choice since the archbishop and the two dukes came to Westminster accompanied by a company of armed men. She may well have had in mind the example of her own husband, Edward IV, who, after the battle of Tewkesbury, had forcibly removed his enemies from the sanctuary of Tewkesbury Abbey.[9] There seems to have been a sense of fatalism (if not fatality) that overcame the queen at this time as she bowed to the inevitable and surrendered the one significant trump card that she still held. The young prince, Richard, Duke of York, was conveyed to the Tower to join his older brother within its stout walls. On gaining possession of the younger prince, Richard now showed his hand and on the same day both the coronation and the Parliament were postponed until the following November.

Intriguingly, no chronicle or record makes any reference to Francis Lovell at this time, all eyes being on Richard and Buckingham. In the light of later events, this is surprising; equally so is the lack of information on Lovell's activities from sources in Oxfordshire. In a letter, dated 21 June 1483, from Simon Stallworth to Sir William Stoner, Lovell's cousin and neighbour, Stallworth discusses the execution of Hastings and the removal of Richard, Duke of York, from sanctuary:

> it is thought there shall be 20,000 of my Lord Protector's and my Lord of Buckingham's men in London this week. To what intent I know not but to keep the peace ... The lord Archbishop of York [and] the Bishop of Ely are yet in the tower ... All the Lord Chamberlains men [Hastings] are become my lord of Buckingham's men.

This letter seems to indicate that no communication with Lovell was available. As the highest placed local source, he would have been invaluable to Stallworth so it is curious that no mention is made of him at this time, especially given his friendship with Richard. This opens up the wider question of Lovell's relationship with Richard, as this is not recorded or even commented upon by contemporary chroniclers; records of the time show only that, as in May 1483, he obtains further commissions as Justice of the Peace – this time for Berkshire and Essex (26 and 28 June, respectively). It is, however, unthinkable that Lovell was not present in Richard's councils at this time, not merely as a friend but as part of the broadening of the political base of support that Richard would have required. This base of support had by now drawn in Viscount Berkeley, whose share of his inheritance had been detained by Edward IV, and the Howards (both father and son), who had been denied their share of the Mowbray inheritance of the duchy of Norfolk. These nobles joined those already committed to Richard. It is more than likely that Lovell was already close to Richard and attending his councils at this time. But why would this not come to public attention? It may, in part, be due to Buckingham's overweening desire to place himself in the spotlight and to maximize his opportunity to act as Richard's spokesman (and, in effect, of the government). Buckingham had endured years of obscurity during which Edward IV had quite deliberately denied him any role commensurate with his rank. Now Buckingham had his chance to shine. His brilliance in this role dazzled contemporaries, leaving little room for other members of Richard's entourage to make an impression. Unlike Buckingham, Norfolk, Nevill and others, Francis Lovell had no grievance that required resolution by Richard; he had no particular animus towards Elizabeth Woodville's family and, unlike other peers, did not harbour any unresolved grievance over his inheritance. Consequently, his lack of presence in official records could indicate that there were no issues for Richard, as Lord Protector, to address, and the evidence indicates that Lovell did not petition for any significant rewards. In fact, Lovell seems to have offered that most rare thing in politics – the counsel and advice of a friend. This is laudable in itself, but recognizing it makes him all the more culpable in the events that would unfold in the summer and autumn of 1483.

It is reasonable to assume that Lovell and Richard had been in contact prior to 4 May, and it is more than likely, bearing in mind their longstanding friendship, that Lovell would have joined Richard in London soon after this date. From then on, it can be supposed that Lovell formed part of Richard's inner circle and was, therefore, aware of his plans and intentions. That Lovell was not publicly rewarded on the same scale as Buckingham would imply that his loyalty did not need to be bought, but was given freely. Having grown up together in Warwick's household, both Richard and Lovell would have been familiar with Warwick's methods and his preferred political way of operating. Warwick's use of force and his resorting to extreme violence against political opponents, removing them without recourse to existing legal practices, would have been part of Richard and Lovell's formative experiences. Whilst Warwick was, at best, a mediocre general, he was a masterful tactician and politician, whose proclamations from 1460 onwards laid great stress on presenting his position by utilizing popular grievances and, by doing so, bringing public opinion into the political arena. Edward IV adopted the use of arbitrary violence in politics and the setting aside of legal norms after the battle of Tewkesbury, when those who were his inveterate enemies had been removed from their sanctuary in the bosom of holy mother church and summarily executed.

The judicial use of violence ultimately impacted on Edward's family itself and revealed itself with what many thought as Woodville-sought judicial murder of the Duke of Clarence. The palpable rise in violence infecting the politics of the country had now been brought within the Yorkist royal family by the queen herself. These were the examples of statecraft and politics by which Richard and Lovell had been moulded; the lessons they had learned and their moral framework were products of the age into which they had been born, and both drew the same conclusions as to their efficacy in the early summer of 1483.

This does not make Richard into the Shakespearian villain of popular imagination, but rather a product of the political culture of the early Renaissance just as were Alexander VI, Cesare Borgia, Francesco Sforza and other historical 'baddies' of the time. The new-found interest in the works of antiquity created within the mind of the early Renaissance a different attitude towards the practice of politics; the works of Sallust, Livy and Tacitus now carried greater weight than the chivalric tales of Arthur and the knights of the Round Table. The inherent cynicism and duplicity of the end of the Roman Republic and an elastic moral outlook represented, for these men, a break with the medieval ideals of chivalry.

A question of legitimacy

All the lessons learned in Warwick's household were put into practice on 22 June 1483. On this date, the secret plans of Richard and his coterie were made public when the popular Cambridge cleric, Dr Ralph Shaw, was wheeled out to preach at St Paul's Cross, the acknowledged place from where royal policies and pronouncements were made public. What Shaw announced to the assembled Londoners was both astonishing and unexpected:

> … that the children of king Edward were not the rightful inheritors of the crown and that king Edward was not the legitimate son of the Duke of York as the Lord Protector was. By this declaration and many other allegations and approbrious reports he [Shaw] then alleged that the Lord Protector was most worthy to be king and no other.[10]

It is from here that Richard's actions now begin to acquire the baleful reputation that was to bedevil the rest of his reign. Richard's act to remove the Woodvilles, long regarded (rightly or wrongly) as being avaricious, venal and licentious, had enjoyed a measure of support amongst the nobility and, indeed, from what we can deduce, the broader nation as well. These events now began to acquire a more cynical and sinister interpretation. Rather than rescuing the young Edward V from the clutches of the queen's low-born, self-interested relations and returning him to the company of the old blood of England, his uncle, Richard now appears to have been taking his first steps in a premeditated bid for the throne. These suspicions would have been confirmed if the wider populace was aware that, at the same time as Shaw's pronouncement, the queen's brother, Earl Rivers, was at Pontefract Castle, making his will in expectation of imminent execution. Richard's extreme action against Hastings, which had lacked even the veneer of legality, was now revealed as the removal of the one person undoubtedly loyal to Edward V and who was capable of mobilizing the young king's household against Richard's bid for the throne. It is immaterial whether Richard acted from fear, self-interest or blind ambition. Those who could have led factions to deny his acclamation and accession to the throne had been, or were about to be, eliminated. Throughout these actions, Lovell had stood at Richard's side, involved in the planning of Richard's progress towards the throne, and fully endorsing Richard's claim.

This proclamation of illegitimacy stunned all those present and did not have the desired effect of endorsing Richard's claim to the throne, for Shaw had a decidedly lukewarm reception among the gathered crowds. To hammer home the legitimacy of Richard's claim to the throne, on 25 June an assembly of lords and those notables who were in London met under the Duke of Buckingham's chairmanship to discuss the shocking news and to be guided by Buckingham, who acted as the principal spokesman of the regime. Buckingham raised another sinister issue when he suggested that Elizabeth Woodville's mother, Jacquetta of Luxembourg, had resorted to the dark arts of necromancy and sorcery to ensnare Edward IV and ensure that he remained under her daughter's spell. In a time when there was widespread belief in magic, this was a serious and unsettling allegation, suggesting that rather than the realm being a reflection of the celestial hierarchy, forces of evil had been called into being, usurping the legitimate power of the Lord's anointed, i.e. the king. At this meeting, those in attendance were invited to meet with Richard, the Lord Protector, at his mother's house of Baynard's Castle, near St Paul's.

> To this assembly [at Baynard's Castle] the duke [of Buckingham] then made an oration, rehearsing the great excellency of the Lord Protector and the manifold virtues which God had endowed him with, and the rightful title which he had to the crown. It lasted a good half hour, and was so well and eloquently uttered and with so angelic a countenance, and every pause and time so well ordered, that such as heard him marvelled and said that never before that day had they heard any man, learned or unlearned, make such an oration as that was. When he had finished and well exhorted the assembly to admit the Lord Protector was their liege Lord and king and they to satisfy his mind more for fear than for love, had cried in small number Yea! yea!, he departed.[11]

The following day, the mayor, the corporation of London and others attended Richard at Baynard's Castle. There, Buckingham presented their petition that Richard become their king while Richard initially appeared to demur before 'modestly' agreeing to become their sovereign. After accepting the petition of the mayor, corporation and assembled notables, who had now played their role in the drama, the newly appointed king, Richard III, rode to Westminster Hall, to be attended upon by the lords temporal and spiritual gathered there. When Richard arrived, he took up his seat upon the king's bench, literally acceding to the throne. All that remained was to formally acknowledge the change of monarch and, following his acknowledgement as king by the lords temporal and spiritual, a hasty provision was made for his coronation on 6 July.[12]

During Buckingham's Guildhall speech on 24 June, the Earl Rivers, Sir Richard Grey (the queen's son by her first marriage), and Thomas Vaughan had been executed at Pontefract Castle. The executions had taken place under the supervision of Richard's northern followers, the Earl of Northumberland and Lord Nevill, who had remained in the north after Richard had progressed south to meet with his nephew at Stony Stratford. Both Northumberland and Nevill had held themselves in readiness, initially to remand the prisoners who had been sent north after the coup on 1 May and later, as letters written by Richard on 10 and 11 June testify, to gather and hold troops and stand in readiness to provide military support for the Lord Protector (as Richard then was). It is quite clear that on 22 June Earl Rivers recognized that his execution, and that of the two other prisoners, was premeditated and inevitable. The composition of his will included an attempt to expunge all earthly debts and insults prior to meeting his Maker – the hour of which he believed was at hand. In this, Rivers was correct: he was executed the very next day.

The execution of the queen's brother and her son were actions that could only be undertaken by men assured that they possessed the legal absolution for their deeds – an absolution that only a king could grant. Irrespective of their rank, Northumberland and Nevill knew that if Richard did not reach for the throne, then their actions would, at the very least, earn them the undying hatred of the queen and her family. In all probability, they would face the vengeance of her son when he came of age. By executing Rivers, Grey and Vaughan, both Northumberland and Nevill acted in collusion with Richard in the full knowledge of what was to occur in London and recognizing that Richard's success would automatically justify their actions at Pontefract.

Northumberland and Nevill were not alone amongst the nobility in supporting Richard's grab for the throne. Richard had been able to mobilize those members of the nobility who had been victims of Edward IV's arbitrary policy towards the descent of inheritances and, in a short time, Richard had created his own party within the political nation. This party was led most conspicuously by the Duke of Buckingham, but also consisted of Lord Howard and Viscount Berkeley as well as Lord Nevill, all of whom had been denied a share of their rightful inheritances. Northumberland had more oblique motives for backing Richard: a king in London, rather than a royal duke in the north, would be more likely to acquiesce in the restoration of his family's position in the north, which had been overshadowed by Richard and the Nevill affinity at Middleham and Sheriff Hutton. Richard's northern supporters, Scrope and Greystoke, could look to the rewards proffered by a king and not just a regional duke. Although not as prominent in contemporary chronicles, John de la Pole, Duke of Suffolk, and his wife, Elizabeth, Richard's sister, would also look warmly upon the accession as that of 'a true sonne of Yorke' shorn of the Woodville pretentions that diminished the duchess' position of sisterly pre-eminence and reduced the duke to regional impotence. Another backer was the recently demoted Earl of Huntingdon, who had been humiliatingly forced to accept a swap of his father's earldom of Pembroke for a scattered inheritance far from his family's areas of influence.

Thus, a significant section of the nobility was prepared to accept at face value the charges that Richard now brought against his brother, Edward IV, and also the supposed licentious behaviour of Elizabeth Woodville and her mother's alleged use of sorcery and necromancy. Added to these charges was the assertion that Edward and Elizabeth's marriage had taken place irregularly and that no banns had been proclaimed or made public. Finally, much was made of the irrefutable fact that Edward IV had been born overseas – in France, of all places – and that he did not resemble his father, Richard, Duke of York, as Richard, now Lord Protector, clearly did. Inevitably, this cast aspersions upon the morality and probity of Richard's own mother, Cecily, and, although these accusations merely re-hashed those made in 1469 by Warwick the kingmaker and George, Duke of Clarence, there can be little doubt that the charges must have been particularly hurtful to the Dowager Duchess of York, known widely as 'proud Cess' and venerated for her piety. This concoction of rumour, half-truths and innuendo had been effective in providing a route to the throne for Richard and one that a significant proportion of the nobility was prepared to acknowledge and (with varying degrees of enthusiasm) to set aside the son of Edward IV, to whom they had sworn binding oaths of allegiance in April of the previous year. On 25 June 1483, Edward V and his brother Richard, Duke of York, were deprived of all their titles and designated illegitimate and therefore unable to inherit the dignities of their father. The reign of Richard III had begun and that of 'Edward, bastard, late called king Edward V ended'.[13]

In only three months, Richard, Duke of Gloucester, now King Richard III, had arrived from the north and destroyed the party and the family of the queen, who had looked set to dominate the government under the young king. Richard had effectively eliminated those household loyalists led by Hastings, who sought to implement the will of Edward IV, and had obtained the crown for himself. In doing so, he had created a Ricardian party of men who were now committed to him and who were prepared to sustain him, having already made a profound investment in his rule. This new Ricardian party stood with the new king and none stood closer than Francis Lovell, who, in early August 1483, was appointed King's Chamberlain.

7 THE MASSACRE OF THE INNOCENTS

A publicly acknowledged heir no more

On 25 July 1483, the reign of Edward V, eldest son of Edward IV, came to an end. The young king was set aside and replaced by his uncle, Richard. The setting aside of a king in medieval England was an extremely rare event, even amidst the relative chaos of the late fifteenth century. What was exceptional in the case of Edward V was that he had been publicly acknowledged as his father's heir since infancy when, on 11 June 1471, he had been officially invested as Prince of Wales, Duke of Cornwall and Earl of Chester. On 3 July that year, he had been presented to the lords spiritual and temporal at a great council by Archbishop of Canterbury, Cardinal Bourchier, who had been the first in a long parade of lords who had sworn allegiance to the infant prince on the Gospels. The words of allegiance used by the archbishop could not have been clearer:

> I Thomas Cardinal Archbishop of Canterbury acknowledge take and repute you Edward Prince of Wales ... first begotten son of our sovereign Lord Edward IV, king of England and France and lord of Ireland to be the true and undoubted heir to our sovereign Lord.[1]

This oath was taken in front of forty-six lords spiritual and temporal, including two archbishops and five dukes. On 14 April 1472, the Prince of Wales was elected Knight of the Garter: underage though he may have been, he was now a member of the highest order of chivalry in the land.

Following the death of his father, Edward IV, on 9 April 1483, all the bonds of allegiance entered into with regard to the young prince eleven years earlier began to unravel. Of the original forty-six lords spiritual and temporal who had sworn allegiance to the infant prince in 1471, thirty-four were still alive and acquiescent in the removal of Edward V from the throne. Years of loyalty were now erased and overwritten by the political realities that had occurred during the spring of 1483. Those nobles now acknowledged the 'superior' claim of his uncle Richard – a claim that only a month earlier no-one had heard anything about.

Richard's dilemma

While Richard III had been publicly acknowledged as king, it did not mean that everyone agreed to his elevation with a clear conscience. Indeed, the betrayal of a sacred oath freely and publicly made would have weighed heavily on the consciences of most men. At this time, the breaking of a sacred oath was a very public stain on honour, reputation and character, and was a burden not lightly carried. Few men could easily cast aside years of loyalty and replace the focus of that loyalty in an instant; neither could Edward V cease to be king merely on the whim of men, despite not having been crowned. Having been acknowledged as king on the death of his father, Edward V had become the Lord's elect, if not the Lord's anointed, and no one then had questioned his right to succeed to the throne; certainly not his uncle Richard, who had led the northern nobility in publicly offering his allegiance to the new king at York Minster sometime between 14 and 23 April. Edward IV's council had written to the new king at Ludlow, acknowledging him as his father's legitimate heir and offering him the crown. These very public acts of affirmation had raised Edward V above other men, only for him to be grievously dashed down on 25 June 1483.

Although Edward officially ceased to be king after that date, it did not make him any less a king in the eyes of many. He had, after all, been the acknowledged son and heir of Edward IV, a reigning monarch who had ruled since 1461 (and had been unchallenged since 1471). As such, Edward V joined the ranks of European monarchs such as René of Anjou who, in a long life of political failure, had claimed to be king of both Sicily and of Jerusalem despite only ruling briefly in one realm and never having set foot in the other. Throughout his life, René was styled 'Le Roi de Naples' and treated with the deference and ceremony due to a reigning monarch because once a king was made, a king was very difficult to unmake. Such a notion made Edward V a danger to Richard III and, as he grew older, an increasing threat.

This was the moral dilemma that Richard faced as soon as he ascended the throne. One source – *The Anlaby Cartulary* – baldly states that even prior to the accession Edward V had been killed, recording that:

> Edward V died on the 22nd of June. He reigned for two months and eight days and was not crowned. He was killed and nobody knows where he is buried.

Almost certainly this date is too early as the boys were later subject to plots to free them and, as a result, actions were taken to increase the security surrounding them. On 9 July, eighteen members of the prince's household who had travelled with him from Ludlow were paid off and replaced by strangers. The last remaining member of the prince's household to attend to him was his personal physician, Dr John Argentine. It is possible that it is originally from Argentine that we have the following description of the young prince, as related by the Italian chronicler, Dominic Mancini, who was present in London at the time:

The physician Argentine, the last of his attendants whose services the king enjoyed, reported that the king, like a victim prepared for sacrifice sought remission for his sins by daily confession and penance because he believed death was facing him.[2]

Here we have an authentic picture of a frightened young boy, aged only thirteen, who clearly anticipates his fate and is making his peace with a world he knows he will be leaving all too soon. Mancini also relates that the prince's brother, the Duke of York, too young to fully recognize the grim reality of their situation and bored with being separated from loyal servants and family, just wanted to play all the time. These vignettes serve to remind us of how all-too human were the young princes at the centre of the ensuing mystery.

From the middle of July 1483, rumours began to circulate in London that the two princes were dead. These were probably a natural reaction to the fact that after 9 July sightings of the boys became rarer and rarer, and were soon to cease altogether. There can be little doubt that the problem of the princes exercised the minds of Richard's councillors at this time and that considerable discussions regarding their fate took place. On 6 July 1483, Richard's coronation took place at Westminster Abbey. The date is important because one of our best sources – the Crowland Chronicle – states that Buckingham, now Great Chamberlain of England, having presided very prominently over the coronation, soon after took his leave of the king, departing westwards, firstly to his palatial manor of Thornbury and, ultimately, to his Welsh stronghold of Brecon. This is important because *The Historical Notes of a London Citizen* relates that 'king Edward IV's sons were put to death in the Tower by the vise of the Duke of Buckingham'. The word 'vise' here can probably be taken to mean by the *advice* of Buckingham rather than by his *design* as it is unlikely that he himself would take the decision to eliminate the princes. It is much more likely that, as king, Richard III was under pressure to resolve the problem that the princes in the Tower most definitely represented. Crowland strongly suggests that it was Buckingham's advice that the dynastic and political threat that the princes represented had to be neutralized.

With the coronation over, Richard was in London with the earls of Surrey, Lincoln, Huntingdon and Warwick, Sir Richard Hussey, a chief justice of the king's bench, and, of course, his chamberlain, Francis Lovell. Also present was the Chancellor, Bishop Russell of Lincoln. Since Warwick was a minor, aged only eight in July 1483, it is highly unlikely that he would have been part of this discussion; similarly, Lincoln was present possibly to represent the interests of his father, the Duke of Suffolk, but he would only have been a junior member (being merely twenty or twenty-one at this stage), not yet assuming the significance he would have later. It is likely that the issue of what to do with the princes would have occupied the minds of these men, all of whom were complicit in Richard's usurpation and *coup de main* in the period of 6 to 21 July when Richard departed on his progress. All were committed members of the new regime and some, like Surrey, had gained significantly from Richard's accession as others, such as Huntingdon, hoped to do. It does not require a great leap of the imagination to hear Buckingham advising the council on a course of action that, although unpalatable, was politically inevitable to ensure the security of them all: both young princes had to be eliminated. Indeed, if the thirteen-year-old boy in the royal apartments could recognize this reality, it would be hard not to believe that the obvious solution did not present itself to those members of Richard's inner council.

There can be little doubt as to the advice offered to Richard by Huntingdon, Surrey and Francis Lovell during July 1483, but, from what we know of Richard's character, he may well have shied away from the obvious solution. He was, after all, their uncle. Thus, he may well have hesitated, beset by qualms of conscience at the immorality of the suggested deed, which conflicted with his idea of himself as a good and pious Christian bound to the boys by the loyalty of kinship. From the chronicled sources, it would appear that Richard's opponents also recognized that time was running out for the princes: there was an abortive and obscure plot to free the boys undertaken by John, Lord Welles, the half-brother of Margaret Beaufort, the mother of the exiled Henry Tudor. The discovery of this plot and the possibility of others pending helped to crystallize minds, and the decision to resolve the issue once and for all was taken prior to Richard and his queen leaving on a royal progress.

Richard and Anne left London on 21 July 1483, travelling first to Windsor and Reading, and then spending three days at Oxford where Richard debated theology with the college dons – a pastime he thoroughly enjoyed. After the royal party departed Oxford, Francis Lovell had the singular honour of entertaining the king and his wife at his home at Minster Lovell. This act demonstrates not only his importance, but also his unique and genuine friendship with the new king for, out of all the other places that Richard visited on his progress, none was a private residence, nor did any other individual enjoy the honour of welcoming the king and queen over their threshold. It is quite clear that, even in the pleasant Oxfordshire surroundings of Minster Lovell, the concerns of politics and state could still intervene. While there, Richard wrote to Bishop Russell, ordering him to increase the security surrounding the princes and urging the chancellor to 'fail ye not hereof'. This letter, dated 29 July 1483, is a reaction to another plot that, as the Crowland Chronicle later recorded, was planned to take place as soon as Richard and the royal party left London on their progress. The alleged plot was supposedly led by John Cheyne, which almost certainly would have meant that the Lancastrian Margaret Beaufort was involved. The details and the nature of the plot were revealed by John Stowe, and a certain John Nesfield was appointed to reinforce security and vet all activity at the Tower. The failure of this plot and the need for closer confinement of the princes were probably the triggers for the rumours of their deaths that swept through London at the end of July.

The royal party, accompanied by the King's Chamberlain – Francis Lovell – left Minster Lovell soon after, heading for Woodstock, Gloucester, Tewkesbury and eventually arriving at Warwick, where the king was met by a Spanish embassy. From here, Richard condemned John, Lord Welles, of treason for a conspiracy based on the Northamptonshire manor of Maxstowe. On 17 August, Richard issued commissions to the Duke of Buckingham to investigate treason in London, Surrey, Sussex and Kent, followed by further investigations in other counties. During this period, Richard stayed at Warwick for a week before leaving for Coventry, Leicester, Nottingham and Pontefract, and arriving at York on 29 August. It was at this time that the Crowland Chronicle recorded that 'a rumour arose that king Edward's sons, by some unknown manner a violent destruction had met their fate'. The persistence of rumours surrounding the boys at this time strongly suggest that they were killed when Richard himself was sure to be away from the capital and able to put as much distance between himself and the actuality of the deed.

It is probably at this point that the irrevocable decision to eliminate the princes was taken and enacted. Polydore Vergil, who had the opportunity to interview reliable contemporaries on what occurred, probably produces an account that comes closest to the truth, despite its dismissal by Ricardians as Tudor propaganda. Vergil writes that Richard '… sent a warrant' to the Lieutenant of the Tower, Robert Brackenbury, 'to procure their [the princes] death with all diligence'.[3] Brackenbury, stunned by this command, naturally prevaricated, asking for further instructions. Richard then commanded his chief henchman and master of his horse, Sir James Tyrell, who had been in Richard's employ since 1467, to ride sorrowfully to London to carry out the king's commission. Polydor Vergil has Sir James Tyrell murder 'those babes of the royal issue'. Writing in 1515 in his *History of Richard III*, Sir Thomas More has the instructions brought to Brackenbury by John Green, who then employed two others to complete the deed. More's account carries more detail and could well be taken from the memories of John Morton, Cardinal Archbishop of Canterbury, who had employed the young More as a page. Interestingly, after the deed was done, More has Green account to Richard how it was done, justifying the decision for the royal party to spend a week in Warwick, a place which, whilst solidly Nevill in its sympathies, had never before held any particular associations for Richard III.

These events taken at face value have an extremely important bearing on Francis Lovell's subsequent career. If this timeline is correct, as suggested by the incidental evidence (Buckingham's rebellion recognized that the boys were no more), then it ascribes to Lovell a central role in the elimination of the princes and explains in part his adherence to Richard and to his legacy. During the period soon after 6 June until the end of September, Richard III's closest and most consistent advisers are the earls of Surrey and Huntingdon and Francis Lovell. Neither Huntingdon or Surrey are spoken of as being as close to Richard as Lovell was, but presumably all were involved in the crucial decision to remove the princes and to forestall them becoming the focus of disaffection and a rallying point for the opposition. In this sense, they were all culpable in the murder of two young boys. This made them political realists who would now be bound together until Bosworth. Despite the fact that Huntingdon would marry Richard's illegitimate daughter, Lady Katherine, it is Lovell who stands out as Richard's confidante and the one on whose advice the king would rely.

Later, in the rebellion of 1487, Lovell did not try to manufacture a Yorkist prince from beyond the grave and present him as one of the princes. Lovell could not do that because, not only did he know the truth about the fate of the princes in the Tower, he had been part of their demise. He, with a few others, knew exactly why the boys were no longer seen after the summer of 1483.

8 *RICARDUS REX*

The coronation of Richard III

On Sunday 6 July 1483, Richard and his wife Anne stepped onto a red carpet that stretched from Whitehall to Westminster Abbey. They walked barefoot, with Richard wearing a rich velvet purple gown, his train borne by the chief architect of the ceremony, Henry Stafford, Duke of Buckingham. At Richard's shoulders stood two bishops accompanying him to the abbey where he would be transformed from a mere mortal into an anointed king. Immediately behind Richard walked the Earl of Northumberland holding the blunt Sword of Mercy, accompanied by Thomas, Lord Stanley, who held the constable's mace. Next in the procession came the aged Earl of Kent and Francis, Viscount Lovell, both bearing the pointed Swords of Justice. Taking his turn next was John de la Pole, Duke of Suffolk, and his young son, John, Earl of Lincoln, bearing the sceptre and the orb of state, respectively. Another father and son – Thomas, Earl of Surrey, and John, Duke of Norfolk – bore the sheathed Sword of State and the crown on a sumptuous cushion. Queen Anne walked behind this assembly of the officers of state with her train held by Margaret Beaufort, Countess of Richmond. Walking in state alone behind the queen and the countess came Richard's sister, Elizabeth, Duchess of Suffolk, followed by twenty ladies of the nobility.

Once inside the abbey, the king and queen were divested of their formal robes and then anointed with holy oil by the Archbishop of Canterbury, Thomas Bourchier. When this was accomplished, the royal couple were enrobed with cloth of gold and the elderly archbishop then lowered the crowns onto their heads. At this point, organ music filled the abbey and a solemn *Te Deum* was sung and high mass celebrated. After the service, both king and queen, followed by the court and attendants, crossed to Westminster Hall, where the royal couple, now seated on a raised dais, received the individual pledges of loyalty of each of the invited 3,000 guests. Before the second course was served, the king's champion, Sir Robert Dymmock, rode into the hall on a destrier and issued the traditional challenge to any who doubted the king's right to rule. The hall reverberated to the affirmative cries of 'King Richard, King Richard!', thus confirming that England now had a new king.

Richard's administration

Soon after his coronation Richard III began to assemble his own government. Now anointed and crowned, Richard had free rein to stamp his authority on the realm and to appoint his own ministers and councillors. While Buckingham had received huge rewards, they had been of a regional nature and firmly concentrated his influence in Wales, the Welsh Marches and the West Country. Buckingham also seems to have been too grand a figure to play a role in the day-to-day mechanism of royal administration, preferring (it would appear) the independent role of the king's chief councillor when needed. Otherwise, he was a man who looked to his own interests in the West, where he enjoyed almost vice-regal authority. Buckingham was Great Chamberlain of England – a largely honorific office that gave its holder a place in the hierarchy of the great offices of state below that of Lord Privy Seal and above the military office of Constable. The general duties at court of the Great Chamberlain were largely undertaken by the Lord Chamberlain of the Household or the King's Chamberlain who was in charge of the royal household, the wardrobe and the court itself – a role to which Richard appointed his closest friend, Francis Lovell.

Richard's new government comprised of about twenty key members – the Chancellor was Bishop John Russell of Lincoln, a scholarly and learned man who would remain in this post until 29 July 1485. The Treasurer was Sir John Wood; the Lord Privy Seal was John Gunthorpe, Dean of Bath and Wells; the Steward of the Household was Sir Thomas Stanley; the Chancellor of the Exchequer was William Catesby from a prominent Northamptonshire legal family. The Chamberlain of the Exchequer was Richard's henchmen, Sir James Tyrell of Suffolk; John Kendall, originally from York, continued to act as Richard's secretary, a role he had held since the king had been Duke of Gloucester. The Duke of Norfolk was appointed Constable of the Realm and Admiral of England. Norfolk seems to have occupied a purely military role, not normally required to act on civic business. As admiral, Norfolk was no doubt aided by the Earl of Arundel who, with his vast Sussex estates, was ideally placed to act as Warden of the Cinque Ports

As King's Chamberlain, Francis Lovell was closest to the king, in charge of the king's chamber, private apartments and, most importantly, with control over who had access to them and the person of the king. He also established the order of the king's business. In drawing up that order, he inevitably controlled what and whose petitions the king would hear and whom the king would receive: in an age of personal monarchy the role of the king's doorkeeper was not only influential, but extremely powerful. Other duties included the enforcing the rules of the court, standards of behaviour and the maintenance of the magnificence and splendour appropriate to one of Europe's pre-eminent monarchies. In this role, Lovell was likely guided by the precedence established by Edward IV and his chamberlain William, Lord Hastings. Upholding the moral standards of the court would have been particularly important to Richard III, who would have sought to draw a line between his new court and that of his brother's – especially because of the charges of indecency and immorality that had been levelled at the Woodvilles and the general licentiousness for which they and Edward had become famous.

The tone of the new court was established early when Richard's government rather spitefully held up Edward IV's mistress, Jane Shore, to public ridicule and shame. Mistress Shore, as she was known, had had a chequered career in royal service as Edward's principal mistress for twelve years. However, during this time she had also embraced the attention of Edward's friend, Lord Hastings and Edward's stepson, Thomas, Marquis of Dorset, causing no little animosity between the two. After the execution of Hastings and during the disappearance of Dorset, Richard's government sought to further blacken the name of Elizabeth Woodville by associating her with the notorious mistress of her husband. Shore, condemned for her immoral behaviour by the Bishop of London, was forced to walk around St Paul's Cross draped only in a sheet and carrying a candle, the punishment of a common whore. However, the plan backfired as she attracted the sympathy of the crowds.[1]

Lovell's growing influence and authority

As one who controlled the court, Francis Lovell also influenced the timbre of government. The processes of government required direct intervention by the king, including determining individual petitions and providing judgment on his subjects' disputes. To obtain a royal judgment, a written petition had to be presented to the king via the royal chamberlain in his role as gatekeeper. Obviously, it was beneficial to be able to present one's petition to the king in person and to, hopefully, obtain redress directly from him. The office of King's Chamberlain was thus extremely important, influential and highly lucrative, attracting as it did many fees and prerequisites alongside the wages drawn from the exchequer. Many nobles felt it worthwhile to offer the King's Chamberlain a retainer to ensure access to the king, giving the postholder more personal influence than many members of the higher nobility.

On 14 August 1483, Lovell replaced the Duke of Suffolk as Constable and Steward of the honour of Wallingford in Berkshire. The honour of Wallingford, in royal hands since the reign of Henry II, was an important centre of royal influence in the Thames Valley, an ancient barony that also held important estates and offices in the Chiltern Hills of Buckinghamshire. In addition to clearly demonstrating who in this area had the king's trust and favour, the grant of Wallingford to Lovell is significant for two reasons: firstly, it considerably enhanced his local power base in his home counties of Oxfordshire and Berkshire and increased his influence in the neighbouring county of Buckinghamshire. Wallingford dominated the area between Oxford and Reading, and control over its offices and estates considerably enhanced Francis' local sources of patronage and reward. Secondly, the grant demonstrated a generational change in policy, with Lovell, now aged twenty-eight, supplanting the older John de la Pole, Duke of Suffolk. Obviously, as a new king, Richard was free to promote his supporters and to remove incumbents at will. While some historians dismiss Suffolk as a nonentity and a noble lacking in substance,[2] there is plenty of evidence to suggest that he and possibly his wife, Elizabeth, Richard III's sister, could be both determined and aggressive when their interests were threatened. This was amply demonstrated when, in the 1470s his dominance in East Anglia was threatened and the then king, Edward IV, received (and ignored) numerous complaints from the gentry of the area. The Suffolks appear to have peacefully acquiesced to the promotion of Francis Lovell to the control of the honour of Wallingford and to his dominance in the Thames Valley to the detriment of themselves, for they had long controlled this area from the manor of Ewelme. That Lovell's elevation was achieved without animosity on the part of Suffolk speaks volumes about the close relations between Lovell and the de la Pole family, originally established by an older family tradition and the strong links forged during Lovell's minority. As such, it was not perceived as the replacement of one duke by a territorial rival, but rather a generational passing of the baton to a close member of the same, extended family. A similar and connected element of this policy was the later promotion of John, Earl of Lincoln, to important offices within Richard III's government.

This was not the end of Richard's generosity to Lovell, for again, on 14 August, another, more intimate grant was recorded at Westminster:

> Grant for life to the kings kinsman Francis Lovell, knight Viscount Lovell the King's Chamberlain of the office of Chief Butler of England, void by the death of Anthony Earl Rivers receiving fees of £100 yearly from the customs and prises of wines and other issues of his office, with all other profits.[3]

The office of Chief Butler of England was again one of the most important and profitable offices of state. The office had arisen during the reign of William the Conqueror and initially gave the holder control of the provisioning of the royal pantry and, more importantly, the royal wine cellar. From this, the office had grown to encompass the organizing and provisioning of the king's coronation and then into control of the customs and excise of all the ports of England. Far from being a mere domestic office, the Chief Butler of England was important in that he appointed deputies to all the principal ports of the realm. Whilst the basic fee was £100 per annum, it was, next to the Treasurer, the most lucrative of the great offices of state, allowing the holder to benefit from contracts to supply the royal household, licensing for shipping, and offering exemptions from customs dues. In addition, the appointments to the office of deputy in regional ports could prove highly lucrative. Thus, well might the Westminster clerk write 'with all other profits' at the end of the grant as a catch-all from the gains that accompanied this office.

More significant is the change in address to Lovell in this grant. At the very forefront of the patent, he is elevated to the status of 'King's Kinsman' – an honorific address that had never been used previously. The actual family link is tenuous, existing through marriage and not blood (Lovell being married to Richard's wife's first cousin, Anne Nevill, who was herself a second cousin to Richard), and so Lovell had no real claim on royal kinship or any family relationship with the House of York. The addition of the 'kinsman' title comes from something more than genealogy or family connections as it was Richard himself who chose to employ the term in recognition of their long association and friendship and also from a wish to ensure that this was publicly acknowledged. This very public acknowledgement of Lovell's friendship and inclusion in Richard's extended royal family fundamentally changed his standing in the realm.

From this time onwards, Lovell held two of the great offices of state and controlled the operations of the royal household, in addition to (in effect) having control over the royal wardrobe and the royal pantry – two departments that allowed intimate access to the king himself. Lovell was now a lynchpin of Richard III's government. As the King's Chamberlain, he was a member of the Privy Council, where he spoke with the king's voice when the king was not present, both composing and articulating royal policies. Lovell also acted as a royal intercessor with parliament, ensuring that parliament was aware of the king's wishes and the direction of royal policy. In this role, he was required to work very closely with the Speaker of the House of Commons, reinforcing his relationship with William Catesby. The significance of Lovell's participation in government and his large portfolio of responsibility has often been eclipsed by a focus on his personal friendship with Richard III.

The royal entry to York

Following Richard's coronation, the court had undertaken a leisurely progress through the Thames Valley and West Midlands, stopping at a variety of locations, including the ominously long residence of one week in Warwick. Throughout August that year, the royal progress continued, with Richard and his queen coming closer and closer to their final destination. The royal couple no doubt looked forward to returning to the north, the land that both had called home since the mid-1470s. The climax of their summer progress came on 29 August when Richard and Anne were joined by their son, Edward of Middleham, for a formal entry into York. The royal family was to be accompanied by five bishops, three earls and Francis Lovell. The royal procession was met by the city corporation and then it progressed to York Minster, where a *Te Deum* was sung. This was followed by two banquets and a feast in the archbishop's palace at which the king and queen sat for four hours receiving the good wishes and traditional homilies from the mayor and his fellow aldermen. Richard reciprocated by presenting gilt figures and relics to the Minster and promising to found a college with one hundred priests. Richard also promised to reduce the city's free farm (the amount paid by the city directly to the Crown to ensure that the Crown upheld its charter of liberties and self-governance – effectively to ensure against royal interference in the city's affairs), a promise that he also extended to other northern cities and churches. The high point of the visit and singular honour for the city of York occurred during the feast of the Nativity of the Blessed Virgin Mary (8

September) when, during a splendid service, Richard's son, Edward of Middleham, was created Prince of Wales.

The Crowland Chronicle states that Richard was keen to establish his 'superior royal rank' to those who were more familiar with him as a mere Duke of Gloucester. The visit doubtless held many pleasurable aspects for Richard, but he never lost sight of its importance as a piece of political theatre in which he took the starring role that summer. The creation of his son as Prince of Wales was a strong political statement of his kingship and his dynasty, a clear assertion of permanence to anyone who may have seen his rule as being a temporary incursion. Also, it would not have escaped notice (in the north, particularly) that his son represented the elevation of a Nevill to first in line to the throne; this act would command the loyalty of traditional supporters of that house and, therefore, continued support of his line in the future.

Richard's council had left little to chance in ensuring the success of the royal visit, having had 13,000 white boar badges made and distributed prior to the king's arrival. Richard's secretary, John Kendall, wrote to the council at York advising them:

> to dispose you to do both pageants and speeches as can goodly … be devised
> … as in the hanging the streets through which the king's grace will come with
> cloths of Arras, tapestry work and other, for there are coming many southern
> lords and men of worship with them which will mark greatly the receiving of
> their graces.[4]

Whilst we are aware of Master John Kendall's correspondences to York and other stops on the royal progress, it must be borne in mind that he was not the architect of these celebrations, but rather the communicator of the plans of others. The responsibility for organizing the king's progress lay with his chamberlain, Francis Lovell. As they enjoyed the festivities and public acclamation of York, both Richard and Lovell had every reason to feel deep satisfaction with the way events had unfolded over the spring and summer. Little did they know that in distant Brecon, treason was brewing in the breast of Buckingham, 'him that had the best cause to be true'.[5]

9 'AND THE WEALD IS UP'

Buckingham turns on Richard

RICHARD, DUKE OF GLOUCESTER, was well liked and respected in York as elsewhere in the north of England. As Lieutenant of the North, he had been the rod that had kept the fractious northern nobility in check, the king's voice and a well-respected arbiter of authority. He also had landed interests in the area through the Nevill estates brought to him by marriage, including residences in nearby Sheriff Hutton and further north at Middleham.

Through his wife's wider family and her extensive cousinage, Richard's presence in the northern capital had brought into attendance a host of northern notables. The Earl of Northumberland was present, as were the Scropes of Bolton and Masham, the Lords Lumley and Dacre, and Francis Lovell's in-laws, the Fitzhughs and the Parrs. These were joined by Richard's direct retainers, such as the Conyers, the Ogles, the Conisburys and the Harringtons. Presiding over this assemblage was Francis Lovell, who would have been involved in organizing the round of official receptions for the king and who would now determine who should gain access to the royal presence. He would have overseen all: those whose allegiance was needed; those whose loyalty was desired; those who could be promoted and brought in to speak; those who could be bought; and those who could be safely ignored. He would also have been in charge of orchestrating the more subtle aspects of altering perceptions: Richard must now be acknowledged as king, not merely as a king's representative; any past familiarity with Richard must now be discouraged as inappropriate as kingship demanded that royal distance be maintained from all subjects, irrespective of status.

As king, Richard enjoyed the adulation of his northern subjects. Meanwhile, his most mighty subject, Henry Stafford, 2nd Duke of Buckingham, was beginning to question Richard's transition from Duke of Gloucester to 'His highness, king Richard III', despite his own part in facilitating this. Buckingham had been crucial in Richard's elevation and he had been handsomely rewarded for it: no noble in medieval England had ever gained as much as Buckingham. He had been given control over all royal castles in Wales and the Marches, plus the stewardship of all royal estates in Shropshire, Herefordshire, Gloucestershire, Somerset and Dorset.

He had the Brecon lordship of Cantref Sylef returned to him and on 13 July was promised the whole of the de Bohun earldom of Hereford, to be confirmed at the first parliament of the reign. He was the Lord High Chamberlain of England, the greatest and richest noble in the realm, a man whose pre-eminence had not been matched since the days of Warwick the kingmaker in the 1460s. He had been invaluable to Richard, both in terms of his military potential and his political advice and support. His relationship with the king was cemented by the coronation, which he had largely orchestrated – since his exposition of Richard's right to the throne at Barnard's Castle before the lords and the Corporation of London at the end of June, he could be viewed as the voice and public face of the new regime. No man, it seemed, stood higher in royal favour than Buckingham when he and the king had parted company during the royal progress in early August 1483.

From London, Buckingham had ridden west to his favourite castle of Brecon, which lay in the centre of Wales, above a bluff, overlooking the river Usk. This was in the very heart of an extensive Marcher lordship comprising rich, fertile, arable valleys and sheep-rearing upland pastures. Here, the thousands of sheep grazing those pastures brought the dukes of Buckingham an income of over £1,000 a year. Equally important was the fact that, within the lordship, the writ of the king did not run, for here, as Marcher Lord, Buckingham did not have to apply the common law of England or admit the king's justices; instead, he appointed and maintained his own laws and his own courts. Surrounded by an extensive lordship in which he was the sole arbiter of justice, Buckingham should have felt at his most secure. Yet the reality was that he felt anything but secure that summer.

As he had ridden westward toward Brecon, Buckingham had become increasingly conscious of the growing disaffection with Richard's usurpation. As Richard and Francis Lovell moved northwards accompanied by a wave of orchestrated acclamation, Buckingham began to sense the true temperature of the body politic. From the end of August onwards, Buckingham had become aware of a number of plots to unseat Richard and to have him replaced. In fact, during September three separate plots began to foment and to coalesce by the beginning of the following month as Richard's court began to wend its way back from York towards the East Midlands, crossing the Trent and moving towards Lincoln.

The first inkling of Buckingham's disquiet came towards the end of September when, swallowing two decades' worth of dislike of his wife's family (whom he had always regarded as being below his own rank and status), he met with his brother-in-law, Bishop Lionel Woodville of Salisbury, at his castle of Thornbury.[1] Lionel was the brother of Buckingham's wife, Catherine Woodville, and of Edward IV's wife, Elizabeth Woodville. Moreover, Lionel was one of the few members of the Woodville family still at liberty and able to undertake some form of political activity. Lionel brought news of a sequence of risings that were planned throughout the south by the Woodvilles and other former members of Edward IV's household who still felt honour-bound to defend the rights of his sons. In the west, Edward IV's brother-in-law, Sir Thomas St Leger, was prepared to rise at Exeter, supported by other former knights of Edward's household such as Thomas Arundel and Edward Courtenay.

Another Courtenay with large influence in Devon, Piers, Bishop of Exeter, had also indicated his support.[2] These plotters hoped to make contact with Elizabeth Woodville's son, the Marquis of Dorset, currently in hiding, but who, through his wife's Bonville estates, was also a power in the region. A further element of the plot was germinating at Newbury in Berkshire, where once again those plotting were former members of Edward IV's household and from the substantial gentry of south-central England, including William Norris, Richard Woodville, William Berkeley and William Stonor, Francis Lovell's own cousin and neighbour. Between Exeter and Newbury, and centred on Salisbury, other household men plotted. These were Walter Hungerford, Giles Daubenay and John Cheyne, all led by Bishop Lionel himself. To the east, in Kent, Woodville relatives and adherents, Sir John Fogge, Sir Richard Haute, Sir Thomas Lewkenor and the Guildford and Gaynesford families, gathered in support.[3]

These plots represented the mobilization of the old Woodville connections, together with retainers of Edward IV's household, who had now recovered from the shock of Richard's *coup de main* at Stony Stratford. Initially, their plan was to restore Edward V to his inheritance with the support of the dowager queen and her family. Acting in conjunction with these plots were the shadowy manoeuvrings of Margaret Beaufort, Countess of Richmond, and her husband, Lord Stanley. Margaret Beaufort almost certainly had in mind the restoration of the fortunes and inheritance of her son, Henry Tudor, still in exile overseas but now supported by Duke Francis of Brittany. Margaret Beaufort and Elizabeth Woodville had been communicating with each other through their doctor, Lewis of Caerleon, and appeared to be united in their mutual antipathy towards Richard III. This Beaufort–Tudor link added another skein to the plots against Richard. Yet none of this explains Buckingham's participation.

One view suggests that Buckingham was actually a rather weak-willed and malleable man who came under the influence of his wily prisoner, Bishop John Morton, at Brecon. Arrested at the same time as Hastings was executed, Morton had already enjoyed a long career. Trained in canon law, he had been Master of the Rolls for Henry VI's government, which had been exiled in France during the 1460s. After the Lancastrian defeat at Tewkesbury, Morton had offered his allegiance to Edward IV. Edward – who recognized talent when he saw it – appointed him Bishop of Ely and Ambassador to France and Burgundy. Widely acknowledged for his talent and diplomatic skills, Morton had remained a member of the Privy Council during Edward V's brief reign. When Richard III had Hastings arrested and executed, Morton had been associated with the former chamberlain in his opposition. Unable to execute a churchman, Richard had ordered his incarceration at Brecon, as far from London as possible and under the watchful eye of the man he assumed to be his most significant supporter. So, was it possible that Buckingham could have fallen under the influence of the more experienced and wily prelate? Not necessarily. Since April 1483, Buckingham had demonstrated his own considerable skills as a political operator who was able to articulate a position, sway others with his arguments, and to formulate and present policy effectively. Thus, he was able to emerge from the political wilderness he had experienced under Edward IV and to claim his place at Richard's court, a place to which he felt that his wealth and rank entitled him. However, his rapid rise up the greasy pole of politics had provoked jealousy and he was now left exposed as a supporter of a king whose own right to rule was being seriously questioned. Buckingham, whose success as a politician was initially built on his ability to use words, was now acutely sensitive to the words being used against the king he had helped to put on the throne.

Buckingham appears to have been a political realist who had initially recognized that Richard's usurpation of the throne represented his best chance of establishing himself as a major political force. His wealth, rank, lineage and proximity to the throne had all made Edward IV wary of him, but Richard's accession meant that these attributes were now viewed in a positive light by the new regime, especially as his ability to put large numbers of men into the field added force to his list of attributes. Nevertheless, all of this would now count for nothing if he were too closely associated with a king who, it was whispered, was now being viewed as a usurper and a tyrant. If the king fell, then Buckingham would be the most prominent victim of the ensuing crash. In the light of cold political calculation, Buckingham began to work out where his true interests now lay, so that when Morton, Bishop of Ely, began to lay out the objectives of the rebels at Brecon, he was pushing at an open door.

More honours for Francis Lovell

For three weeks from 29 August, Richard III and his court sojourned at York where, as the Crowland Chronicle states, Richard III exhibited his 'superior royal rank'. One happy consequence of that 'superior royal rank' was the ability to promote friends and those closest to the Crown. Nothing proclaims the friendship of Richard III and Lovell more than Lovell's appointment as Knight of the Garter, probably in the autumn of 1483. With this, Lovell became a member of the oldest and most prestigious chivalric order of knighthood in England, its members including such European luminaries as the Holy Roman Emperor and men of conspicuous valour and military accomplishment, such as Lovell's own kinsman by marriage, Sir William Parr. Membership was limited to twenty-four individuals, including the king and the young Prince of Wales. Lovell was the first Knight of the Garter to be appointed by Richard III and he filled a vacancy that had existed since the death, on 10 September 1482, of the illustrious Italian mercenary entrepreneur, Frederigo Montefeltro, Duke of Urbino. This honour speaks volumes of Lovell's closeness to Richard, but is also testament to his military and chivalric capabilities. Appointment to the Order was highly sought after and sparingly awarded; such was its prestige that the Portuguese Prince Henry, known as 'Henry the Navigator', had been buried in full Garter robes.

The uprising in Kent

Richard III, Lovell and the royal court, including Margaret Beaufort's husband, Lord Stanley, were at Lincoln when news of the rebellion broke. Reports arrived that the men of Kent had risen, perhaps prematurely, in an attempt to gain control of the capital before the king returned. The Duke of Norfolk and his son, the Earl of Surrey, were at this time viewing their newly acquired estates in the area and they immediately took command of the situation. Orders were sent by Norfolk to prepare the defences of the capital and to ensure that the Thames crossing at Gravesend was held by a trusted retainer, John Middleton, and 100 men. Norfolk also instructed Lord Cobham, a Surrey peer, to gather his retinue and advance against the rebels.[4] Richard immediately sent out summons to his supporters in Yorkshire and Lancashire, where he hoped that Lord Strange, Stanley's son, at Lathom would declare for him.

Richard was faced with a dilemma; as yet he was unsure of where the centre of the revolt lay, its focus, and who was involved. The rising in Kent was clearly that of old Woodville familiars, but Richard could not be certain that the revolt only comprised of the usual suspects. No period of fifteenth-century politics is more opaque than that of 1483–87, and it must have appeared doubly so to Richard and his entourage as they laboured south in early October 1483, surrounded by a haze of speculation and suspicion. One thing that Richard appears to have been sure about was that the leader of the revolt and the mainspring of discontent was the Duke of Buckingham; all of Richard's proclamations appear to focus primarily on Buckingham and then the Marquis of Dorset. This is interesting, for if Buckingham and Dorset were indeed the main protagonists, who did they have in mind for king in Richard's stead? No contemporary account posits Henry Tudor as putative king at this point, Margaret Beaufort and Henry Tudor appear as participants in the rebellion, but not as its focus. This initial rising is in support of the two princes, Edward V and his brother, Richard, Duke of York, both assumed to be alive, despite rumours to the contrary. Therein lay the danger to Richard and his supporters.

Richard III began to mobilize his forces, calling for a general muster at Leicester on 23 October. If not the experienced campaigners of Ricardian belief, Richard, Lovell and members of his household were, at the very least, competent soldiers who, apprised of the facts, were quickly able to construct a cohesive military strategy in response. Richard was acting on information brought in by spies, informants and well-wishers. While the men of Kent had revolted prematurely on 11 October, a more co-ordinated revolt had erupted in southern England on 18 October. This is the date recorded by the Act of Attainder, although planning and preparations had obviously pre-dated the act by some time, most notably at Salisbury and at Brecon and Exeter. Recognizing this, Richard moved south west from Leicester to Coventry, arriving on 24 October. Before departing for Coventry, on 23 October Richard issued a 'General Commission of array to the king's kinsman Francis viscount Lovell, for the resistance of the rebel Henry, Duke of Buckingham by word of mouth.' The last words of the commission reveal the urgency of the situation: no warrant or seal is used – the king gave instruction by word of mouth as his household was now placed on a war-footing. Acting on this instruction we have one of the few documents to survive, attributed directly to Francis Lovell, who writes directly to his neighbour and kinsman, Sir William Stonor:

> I commend me to you as heartily as I can. Forasmuch as it pleases the king's grace to have warned you and all others to attend upon his grace and your company that you will come in my command and my company will be with. And I am sure it will please his grace best and cause me to think that you love my honour and I trust shall be to your security.[5]

Lovell's summons to Stonor was part of this mobilization, gathering support for the king en route and bringing in his connection from the Lovell heartlands. As he and the king headed south from Coventry to Oxford, Lovell seems to have been confident of meeting a muster of his own retainers and gentry supporters from Oxfordshire and Berkshire, bringing the Thames Valley to the king's standard. He clearly anticipated the support of his retinue at this time, also writing to the Harcourts requesting that they muster their men and join his company as it headed south through Oxfordshire. This was not really a request, but a veiled command to join with Lovell's already half-mobilized retinue. In this, Lovell was to be gravely disappointed for he had failed to recognize that Stonor and other members of the Oxfordshire gentry had, over a long time, developed close links not only with William, Lord Hastings, but also with Elizabeth Woodville's son, the Marquis of Dorset. These earlier loyalties now took precedence as Stonor took the information regarding the date and the location of the king's muster to the rebel encampment at Newbury. This episode reveals a certain political naivety on Lovell's part and an inability to recognize that others' political associations and calculations were not viewed through the same prism of personal friendship as his own.

Richard III's strategy was to move from Leicester to Coventry and on to Oxford, towards the centres of rebellion at Newbury and Salisbury. This would isolate the rebels from Buckingham's forces, which were mustering at Brecon and would have to cross the river Severn if they were to join with the others. Those at Exeter were also awaiting the arrival of a fleet from Brittany bringing professional Breton troops led by Henry Tudor and his uncle, Jasper. In this light, Richard's strategy was militarily sound, seeking to eliminate the rebel conspiracies before they could become concentrated in one area. As he came further south, Lovell's knowledge of the area, his connections with the gentry and prominent county officials, together with his own retinue, would have been invaluable to Richard, whose own experiences and connections were heavily focused on the north. Lovell and the Duke of Norfolk would be crucial intermediaries between the king and local society and necessary enforcements of newly formed alliances. By 28 October, Richard was in Oxford, in the heart of Lovell country, and must have been highly satisfied with the progress of the campaign thus far. Norfolk had been easily able to retain control of the capital and his son, the Earl of Surrey, had been able to disperse the rebels who had risen in the Weald of Sussex and East Kent. Here Richard was aided by Lord Cobham. He was also aided by the appalling weather, especially in the English Channel, which, from 15 to 25 October, experienced continuous wind and gales that would prevent Henry Tudor sailing from Brittany.

The weather had more drastic consequences for the rebels in the west, causing the river Severn to rise in spate and become impassable. Stranded on the west bank of the river and suffering unseasonably torrential and unrelenting rain, Buckingham's forces began to melt away. Buckingham, seen as being a 'hard driving' man, was unpopular with his Welsh tenants; he was also unable to control his own core territories and evidence of his unpopularity prompted the Vaughan family of Tretower (no doubt with the encouragement of William Herbert, Earl of Huntingdon) to sack his castle at Brecon, ensuring there was no retreat available. With his forces wasting away, Buckingham sought to escape in disguise. Hiding in Shropshire, he was betrayed by Ralph Banaster of Wem, an old servant, for the huge reward offered by Richard III.

Buckingham was now brought as a prisoner to the king at Salisbury. Buckingham sought a private audience with Richard, no doubt relying on his eloquence to get him out of this rather tricky situation. His request was denied, presumably by Francis Lovell as the King's Chamberlain. The denial was wise as accounts suggest that Buckingham had secreted a knife in the sleeve of his doublet and he was planning to kill Richard. On 2 November 1483, Buckingham was brought into the market square at Salisbury and beheaded, ending his participation in the rebellion that bore his name.

The execution of Buckingham exposed the remaining rebels to the full force of royal wrath. At Exeter, Richard III's brother-in-law – Sir Thomas St Leger, the Marquis of Dorset – Edward Courteney and his cousin Piers, Bishop of Exeter, were now standing alone as the king with the royal army drew near. St Leger, Dorset and their cohorts had been anticipating support from Buckingham, whose forces had never crossed the Severn, and from Henry Tudor, who was rumoured to be arriving in the West Country with a Breton army 5,000 strong. There is no evidence that Henry Tudor had expectations of the crown at this point, but rather had joined the conspiracy to return to England and to assume his father's title and estate (the earldom of Richmond). Unfortunately for the rebels, severe gales and bad weather in the Channel had prevented Henry Tudor from sailing and by 30 October he was still anchored in Breton ports. Henry did not sail for England until the first week of November, when it was too late and the rebellion was dead in the water. In fact, Henry had been lucky to avoid a trap at Plymouth by Richard's supporters and soldiers masquerading as rebels trying to induce Henry to land, a ruse which failed as the ever-cautious Henry turned about and returned to France. The last act of the rebellion occurred on 3 November at Bodmin, where men congregated outside the town to call for a new king (though contemporary sources seem unsure as to who that new king should be).

A 'revolt of the establishment'

Richard III arrived at Exeter on 6 November to bring summary royal justice to the West Country where the feared punishments for treason were now meted out. On 13 November, Richard's brother-in-law, Sir Thomas St Leger, by all accounts a valiant soldier, was brought into Exeter castle where, with two others, he was beheaded. His punishment was part of a royal retribution that encompassed a total of 103 attainders proclaimed throughout south and central England, including eighteen in Devon. Standing at his sovereign's shoulder as these punishments were meted out was Francis Lovell, who, on the same day as St Leger's execution, was given a commission with Richard Harcourt, William Catesby, esquire of the body, and Edward Frank, to arrest and imprison all rebels in the counties of Oxford and Berkshire.[6] This commission was issued in Richard's presence and is indicative of Lovell's standing in Oxford and Berkshire, which formed the core of his 'countrie'. Whilst it was clear that Lovell held the king's ear, he was to discover that this in itself was insufficient to command the obedience of local society. During his minority, established families such as the Harcourts and the Stonors had found patrons other than the Lovells and these associations were now proving more significant than Lovell's appeal on behalf of the king. The Stonors had been clients of Clarence, and later Hastings, and it was to be these older loyalties that would prevail, bringing both families out in support of the rebels. Nonetheless, Lovell was able to mobilize his retinue from Oxford and Berkshire on the king's behalf, and was supported by Edward Frank, the sheriff of Oxford. This event also represents the first recorded association of Francis Lovell and the Northamptonshire lawyer William Catesby, who would soon be pilloried by Collingbourne as 'the catte'. This association signalled a change in the politics of Northamptonshire as the Woodville interest in that county was now superseded by Lovell and those faithful to Richard III.

Whilst Buckingham's rebellion had been named after the most senior peer to come out against Richard, it could be argued that Buckingham was by no means the most important element in this revolt. One hundred and three attainders across the country suggests that the conspiracy was far greater and more widespread than that centred on one magnate, no matter how important he was. What Richard and his closest associates faced was what has been termed the 'revolt of the establishment'.[7] The revolt was the creation of the men who had served Edward IV for years and who had been his most effective supporters in the shires: men such as St Leger, John Cheyne, Giles Daubenay, the Hautes, the Fogges and Sir William Brandon. From Norfolk to Cornwall, these men had been the sinews of royal government; they were local men of substance who stood high in the king's favour and who translated the royal will into action throughout England. These men had shared many prior affiliations to the queen, the wider Woodville family and Lord Hastings, but more than this, all had been loyal to the House of York and, ultimately, to Edward IV. They rejected Richard's justifications for assuming the Crown and his displacement of Edward V; they were determined to bring down Richard's revolution. Initially, that had meant forming a plot to free the young princes, but at some point it became clear to them that the princes were no longer capable of being freed. From this point on, Richard had no legitimacy in their eyes, being viewed as a usurper, tyrant and now a murderer. This widespread hostility had caused them to rise in such numbers in a revolt that had ultimately proven futile. It had, however, changed the nature of government from a broadly Yorkist one, based on a political and dynastic consensus after 1471, to a narrower northern, Ricardian-based rule that was increasingly reliant on those who enjoyed a direct personal relationship with the king and who now had a considerable investment in the continuation of his reign.

10 'GREAT ABOUT THE KING'

The aftermath of the uprising

By 13 November 1483, Richard III could congratulate himself on his success in quelling the fires of rebellion. Whilst the embers of revolt stuttered into the New Year, all of its principal leaders were either dead, had fled or were now penniless exiles. Henry Tudor, having failed to make landfall at either Plymouth or Poole, had retreated to the coast of Normandy, from where he returned to Vannes in Brittany. Whatever role he had hoped to play if the rebellion had succeeded is now lost to us. What he did become on his return to Brittany was a figurehead for all those still committed to forming an opposition to Richard. In Brittany, Henry Tudor was joined by Elizabeth Woodville's eldest son, Thomas Grey Marquis of Dorset, Lionel Woodville, Bishop of Salisbury, Peter Courtenay, Bishop of Exeter, also Thomas Brandon, Sir William Norris, Sir William Knevet and others. Henry's small court now came to number approximately 1,500 exiles, now all lodged as guests of Duke Francis II of Brittany, living a precarious existence away from home, hearth and livelihood, subsisting on a pension sparingly doled out by Duke Francis' officials. In close contact with Henry was that other prominent Ricardian dissident, John Morton, Bishop of Ely. Having escaped from Brecon, he had made his way to the Burgundian Netherlands. This may seem to be a rather strange destination for an enemy of Richard III since prominent in the government of the Netherlands was Richard's sister, Margaret, Dowager Duchess of Burgundy. However, Morton appears to have resided in her dominions unmolested.

Richard's household had demonstrated its capacity to organize and direct a military response to the rising, successfully gathering and deploying its own resources whilst at the same time denying the opposition any opportunity to concentrate its own forces. Richard's leadership had been energetic and forceful with a sound grasp of tactics and strategy. In just three weeks he had assembled his forces and had descended from the Midlands to the West Country before the rebels could gather and before Henry Tudor and overseas support could arrive. Granted, the weather had been on his side, but Richard had not relied upon this in his planning, and he had instigated local counter-attacks led by capable subordinates such as the Duke of Norfolk, the Vaughans and the Stafford brothers in Worcestershire.

Richard viewed the rebellion as a continuation of the opposition of the Woodvilles and their supporters, and would present the rebellion to the forthcoming parliament in this light. Although Richard may have been genuine in his perception of the Woodvilles as the focus of the rebellion, the size and scale of the revolt should have disabused him of this. The rebellion had brought together three strands of opposition to Richard's ascent to the throne. The first and most significant had indeed been the Woodville-led revolt of the Edwardian establishment, which had been widespread and deep rooted throughout southern England. It had been joined by Buckingham, who seems to have had his own agenda in joining the revolt and whose opposition to Richard seems to have sprung from personal political calculation. In addition to this, the rebels were joined by Margaret Beaufort and her son, leaders of what remained of the Lancastrian faction. All of these were united and formed common cause by their enmity towards Richard. As the revolt ended, Margaret must have counted herself lucky to retain the liberty that she continued to enjoy, having been punished by being placed into her husband's custody and having her estates assigned to him.

During the winter of 1483, justices and commissions of Oyer and Terminer scoured the realm, especially in southern England. Swathes of the higher gentry were rounded up, including Sir William Daubenay, Sir John Cheyne and William Stonor. Edmund Hampden and John Harcourt, both neighbours and previous associates of Francis Lovell in Oxfordshire and Berkshire, were attainted. Those attainted had been estate officers, officers of the Crown and prominent members of the household of Edward IV : men such as Richard Guildford, Edward Poynings and John Darrell of Kent, who now fled overseas.[1] Lesser punitive measures included the imposition of fines, bonds and imprisonment. William Knyvet escaped attainder, but had to make over four manors in Norfolk to Richard's henchman, Sir James Tyrrell, as well as 800 marks, if he 'had not agreed he should have lost his life, livelihood and goods'.[2] A clearer case of high-level extortion would be difficult to find.

Yet Richard could be merciful. Whilst many were condemned, still more were to be pardoned and Richard began to draw up lists of who might approach him to seek pardon under the Great Seal, presumably with the support of the Privy Council, firstly at Beaulieu Abbey in November 1483 and at Nottingham in the spring of 1484. From these pardons we can gain a clearer picture of the scale of the revolt. Pardons were obtained by twelve nobles, forty-six knights, 170 squires, 191 gentle-men, fifty-seven merchants, 201 ecclesiastics and 201 yeomen. The nobles included Lords Abergavenny, Stourton, LaWarre, Audley, Dudley and Stanley. We can perhaps detect Lovell's intervention here in the pardoning of his kinsman John Norris, who escaped attainder and who was subsequently summoned to appear in person before the king 'in all goodly haste'.[3]

The proscription and attainder of so many members of Edward IV's corpus of local government created a political void that now had to be filled. Richard's solution was to replace those who had rebelled or who could no longer be trusted by those who could, principally members of his northern-based household. Alongside punishments and confiscations for those he saw as traitors came rewards for loyal supporters. From the spring of 1484, men loyal to the king now became prominent in the government and administration of the southern counties, men primarily loyal to the Crown and the centre and not the locality. These replacements brought with them their own trusted officers, family and servants so that the local body politic was now skewed to accommodate an alien growth. Gentry society and its links were broken; centuries of alliances, connections and trust were replaced with a new political grouping. The Crowland Chronicle summed up the mood, recording that Richard

> planted [his men] in every part of his dominions ... to the 'shame' of the Southerners who murmured ceaselessly and longed more each day for the return of their old lords in place of the tyranny of the present ones.[4]

The Crowland Chronicle's antipathy towards northerners reflects a longstanding preju-dice felt by southerners against those in the north, who were viewed as harsh, cruel and warlike because their blood was thought to be colder! The invasion of the south by Margaret of Anjou's northern army in the winter of 1460 was still remembered with dread in southern folk memory, despite no modern evidence of any great destruction. Nevertheless, the Crowland Chronicle's words do reflect a political reality, Richard did extend his power base into the south by inserting his trusted followers into posi-tions of power there, and whilst these were not all northern, all were alien, unwelcome and unfamiliar with the territories they now inhabited.

At least seven prominent Ricardian supporters were rewarded with estates and offices in southern England: Henry Percy, Earl of Northumberland, received author-ity to take possession of castles and lordships from Kent to Pembrokeshire; John, Lord Scrope, became steward of the temporalities of the bishopric of Exeter; Sir Ralph Ashton received land in Kent to the value of £100; Sir John Saville of Thornbury, in Yorkshire, became Lieutenant of the Isle of Wight; Sir Marmaduke Constable of Flamborough, in Yorkshire, became steward of the lordship of Tunbridge in Kent and Tutbury Castle in Derbyshire; Sir Thomas Worthey received land in Kent and Staffordshire; Sir Ralph Bigod of the East Riding became a justice of the peace in Kent. Even so, the greatest grants in land and money went, not to northerners, but to the East Anglian father and son, John Howard, Duke of Norfolk, and Thomas, Earl of Surrey, despite Richard already having rewarded Norfolk with his share of the Mowbray inheritance and the ducal title on 21 August 1484. Surrey received an annuity of £1,100[5] from the duchy of Cornwall during his father's lifetime. Similarly, William Herbert, Earl of Huntingdon, who married Richard's illegitimate daughter, Dame Katherine Plantagenet, received an annuity of £400[6] from the confiscated Buckingham lordships of Brecon, Newport and Hay. The king's nephew, John de la Pole, Earl of Lincoln, received confirmation of his title, plus lands worth £156 and an annuity of £276.13s.4d, as well as reversions on Margaret Beaufort's estates worth £203.[7] The greatest of these rewards was reserved for Richard's close adherent and henchman, Sir Richard Ratcliffe, who received the unprecedented gift of twenty-three manors and lordships in Devon, Somerset, Wiltshire, Lincoln and Cumberland. The elevation of a county knight into one of the greatest barons, by a single grant worth £662 per annum was unprecedented. In particular, the grant of the lordship of Tiverton and its outliers was astonishing in that it represented the caput, or administrative centre, of the Courtenay earldom of Devon, whose previous holders had been close members of the Yorkist family such as John, Marquis Montague, and George, Duke of Clarence. The fact that Ratcliffe was charged a modest rent of £50 per annum for this princely reward did little to assuage the jealousy of the broader political nation or the antagonism of Courtenay loyalists in Devon.

It can be argued that Richard's rewards were injudicious and extreme and that in this they demonstrate the fragility of his position as the normal rules of patronage were ignored in a rush to purchase loyalty rather than to reward service. Equally, it could be said that, in the aftermath of rebellion and amidst simmering resentments, Richard's policies were pragmatic as he utilized the personnel he could depend upon. The revolt of 1483 split asunder the Yorkist support that had propelled Edward IV to the throne in 1461 – support that had remained true throughout the vicissitudes of 1469–71 and after the battles of Barnet and Tewkesbury, coalescing into the broad consensus that Edward IV had enjoyed during the stability of his second reign.

Richard's capture of the throne had displaced the Woodvilles and their supporters and initially seemed to ensure that the older element of Yorkist support would now prevail. When it became apparent that the son of Edward IV was to be displaced by Richard III, opposition had formed around Lord Hastings. His execution had deprived what remained of Edward IV's household of a leader capable of organizing effective opposition to Richard. However, that opposition had not gone away. It took time for members of the household to recover from the shock of Hastings' execution and to reorganize. They had not, however, relinquished their hope that both the princes remained alive and that loyalty required that they at least try to free them and restore them to the throne. This did not appear to be a forlorn hope in September 1483, and it is for this reason that the rebellion broke throughout the south of England. Remarkably, apart from Buckingham, who had never been part of the apparatus of Yorkist government, no other major magnate had joined the rebellion. The lords had rather acquiesced to Richard's usurpation with greater or lesser demonstrations of enthusiasm. Their unwillingness to mobilize their retinues against him ensured the failure of the rebellion, which was now restricted to the functionaries and the office holders of the previous reign.

The new parliament dominated by Richard's supporters now exacted retribution on those it saw as traitors. An unprecedented 103 sentences of attainder were passed, mostly against the gentry of the west and the south. As if that were not enough, a further 421 applications for pardon were made as men hoped to make their peace with a vengeful king before his commissioners had a chance to look into their recent activities. Government was now formed by those men who were committed to the Ricardian settlement and had an investment, not only in the person of the king, but also in his government. Their loyalty had been forged and strengthened in the suppression of rebellion; in a crisis of duplicity and betrayal, they had stood by their king and faced down threats and, in their eyes at least, had saved the realm from traitors.

As for Richard, after 26 July he was now a duly consecrated king, irrespective of how he had achieved this, and would now confer largesse not just for past loyalties but in expectation of those to come.

John Howard, who had become Duke of Norfolk, now became Admiral of England, partly because of his service to Richard and experience during the Scottish campaign of 1482. Lord Stanley, a power in the north-west, became Constable of England, a role vacated by Buckingham, and the Earl of Northumberland became Steward of England; all were high offices previously occupied by great nobles like themselves and associated with warfare and chivalry.

With this triumvirate of nobles stands Francis, Viscount Lovell, for, as the role of the king's household expanded into the direct governance of some of the southern counties, so did the role of the King's Chamberlain. This is exemplified by Edmund Chatterton, treasurer of the chamber, who was given personal charge as receiver and surveyor of the forfeited lands of Buckingham. As treasurer of the chamber, Chatterton reported directly to Francis Lovell, as did Sir Robert Brackenbury (once Richard's ducal treasurer). These men, who controlled the king's chamber and finances, now came under the authority of the new King's Chamberlain, which placed Francis Lovell at the heart of government.

During Richard's reign fifty-four men were to serve as councillors; of these, twenty-six were appointed during the reign, and it was upon these men that the burden of government now fell, and from whom an inner privy council of trusted associates was selected. Parliament met on 22 January 1484, having been post-poned from the previous November in the wake of the rebellion. Its role was now to provide a platform to articulate the ambitions of the new reign. Lovell, as King's Chamberlain, had to present the requirements and wishes of the king to the Lords and the Commons and to obtain, as far as possible, a compliance with those wishes. As the first parliament of the new reign, it was important that the new king made a good impression as he had come to the throne under unusual circumstances and had survived and suppressed a rebellion against his rule. Richard now had to appear regal, firm and yet conciliatory, particularly as so many members of the Commons knew or were related to those who had been proscribed or attainted as traitors, executed or who had fled into exile. Resentments had to be eased and anger mollified. Equally, Richard had to be seen, not only to be reaching out a conciliatory hand to those who were not his active supporters, but to be positively embracing them.

Richard's first and only parliament

Richard's government, no doubt with, some judicious arm-twisting by Francis Lovell, gained its first victory with the appointment of the royal councillor, William Catesby as Speaker. Catesby was born in 1450 to Northamptonshire gentry and had trained in law at the Inner Temple; previously he had found preferment in the service of Lord Hastings. He had married the daughter of William, Lord Zouche, and had gravitated to the service of Richard, Duke of Gloucester, and, in 1483, a seat on the royal council. In January 1484, he was elected as Speaker of the House of Commons – a very unusual step because he had never been an MP and was therefore unfamiliar with parliamentary procedure. His appointment underlines the influence the Crown had over parliament and particularly Lovell's influence in, not only suggesting Catesby as Speaker, but also being able to engineer his election.

With Catesby in place as Speaker of the Commons, and Lovell as Chamberlain and a leading voice in the Lords, the business of parliament could now begin. The principal business was to pass the Act of Titulus Regius (Royal Title) under which Richard declared his right to the throne. Whilst large elements of the act repeat the provisions of the acclamation of Richard enunciated by Buckingham in June 1483, the discussion of its provisions and its passing by parliament gave its content legal force. The act reiterates the declaration made the previous summer that the claim to the throne by Edward V was invalid since, at the time of his parent's marriage, Edward IV had not been free to marry Elizabeth Woodville, having previously entered into a pre-contract (a promise of marriage) with Eleanor Butler, daughter of the Earl of Shrewsbury. This rumour, which had been in the public domain since 1469, now became parliamentary statute and legally invalidated both Edward's marriage and, therefore, the rights of his children. The Act itself stated:

And how, that at the time of the same pretended Marriage and before and for a long time after, the said King Edward was and stood married and both plight to one dame Eleanor Butler, Daughter of the old Earl of Shrewsbury with whom the same King Edward had made a pre-contract of Matrimony, long time before he made the said pretended Marriage with the said Elizabeth [Woodville] Grey in manner and form above said.[8]

Thus, Richard's right to the throne was presented to Parliament, which was now required, not only to agree to his title but to endorse it with full legality; Richard's right to accession now acquired the veneer of law in what was in effect, the highest court in the land.

The parliament of 1484 can be regarded as fairly representative with a house containing 296 MPs, and we can be relatively confident that the Crowland Chronicle's assertion that 'such terror affected even the most stout hearted among them'[9] was a later exaggeration. Nevertheless, men would have been wary of nay-saying a king who had just suppressed a major rebellion and who now seemed to sit quite comfortably on the throne. The first act of the parliament, following the passing of the Titulus Regius, was to confirm Richard's acclamation as king by the three estates of the realm – the lords, the commons and the bishops.

Richard's one and only parliament then passed a number of public acts upon which his reputation as a conscientious ruler now rests. In these we see some enlightened notions, such as bail for suspected felons, property qualifications for jurors and the condemnation of illegal and arbitrary taxes and gifts, known as 'benevolences', by the Crown. He also introduced a thorough review of the existing regulations affecting the cloth trade, at that time easily England's biggest export, and related to this were a number of actions against foreign merchants reflecting a xenophobic attitude towards trade, which stretched back through Edward IV's reign into that of Henry VI.

Accommodating Richard

These actions, although interesting to economic historians and jurists (not to mention Ricardians in general) were overshadowed by the most dramatic event of Richard's parliament. On 1 March 1484, the realm received the sensational news that the Dowager Queen Elizabeth was to allow her five daughters, aged between eighteen and three to leave sanctuary at Westminster. These were Elizabeth (aged 18), Cecily (aged 13), Anne (aged 9), Katherine (aged 5) and Bridget (aged 3). The same day the king swore an oath in public before lords, churchmen, the mayor and aldermen of London that if the girls left sanctuary they would 'be in surety of their lives'[10] and would not be imprisoned in the Tower. He also swore that they would be placed in 'honest places of good name and fame' and that each would be married to gentle-men born, and that he would provide them with dowries of 200 marks. In addition, 'Elizabeth Grey, late calling herself queen of England' was to receive a pension of 700 marks a year, paid through John Nesfield, a longstanding officer of the royal household, into whose charge she would be placed.

Elizabeth Woodville has been condemned for reaching an accommodation with the man who had executed her brother (Earl Rivers) and her son (Richard Grey), bastardized all of her children by Edward IV, and driven her eldest son, the Marquis of Dorset, into exile. She would also be forced to swallow the well-nigh impossible notion of reaching agreement with a man that she must certainly have thought was behind the murder of her other two sons. Yet this ignores the realities of the position in which she found herself and the political realities that the parliament of 1484 now legalized. Elizabeth faced an isolated and bleak future in opposition to Richard III; bereft of allies in England, she had little alternative but to respond to Richard's offers. The princes in the Tower were almost certainly dead and the rebellion had failed; Richard III was aged only 31 and appeared in good health; she and her daughters could not stay in sanctuary indefinitely, and it is unlikely that she seriously contemplated that they would all take the veil. Acceptance of the king's offer was a pragmatic decision and, realistically, the only viable option left to her if she did not want to accept the gloomy alternative of ossifying in the well-guarded precincts of Westminster.

Elizabeth Woodville's acquiescence was a triumphant coup for Richard and his council; a potentially prickly problem in the form of Elizabeth and her daughters, particularly by virtue of their ages and gender, had been resolved. No king could preserve his reputation by allowing harm to befall 'weak' and friendless women and children, even if he were responsible for removing all their male protectors in the first place. It would be politically injudicious for Richard to bring legal proceedings against the daughters, the most important members of the family, since they were not guilty of any crime and could not be blamed for the actions of their parents. Despite the aspersions now thrown upon their legitimacy, their parentage had never been in doubt and their father had been a crowned king of the realm. So, whilst their very being was overtly political, the king and his council were constrained in what they could do to challenge this. Thus, a compromise in which the girls were accorded a degree of respectability and positions at court was a sensible option for both parties and a political triumph for Richard. With the voluntary surrendering of Edward IV's daughters into his care, Richard had eliminated the last vestige of opposition in England. More crucially, he was now able to pull the rug from under those who sought to replace him by marrying off the eldest of the Woodville girls, Elizabeth of York. His ability to sponsor the marriages of the girls was a political coup of the first order, enabling him to neutralize the aspirations of Henry Tudor and ensure his continued impotence.

The political reconciliation with the former queen, Elizabeth Woodville, ensured Richard's domestic supremacy. He had seen off his enemies whilst successfully calling together the political nation in a parliament. With judicious use of patronage, he had been able to convert the majority of the higher nobility into supporters of the new regime. Of the two remaining dukes, one – Norfolk – owed his title and his lands to Richard's active patronage and so both he and his son, the Earl of Surrey, were now active supporters and, indeed, both members of the king's council. The other – Suffolk – had been Richard's brother-in-law since 1457 and was, therefore, a close family associate. It was not deemed necessary to reward the now elderly duke but his son, Richard's nephew, John, Earl of Lincoln, had been well rewarded, with lands worth £333.2s.5d annually and a pension from the Duchy of Cornwall of £176 a year. In addition, Lincoln held the office of Lord Lieutenant of Ireland and would soon become the king's replacement on the Council of the North. The Earl of Northumberland was not only confirmed in his family's traditional offices in the East March towards Scotland, but Henry Percy was able to regain family property, which had been alienated from them since 1418.

Richard's son-in-law, the Earl of Huntingdon, was now brought into the extended royal family and materially bolstered by a grant of land of £400. In addition, Richard partially restored William Herbert to his father's pre-eminence in the principality of Wales by making him once again Chief Justice of South Wales and a guard against residual Tudor loyalty in that area. Of the remaining earls – Westmorland, Arundel, Nottingham and Kent – Richard had rewarded where necessary and conciliated where not. Westmorland was elderly and his son, Lord John Nevill, was a long-time supporter of Richard who was to succeed his father in 1484. Likewise, Arundel was old and his son, Lord Maltravers, was rewarded and viewed favourably at court. Kent was also old and had been politically inactive for a number of years, so could safely be left in peace. The Earl of Nottingham was childless and eccentric, an inveterate collector of titles who owed his greatest (that of the earldom of Nottingham) to Richard's support for his claim on the Mowbray inheritance.

Of the lords, a significant number were either family members or members of Richard III's existing northern affinity. These included Scrope of Bolton and Scrope of Masham, Lovell's brother-in-law, Lord Fitzhugh, and Lord Dacre of Gilsland. Other northern lords, such as Lumley and Greystoke, were longstanding adherents of the Nevill family, with strands of loyalty going back generations to Warwick the kingmaker and beyond. Lord Ferrers came from a family with strong ties to the Herbert family and also with close links with the House of York. Other traditional supporters of the House of York were Audley, Cobham, Dudley and Dinham, all of whom could be relied upon.

All in all then, Richard's government could count on the support of over sixteen members of the House of Lords – more than half of the parliamentary baronage.[11] This provided Richard with a firm base of support for any actions within parliament, especially since these lords were all sponsors of many members of the House of Commons as well. They also ensured that the king's influence extended beyond the court into the localities where they were justices of the peace and leaders of traditional country society. Whilst these new men were resented in areas where they had displaced traditional elites who had either perished or chosen exile after Buckingham's rebellion, there was, in reality, little alternative to loyalty.

The one lord who stood apart from this rather pleasing picture was Sir William Stanley. The Stanley family had come to occupy a predominant position in southern Lancashire and Cheshire as the previously strong Lancastrian affinity had slowly disintegrated during the childhood and reign of Henry VI. Through the assiduous use of offices and resident local influence, the Stanley family had risen to a position of pre-eminence in the north-west since the 1440s. Strongly rooted in their area of influence, the Stanleys had woven a judicious political path through the turmoil of the 1450s and 1460s to dominate Lancashire by 1483. The Stanleys' relationship with Richard in the past was strained, to say the least, when, in 1467, Richard, as Duke of Gloucester, had joined with the Harrington family to hold Hornby Castle in northern Lancashire against the Stanleys. Despite this and Stanley's equivocal attitude towards Richard, their relationship had survived the crisis of June 1483 when Stanley had been wounded during the arrest of Hastings and when he himself had been imprisoned briefly. Although resolved, this left each party rather wary of the other; Stanley had remained loyal (or, more accurately, inactive) during Buckingham's rebellion and had been handsomely rewarded with land worth £687 per annum, including Buckingham's palatial manor of Thornbury in Gloucestershire. Stanley's inaction had in itself been hugely valuable given the prominent role his wife, Margaret Beaufort, had played in not only organizing, but in brokering, the intervention of her son, Henry Tudor, from Brittany during the recent rebellion.

The actions of Margaret left Richard in a quandary. He could not exhaust his already low political capital by executing a woman, adding to his already unwholesome reputation; but neither could he allow such a prominent rebel to get away scot free. He therefore resolved to act in a balanced way that would deprive Margaret of both her estates and income whilst at the same time rewarding the wavering support of her husband. As such, Margaret was deprived of her estates and her liberty, both of which were entrusted to her husband, who would now be closely watched. In this respect, Richard had brought a recalcitrant rebel to heel without attracting the odium that would inevitably accrue at the execution of a famously pious middle-aged woman. Whilst it was a calculated risk, it is difficult to see what else Richard could have done, short of Margaret taking the veil. Placing Margaret under the government of her husband, Richard was conforming to the accepted gender roles of the time. From Stanley's point of view, when Richard vested his wife's estates in his hands directly, he made him a provision of lands worth over £1,300 per annum and greatly increased his national profile. In this way, Richard seemingly neutralized his one existing threat in the kingdom whilst keeping an eye on the potential threat emanating from Henry Tudor who, with his uncle, Jasper Tudor, was once again a pensioner of the Duke of Brittany.

Henry Tudor

Ironically, the failure of Buckingham's rebellion had considerably strengthened Henry Tudor's hand, if only in the raising of his profile amongst the English nobility. In fact, prior to Buckingham's rebellion, Henry and Jasper had been largely forgotten. Indeed, there was nothing that could have been seen to constitute a Lancastrian party in England in 1483. The House of Lancaster had died with the death of Henry VI's son, Edward, at Tewkesbury in 1471. After that, even diehards such as the Butlers had reached an accommodation with Edward IV. There were some irreconcilables, such as John de Vere, sometime Earl of Oxford, and Jasper Tudor, and, indeed, others such as Lord Clifford (who lived in such obscurity on the Lancashire moors that he was known as the shepherd-lord) or Viscount Beaumont (who was allowed to reside in England but was deprived of his lands and titles). These families may have harboured grievances, but they were isolated and no longer part of a dynastic party.

Margaret Beaufort, having lost three close relatives in the dynastic conflicts of the 1460s, had reached an accommodation with Edward IV in 1471 and from then on had assiduously campaigned for the return of her son, Henry Tudor, as Earl of Richmond. This was a title and lands to which he was legally entitled, never having been arraigned or attainted. Indeed, Edward IV had considered Henry's restoration as earl on a number of occasions during the 1470s, but ultimately he had not relented and Henry remained in exile. Here, he and his uncle, Jasper, were political pawns for a cause that was receding further and further into memory with each passing year. Jasper, in particular, whilst still a 'Prince of the Lilies', was increasingly becoming an ornament of earlier conflicts.

This changed when Henry Tudor had agreed to participate in his mother's plotting against Richard III. His escape from royal forces at Plymouth, when he had not been deceived by Richard's soldiers' false assurances to come ashore, had been fortuitous, but it had not altered his material circumstances. What did, though, was the arrival of other refugees from the failure of the revolt. During November and December 1483, 'a great number of English gentlemen came to Vannes to "seek out" Henry.'[12] Ultimately, they would number 1,500 and included such notable figures as Thomas Grey, Marquis of Dorset, Sir Giles Daubeney, an intimate member of Edward IV's household, Sir John Cheney, Edward IV's standard bearer and master of his horse, Lionel Woodville, Bishop of Salisbury, Sir John Harcourt, Francis Lovell's neighbour and cousin and previously a prominent member of Lord Hasting's affinity. These and many others, such as Sir William Brandon, were now summoned by Henry to the ducal capital of Nantes, where much deliberation and discussion took place. It must have seemed strange to these men to now be answering the call of a penniless Welsh exile who had not trodden the soil of England in over twelve years and who they and their relatives had originally driven into exile. At the negotiating table was Jasper, once Earl of Pembroke, whose resentments went back further, to the 1450s and whose brother and half-brother (Henry VI) had suffered and died at the hands of these men and their families. For Jasper, thirty years of hurt had to be assuaged to reach any form of compact with such men.

For the members of Edward IV's household there must also have been much contemplation and reflection. Less than a year earlier, they had all been men of standing and position, with the affection of the king and important roles in the state. Now here they were in a foreign land, bereft of status, wealth and rank, and supplicants to a penniless exile. Such, as the fifteenth-century mind would have it, was the turning of fortune's wheel. Both parties were brought together by desperation and another hoped-for throw of the dice. On Christmas Day 1483, this desperate bond was formalized into an alliance of the disaffected, before the Duchess of Brittany in Rennes Cathedral, as noted by the Italian humanist, Polydore Vergil:

> the day of Christ's nativity was come upon, which meeteth all in the church, they ratified all other things by the plight in of their truths and solemn covenants; and first of all Earl Henry upon this oath promised that, so soon as he should be King he would marry Elizabeth, King Edward's daughter, then after they swore unto him homage as though he had already been created king, protesting that they would lose not only their lands and possessions but their lives before they would suffer, bear or permit, that Richard should rule over them and theirs.[13]

It was an oath made with the full knowledge that they had already lost their lands and possessions and that Richard ruled over the kingdom they had left behind. On the other side of the Channel during Christmas 1483 it looked as if Richard's reign was secure, as was the future of Francis Lovell, who stood by his side.

11 'TWICE BASTARDIZED RICHMOND'

More honours

IN FEBRUARY 1484, FRANCIS Lovell could look upon his career so far with some satisfaction. He now stood at the king's shoulder as his chamberlain and butler, but, more importantly perhaps, he had helped to secure the crown for his friend, Richard. As a staunch supporter of Richard, Francis had been materially rewarded and his position in his core lands of Oxfordshire and Berkshire bolstered. This, however, paled in comparison with the less tangible rewards that accompanied his role in constant attendance upon the king, who clearly valued his advice and support as well as his friendship. As chamberlain, Francis was a constant presence at court and at the king's side in Westminster, the proximity of his principal landholdings in Oxfordshire and the Thames Valley allowing him to spend more time with the king than the other great magnates, such as Norfolk or Northumberland, referred to in contemporary chronicles. Both of these peers had particular regional responsibilities that would have absented them from court for long periods of time. John, Duke of Norfolk, had only recently obtained his title and lands and so had to spend time building up and maintaining his connection in East Anglia. He also had to overcome a reluctance on the part of the local gentry to look up to one who had only recently been a member of the gentry like themselves. This meant that Norfolk, having acquired a substantial share of the Mowbray inheritance, had to make his regional standing a reality. This required the assiduous cultivation of local gentry and, therefore, a prolonged presence amongst them. It also required him to tread carefully in an area where the Duke of Suffolk had previously held a dominant position since 1476. There is no evidence that the two dukes had anything other than an amicable relationship, yet Norfolk must have been acutely aware that he had his work cut out to build up his own influence without alienating Suffolk and reducing East Anglia to the level of disturbance that had existed in the 1450s.

If Norfolk's attendance at court was intermittent, the same could be said of Northumberland, who had even greater commitments. For the Earl of Northumberland, Richard's accession removed the hand of a royal duke from the direct governance of the north. When Richard went south to claim the throne, Northumberland saw a chance to re-establish the authority that his family had once held in the north. Northumberland, based on the East March, could now look forward to dominating large swathes of the north and Yorkshire without, he hoped, having to look over his shoulder for the agreement of a resident royal duke. As Warden of the East March, Northumberland had direct military responsibilities, defending the north against Scottish incursions and raiding. As king, Richard had rewarded his northern supporters with lands in the south and the Midlands, so these men, such as the Scropes and Fitzhughs, took on a new role, beyond their traditional spheres of influence; thus, Northumberland became more and more important in holding the line in the north. This meant that his attendance at court was even more sporadic than that of Norfolk, denying him a major role at the centre of affairs by virtue of his other offices and distance.

Northumberland was a major regional power whose standing in northern society was not diminished when Richard appointed his young nephew, John, Earl of Lincoln, as Lord of the North and president of the Council of the North. Even so, Lincoln's surprise appointment must have shocked Northumberland because the only advantages Lincoln brought were his relationship with the king and his high birth. Lincoln had spent the majority of his life in East Anglia and the Thames Valley, and was both young and relatively inexperienced; nor, despite his high birth, did he possess any land, estates or following in the north. This required or allowed Northumberland to take up an increasing leadership of northern society and to place his family's resources at the disposal of the Crown, ensuring peace in the north.

The other counsellors mentioned in the chronicles of the time and known to be close to Richard were Sir Richard Ratcliffe and William Catesby, who were well regarded and trusted. Both men were highly regarded by Richard personally, but were, in fact, no more than functionaries and henchmen. Like Sir James Tyrrell, their role was to enact their master's wishes and to perform the duties and obligations required of them. They did not possess either the social standing or status to challenge Francis Lovell's friendship with the king. Although well respected, they did not inhabit the same social milieu as the greater nobility, nor did they possess the same value system or ingrained sense of caste shared by the king and these higher nobles. This became more apparent when, as the Crowland Chronicle records, Richard came to emphasize his own sense of majesty. This inevitably reduced the circle of friendship that he had enjoyed previously and altered the roles of those about him.

Despite his moralizing, Richard was as much in thrall to display and magnificence as his brother, Edward IV, had been. Despite making the point of condemning Edward's excesses and extravagances and those of the Woodville family, Richard recognized the importance and value of display to a king. The only near contemporary portrait of Richard III in the National Gallery shows him richly adorned in furs with his doublet fashionably and deliberately slashed to reveal a lavishly embroidered lining and under-mantle. On his right hand he wears three rings, which he appears to be toying with either nervously or absent-mindedly; his shoulders are adorned with a chain of gold encrusted with pearls and rubies whilst his hat has a similarly ornamented brooch and a hanging pearl fashionably in place. Richard recognized that conspicuous display was required of a monarch and so ensured that his court was praised for its magnificence with him resplendent at the centre of it. The pronounced focus on formal etiquette and manners for which the Burgundian court was famous was also reflected at the English court. This fashion for finessed behaviour, elaborate ceremonial and chivalric display needed a choreographer in the person of the King's Chamberlain, a role occupied by Francis Lovell, who was responsible for projecting the king's image to his subjects. The ideal was a sense of awe-inspiring majesty. Indeed, 'Nobody was the king's equal, not even his relatives or favourites. All had to abase themselves.'[1]

This use of magnificence and ceremonial was part of the process used to manage the realm. It was meant to both appeal to and to overawe Parliament. It demonstrated to foreign visitors and observers the wealth and power of the English Crown. It also demonstrated to the people that their king was worthy to wear the crown and possessed of sufficient majesty to rule. The joint enterprise to maintain the façade and the construction of this public persona inevitably brought Richard III closer to Lovell whilst increasing his attachment to this older friendship that harked back to less complicated times. As Richard and Lovell surveyed England in March 1484, they would have had every reason to be satisfied: after the recent rebellion, successfully put down, the realm was now quiescent and firmly under the king's control; there was peace on the northern frontier; and Parliament, as well as the higher nobility, had endorsed Richard as king. In addition to which, Elizabeth Woodville had also returned to court and placed her daughters under the king's tutelage.

A personal blow with dynastic consequences

Having seemingly overcome all threats to his rule and having crushed his domestic enemies, Richard was unprepared for the devastating repost that fate had in store for him. On 9 April 1484, Richard and his queen were at Nottingham Castle when they received the devastating news that their only child, the ten-year-old Prince of Wales (known as Edward of Middleham) was dead. It would appear that the boy had not enjoyed particularly robust health, but at no time had his parents any genuine reasons for concern, and his sudden death was a terrible shock to them both. The Crowland Chronicle recorded the highly charged atmosphere as both parents were told of the death of their only child and the king's heir.

> On hearing the news of this at Nottingham, where they were then residing, you might have seen his father and mother almost bordering on madness by reason of their sudden grief.[2]

The death of their son was a devastating, personal blow for his grieving parents. It also had profound political and dynastic consequences for them. Richard could no longer promise a dynastic investment in the future and with no such promise, there could be no stability for the realm. Enough was known of the queen's health for the political nation to be aware both of her indisposition and to recognize that a further heir was unlikely. Anne Nevill was not yet thirty, but few seem to have doubted that she was unlikely to have any more sons. Both of Warwick's daughters were descended from the Beauchamps, who had themselves failed in the male line. Warwick and Anne Nevill (Richard's mother-in-law) had produced only two daughters and through them the previously fecund Nevill family had come to dynastic grief. The same was now happening to the House of York. Anne Nevill had been childless for the previous ten years and most thought it extremely doubtful that she would once more become fertile. A longer shadow in more ways than one may well have been the early signs that she may have been suffering from the tuberculosis that would eventually kill her.

The death of Richard's son immediately altered the political situation. In an age that strongly believed in signs and portents, the death of Edward of Middleham was seen as a divine judgement: a clear case of biblical justice for the Yorkist Herod with an eye for an eye and a tooth for a tooth. Here was evidence that nothing eluded an all-seeing God who knew what had really happened to the two princes in the Tower and had now taken appropriate vengeance. Throughout England there were those who saw only too clearly that the hand of Providence had reached out and plucked the king's only son from the bosom of his family. This, despite the efforts of Richard and his government, was clearly seen as evidence of the king's complicity in the death of his royal nephews. Edward of Middleham's death was not merely dynastic, but had widespread political effects that even the simplest person in the kingdom could understand. It eroded the obligation of loyalty towards a king that even God had turned against.

With the death of his son, Richard now appeared, domestically and internationally, to be a self-seeking usurper whose actions only served himself and not the realm. This weakness now began to open up divisions that only a couple of months earlier had seemed closed. The abscess of suspicion and conspiracy, which had existed before Buckingham's rebellion and which the king had thought he had lanced, now began to gather again. Those who had seen their aspirations crushed and their hopes dashed now began to see them revived. Instead of an all-victorious king with a son on the verge of adolescence offering dynastic succession, Richard III was now reduced to the figure of an isolated individual only a blade away from being overthrown. If the death of Richard's son had produced paroxysms of grief at Nottingham, in Brittany it had produced cheers and a renewal of hope.

Henry Tudor's renewed hopes

The death of Edward of Middleham was the one piece of good news that Henry Tudor's small band of exiles heard that spring. Middleham's death had bolstered Henry Tudor's precarious position, which had become markedly worse since the previous Christmas. Richard III's rapproachment with Elizabeth Woodville had effectively pulled the marriage rug out from under Henry's feet, irrespective of any oaths sworn on Christmas Day in Rennes Cathedral. King Richard's possession of Edward IV's daughters effectively took them off the board as marriage pieces. The hope of a successful invasion and a unifying marriage began to look more and more remote in March 1484. There were also other consequences as one of Henry's most notable supporters now began to exhibit the strain of conflicting loyalties. Thomas Grey, Marquis of Dorset and the eldest son of Elizabeth Woodville, was the most prominent member of the wider family of Edward IV. He was the living reminder that Henry Tudor represented a wide coalition of interests bound together by a shared hatred of Richard III. Without Dorset and his followers, Henry would revert to what he had been for the previous thirteen years: merely the figurehead of a Lancastrian rump increasingly marginalized by English politics. Dorset's adherence to the Tudor cause had to be cemented and any thoughts of his defection stifled. When Dorset attempted to travel to England, Henry's servants ensured that he returned to Henry, who placed him under close supervision. Dorset's attempt at defection infected his relationship with Henry with a strain of suspicion that was never completely extinguished. From Dorset's point of view, if his mother had made peace with Richard III, what gains was he likely to obtain by continued opposition overseas? In addition, Henry's failure to make a successful landfall in England had rebounded on Brittany's government, which now began to question the value of its political investment in Henry Tudor. These doubts were confirmed when the government of Richard III began to apply pressure on Brittany for its support of Henry. The early months of 1484 saw the appointment of John, Lord Audley, to the command of a squadron of royal ships that began to aggressively patrol the English Channel. Duke Francis II and his leading councillor Pierre Landais could not afford to alienate England, whose support they needed to retain a large measure of independence from France. These concerns meant that Duke Francis's government held back from offering Henry Tudor further military support for the present. Nevertheless, with the death of Edward of Middleham, Henry Tudor and his supporters recognized that the political situation in England had irrevocably changed. Richard now appeared as a king marked by earthly suspicion and heavenly condemnation. Such attitudes had a corrosive effect on the body politic of the realm.

A grieving Richard fights back

The danger was recognized by Richard himself, even while mired in grief. His spies on the continent were looking at the affairs of those dissidents in Brittany and elsewhere, and he would have been well informed of Henry Tudor's actions. Richard would also have been aware of hostile French attitudes towards him and his regime after the French Chancellor Cardinal Rochfort told a meeting of the French estates general at Tours in January 1484:

Regard the events which have occurred in that land [England] since the death of king Edward. See how his children already quite old and brave have been murdered with impunity and the crown has been transferred to their assassin by the consent of the people.[3]

Whether this was a feigned or real attack, Rochfort was clearly voicing continental suspicions regarding Richard's path to the throne that also conveniently served to further blacken the national character of France's traditional enemy. Even so, the terms 'murder' and 'assassin' were undiplomatically precise.

Therefore, Richard had to attempt to shake off the lethargy of grief and make appropriate political and military preparations. No doubt consulting with his council, Richard began to make his dispositions. On 1 May 1484, Francis Lovell was appointed Commissioner of Array for Buckinghamshire, Oxfordshire, Berkshire and Northamptonshire. Lovell was clearly the most powerful person within these counties and the only peer summoned, indicating that his pre-eminence within these counties was unchallenged. It is also indicative of his local standing how many knights were arrayed to serve with him. These included old Yorkist supporters such as Sir John Down and Drew Burdinell and household men such as Robert Pemberton (of Northamptonshire) and Thomas Fowler. The only person on these commissions who was close in rank or authority to Lovell was Sir John Grey, son of Lord Grey of Wilton, a minor peer. Edward Franke and Richard Rugge, recently appointed sheriffs of Oxfordshire and Northamptonshire, were also included, but both men were already close adherents of Lovell and likely to abide by his instructions. Legal expertise was given by the ubiquitous William Catesby, whose family relations were particularly prominent on the commission for Northamptonshire. These men could be regarded as forming Lovell's connection and, between them, they would have dominated the area. The commission also demonstrates Lovell's importance to Richard's government and his integral position as one of the premier nobles of the realm. Like the Percy family and the Stanleys, Francis Lovell had a position of dominance in the Thames Valley and the Chilterns, and his dominance there was as much part of the political mosaic of power of Richard III's reign as the Stanley dominance in Lancashire and Percy rule in Northumberland. Like Hastings before him, Lovell represents a classic case of bastard feudalism able to utilize land office and proximity to the king to form a nexus of local and national power. These actions – those of government, of the impersonal, the objective and the calculated – must have brought some relief to Richard III, who must have been suffering the mental agonies of self-doubt and personal recrimination at this time.

Sowing 'the seed of noise and slander'

If Richard III's enemies could not immediately take advantage of his loss by launching an attack from abroad, they could try to capitalize on Richard's newly exposed domestic vulnerability by launching a propaganda offensive within the realm itself. Richard and his government were only too aware of the destabilizing effect of the placards and proclamations that were now becoming increasingly common, and their effect on the mind of the ordinary subject.

> So that divers seditious and evil disposed persons both in our city of London and elsewhere within our realm enforce themselves daily to sow seed of noise and slander against our person.[4]

The fact that Richard and his government felt the need to issue these prohibitions demonstrates how prevalent the rumours were and how easily they were believed. Those writing on behalf of the king condemned the rumours and slander, fearing these would divert people's loyalty away from the king by, as Richard said, 'the sending forth of false and abominable language and lies, some by bold and presumptuous open speech'.[5]

This form of propaganda had become so pervasive and common that the king ordered it to be confiscated and sent to him unread. (It does beg the question that if the propaganda had not been read, how did anyone know it was seditious?) These petitions and proclamations were not only aimed at Richard himself, although as king he was the focus of most of the opprobrium. Those who were members of his government were equally mocked and were condemned by those who wished to denigrate the regime itself and question its moral and legal legitimacy. The most memorable of these barbs was pinned onto the great door of St Paul's Cathedral on 18 July 1484:

> The catte, the ratte, and Lovell our dogge
> ruleth all England under a hog.

This rhyming couplet had been placed on the door of St Paul's in imitation of a theological argument by William Collingbourne, a disgruntled Wiltshire gentleman who had been a servant of both Edward IV and his mother, Cecily, Dowager Duchess of York. Collingbourne was already in communication with Henry Tudor and was plotting to raise Dorset on his behalf, offering up the port of Poole as a potential landing site. He had recently been removed from sitting as a justice of the peace on the Wiltshire bench and his doggerel may well have been a personal grievance against Ratcliffe, Catesby and Lovell, the men who he may have thought monopolized court patronage and whose influence had prevented him from rising in county society. Collingbourne's malicious rhyme is remembered for its simple effectiveness; the immediacy of the caricatures, the animalistic allusions that both simplify and denigrate, all wrapped up in the singsong cadences of a nursery rhyme. Yet this hides the extremely pertinent political point that the figure and the authority of the king, the Lord's anointed, can be reduced to resembling nothing more than a rutting hog; that the royal majesty could now be likened to the farmyard and the venality of the creatures within it. Collingbourne's barb perfectly pricked the aura of majesty and left the government naked before public judgement. The rhyme is only the most famous and well-remembered of a plethora of anti-Ricardian propaganda that began to flood into England from abroad. So far as Richard's government was concerned, such propaganda found a far too willing audience amongst the common people. Richard's political stock in the eyes of his subjects had fallen so low that few things were regarded as too extreme to be attributed to the king. Well might Richard lament that:

> innocent people which would live in rest and peace and truly under our obe-siance, as they ought to do, are greatly abused and oft put in danger of their lives, lands and goods ... As oft that follow in the steps and devices of the said seditious and mischievous persons.[6]

Richard's foreign policy

As Richard coped with the emotional and political ramifications of the death of his only son in the spring of 1484, he also sought to formulate a more aggressive and forward-looking foreign policy for England. Since the death of Charles the Bold, Duke of Burgundy, at the battle of Nancy in January 1477, north-western Europe had been convulsed by warfare as the kings of France had tried to wrest back territory on the north-eastern frontier that had previously been held by the dukes of Burgundy. In this, Louis XI had been partially successful capturing the original duchy of Burgundy and the provinces of Picardy and Artois. Eventually, Louis XI had been thwarted by Edward IV's sister Margaret, Dowager Duchess of Burgundy, who, in support of her stepdaughter Mary and her husband Maximillian, had managed to maintain the independence of the rest of the Burgundian lands and to fight off France's more predatory aims. Throughout the early 1480s, Margaret and Maximillian had appealed to Edward IV for assistance. Edward, hoping to secure both a marriage and a pension from Louis, had sidestepped their appeals. However, the accession of Richard III prompted a more vigorous foreign policy. Richard, whom the French knew had not acquiesced to the Treaty of Picquigny in 1475, was determined to adopt a more proactive foreign policy than that pursued by his brother. Richard was antagonistic towards France and probably needed little encouragement from his sister to begin to look favourably towards reaching an accommodation with Burgundy as a way of rectifying the diplomatic isolation experienced by England during the last years of Edward IV's reign. At Whitsun 1484, Richard formally received from Archduke Maximillian an emissary, Nicholas von Poppelau, to begin negotiations for a more active collaboration between England and Burgundy.

Nicholas von Poppelau has been called variously a German traveller or a wandering knight, but this has been to misunderstand his status and the reason for his visit. Originally from the German duchy of Silesia, he was far from being a

mere traveller – he was a *ministrales* (or household knight) of Frederick III. Frederick
was the father of Archduke Maximillian, who was the regent of Burgundy for his
young son Philip. But Frederick was not only Maximillian's father, he was also his
emperor, his feudal overlord. As Frederick's emissary, von Poppelau would try to gain
an alliance with Richard, or at least tacit support for Frederick's son in his conflict
with France. Richard received von Poppelau at Middleham Castle at Whitsun 1484
in a visit that lasted for eight days, during which Richard allowed von Poppelau the
singular honour of setting a place for him at the king's own table, a reflection of his
status and the importance Richard accorded his mission. Von Poppelau has left us
one of the very few intimate descriptions of Richard and his court: 'The table was
covered all around with silk cloth embroidered with gold'.[7] Von Poppelau describes
the king as 'three fingers taller than himself but that he was thinner, less thick-
set with delicate arms and legs and had a great heart'.[8] He was also struck by the
music that accompanied the royal mass he heard on 2 May, an art form for which
England was internationally renowned and which Richard strove hard to maintain,
at one time issuing a warrant 'to seize for the king all singing men he can find in all
the palaces, cathedral, colleges, chapels and houses of religion'.[9] The most revealing
element of von Poppelau's description of Richard III is the following statement:

> that he [Richard] wished his kingdom lay upon the confines of Turkey: 'with
> my own people alone and without the help of other princes I should like to
> drive away not only the Turks but all my foes'.[10]

Here we catch a glimpse of Richard's true psyche; a man surrounded by innuendo
and suspicion, burdened with personal grief, striving for some immediate and simple
physical remedy to relieve his mental anguish. His wish to take a crusade against the
growing power of the Turks fits in well with Richard's pronounced piety and his pref-
erence for direct physical action. Can it be any coincidence that what Richard sought
was atonement for his sins through the path of the penitent crusader? Since Richard's
accession, Archduke Maximillian, backed by Richard's sister Margaret, had pushed
for a formal alliance against France. Richard, whilst sympathetic, had equivocated,
but now was more sympathetic to Maximillian's requests.

Richard was also undertaking a more strident tone towards Brittany, seeking to
achieve three things: to ensure his own security; to apply pressure on France; and to
draw troops away from the Burgundian theatre. This involved dealing with Pierre
Landais who, as Chancellor of Brittany, ran the affairs of the duchy while Francis II
was incapacitated. Brittany, like Burgundy, was fearful of a powerful France assert-
ing her feudal rights over the duchy. To this end, it was part of Brittany's foreign
policy to retain the friendship of England so that it could be called into play if the
independence of the duchy was imperilled by France. In 1484, moves were afoot by
the French government, headed by the regent, Charles VIII's elder sister, Anne of
Beaujeu, to bring about the marriage of Francis' daughter and sole heir, Anne, to
the young king, Charles, thus eliminating the duchy's independence and joining

it in a personal union with the crown of France. Pierre Landais and others at the Brittany court now canvassed support for allies of an independent Brittany. Landais pointed out the threat that a united Brittany and France would present to England, not only to English shipping in the Channel but also those ships ploughing their way south to Spain or the Mediterranean. Richard III saw the opportunity to combine personal and national interests by supporting the government of Brittany, but the price for that support would be the handing over of Henry Tudor and his group of exiles. To this end, Richard sent envoys to Brittany to negotiate a truce and to call a halt to English wafting – a form of semi-authorized piracy, which had been going on for some time against both French and Breton shipping. On 8 June 1484, it was agreed that a formal truce between England and Brittany should last until 24 April 1485.[11] A significant element in the agreement was that Richard would furnish a force of 1,000 archers to serve for three months in Brittany at Richard's expense. A secret clause called for the arrest of Henry Tudor and the exiles whom Duke Francis had in some cases sheltered for the last thirteen years.

An unexpected danger for Henry Tudor

Richard III was extremely quick to implement the terms of the agreement and on 26 June a commission was issued to Francis Lovell. This commission empowered Lovell to act alongside the king's attorneys, William Catesby and Morgan of Kidwelly, to go to Southampton 'with all haste and certify that John Grey Lord Powys was dispatched to Brittany with 1000 archers'.[12] In some ways, the appointment of Lovell is strange since one would have assumed that the despatch of 1,000 troops from Southampton for Brittany would have come under the authority of the Lord Admiral, Thomas Howard, Earl of Surrey. However, this would be to view the despatch of the expedition as a purely military operation, which it was not. The archers being sent to Brittany were part of a more complicated plot that had a number of different objectives. The archers represented the first tranche of a policy of engagement by England in continental affairs that would bolster Breton independence and forestall any immediate attempts to marry Anne of Brittany to the young Charles VIII of France. It would demonstrate to the French court that the policy of impotent appeasement adopted in Edward IV's later years was at an end. It also offered indications to Richard's sister, Margaret of Burgundy, and her stepson-in-law, Archduke Maximillian, that under Richard, England would look favourably on negotiating an alliance with the new Hapsburg rulers of the Netherlands, returning to the policy of balancing French aggression by stirring up difficulties amongst France's great princes.

Alongside this resumption of traditional English policy towards France was, however, a domestic *quid pro quo* that explains what Francis Lovell and others of Richard's intimates were doing in Southampton overseeing the embarkation of Lord Powys. Powys was Lovell's neighbour in Northamptonshire and he had served with him as a justice of the peace that county. In line with the secret clause of an otherwise very public agreement, Pierre Landais was prepared to hand over Henry Tudor to Richard III's representatives. Richard personally promised Pierre Landais the revenues of those exiles with Henry Tudor at the Breton town of Vannes. However, it is possible that this may have been a misunderstanding; it is more likely that Richard promised to restore to the dukes of Brittany the earldom of Richmond, which until 1435 had been held by the second son of a Duke of Brittany. This would have had the double benefit of returning to Brittany an appanage of the duchy that had been held by the duke on and off since the Norman Conquest. It would also deprive Henry Tudor of his own dignity, since he also claimed the earldom in the right of his father, Edmund Tudor, who had died in October 1456. This would have been convenient for Richard since the bulk of the earldom had been in royal hands since the death of his brother Clarence in 1478. To secure the person of Henry Tudor, during the summer of 1484 Richard sent to Vannes his trusted henchman Sir James Tyrrell, who was already on the continent as captain of Guines Castle.[13] The use of Lovell to oversee the initial despatch of troops in June and the presence of Tyrrell at Vannes in August and early September strongly suggests an organized governmental action sanctioned at the very highest levels. Landais was at this time finalizing his plans to put specially chosen men under the command of trusted captains to seize Henry Tudor and accompany him on his return to his homeland.[14]

It was through the good offices and even better intelligence network of John Morton, one-time Bishop of Ely, that Henry got wind of the plot that was beginning to close about him. Morton had, since the failure of Buckingham's rebellion, been living an exile's life in Burgundy, presumably because he was regarded as being rather harmless. That was a gross underestimation of Morton's intellect and connections. Morton was a great survivor of the Wars of the Roses and had risen to prominence in the service of the Lancastrian Earl of Wiltshire, then of Margaret of Anjou, whose chancellor he had been before transferring his loyalties to Edward IV after the Lancastrian defeat at Tewkesbury. Morton had served Edward diligently until 1483 and had an extensive network of connections in England that stretched all the way back to Margaret Beaufort. It is probably from Margaret's husband, Lord Stanley, a member of the Privy Council, that Morton learned of the plot against Henry Tudor. The information can only have emanated from the Privy Council or those closest to the king since the coordination of the operation was in the hands of such highly trusted confidantes as Francis Lovell and Tyrell. As soon as he became aware of the plot, Morton sent Christopher Urswick, one of Margaret Beaufort's chaplains who was with Morton in Flanders, to Henry Tudor warning him 'to get himself and the other noble men as soon as might be out of Brittany and into France'.[15] Henry heeded the warning and entrusted the information to very few of his followers. His uncle, Jasper Tudor who, being half-Valois was regarded as a 'Prince of the Lilies', was instructed to pretend to visit Duke Francis, who was recuperating near the French border. When he was almost at the border, he was to turn directly towards France and cross the frontier into the French province of Anjou. Jasper, with his close links in blood to the French court, was a good choice to prepare the ground in France for Henry himself. Two days later, Henry left Vannes with five serving men, ostensibly to visit a sick friend who lived in the countryside nearby. Outside the city he changed into 'a serving man's apparel',[16] and then disappeared along country tracks until he re-emerged in French territory. When Pierre Landais became aware of what was happening, he sent men in hot pursuit. They arrived at the French frontier scarcely an hour after Henry Tudor had crossed into France.

Countering a real and credible threat

Despite the best efforts of Richard III's government, Henry Tudor, one-time Earl of Richmond and erstwhile fiancé of Elizabeth of York, had eluded them. Richard gnashed his teeth in disappointment and for the first time publicly acknowledged the threat posed by Henry Tudor, a man he had in the past publicly refused to recognize. Having failed to capture Henry, Richard now opened a propaganda war against him and the exiles who had joined him after Buckingham's rebellion. These men were now condemned for joining with England's ancient enemy against their fellow countrymen. For the first time, Richard disparaged Henry Tudor personally. In a proclamation issued in the autumn of 1484, Richard castigated Henry's supporters as 'rebels and traitors [who] have chosen to be their captain … Henry late calling himself Earl of Richmond'.[17]

In a further proclamation, one that reflects Richard's growing strident attitude towards immorality, Henry Tudor was condemned by his Beaufort lineage as being unfit for the throne. His mother's Beaufort ancestors, through whom Henry made his claim to the throne, were described as being the illegitimate offspring of John of Gaunt. The proclamation then cast doubt on the secret marriage of his grandfather, Owain Tudor, to Catherine de Valois, the widow of Henry V. This is the first official declaration to question the legitimacy of this admittedly obscure marriage.[18] Richard's propaganda pointed to the secrecy of the marriage and stated that the marriage was not properly conducted, making the offspring illegitimate. This allegation made Henry Tudor illegitimate on both sides of his parentage, not only barring him from the throne, but making him morally unsuited to wear the crown. These proclamations against Henry Tudor are comparable to Titulus Regius: in both instances Richard was seeking to denigrate the claims of his opponents by blaming them for what was seen as the moral failures of their parents and antecedents. The use of moral inadequacy to castigate birthright is a recurring theme in Richard's propaganda. In it we can see the extension of Richard's somewhat rigid piety into the field of politics and its use to bolster his own claims in comparison with the supposed moral failures of his opponents.

On 7 December 1484, Richard III issued a proclamation against Henry Tudor, the Marquis of Dorset and others,[19] who were called 'rebels, traitors, disabled and attainted by the High Court of Parliament'. In addition, they were condemned as murderers, adulterers and extortioners 'who had forsaken their natural country'.[20]

This proclamation against men who had been condemned as traitors over a year earlier continues the themes of Richard's propaganda. It is insufficient for these men to be proscribed simply as traitors – a crime heinous in itself – their names had to be blackened with the accusation that they were murderers, adulterers and extortioners, thus morally unfit to offer any form of leadership for the country. Equally, we can see that Richard hoped to stoke up a xenophobic rejection of Henry Tudor and his associates with an appeal to bluff patriotism exemplified by the phrase 'who had forsaken their natural country', denying that they had any claim on the loyalties of true Englishmen.

In this febrile war of words, Henry Tudor now became 'twice bastardized Richmond', a viper who resided in the bosom of England's traditional enemy. Richard and Francis Lovell had taken the first steps on the road to Bosworth.

12 THE ROAD TO BOSWORTH

Instability and mistrust

THE HIGH SUMMER OF 1484 saw Richard III and Queen Anne try to come to terms with the tragedy of their son's death. Richard was aware that the boy's demise exposed the increasingly precarious nature of his rule. Support now began to ebb away as the nobility and the gentry slowly withdrew from court to their localities to await events. The stability that Richard had promised and his guarantee of good governance now seemed to be ephemeral. Richard was left exposed as an isolated figure, over-reliant on the small coterie of trusted supporters who had been rewarded to an unwarranted degree. The wholesale promotion of Richard's trusted servants had resulted in the breakdown of the traditional fabric of county society throughout south and central England. Such partisan behaviour was bound to rouse the ire of local society and also to disquiet the higher nobility who saw their birthright and their property threatened by such arbitrary over-promotion.

Behind this sense of political unease and unresolved tension, a cloud of suspicion surrounded the king regarding the fate of his nephews, the young princes in the Tower. As the summer of 1484 rolled around, men were reminded that neither of the princes had been seen for over a year and no sightings had occurred since late July 1483. As the mutterings grew louder, Polydor Vergil, writing in the reign of Henry VII and therefore susceptible to the charge of political and dynastic bias, is nevertheless surely correct when he stated that 'people understood that no male issue of king Edward to be now left alive'.[1] Vergil goes on to relate:

> but when the fame of this notable foul act was dispersed through the realm, so great a grief struck generally to the hearts of all men, that the same subduing all fear they wept everywhere.[2]

Vergil may exaggerate, but it is difficult to dispute his conclusion that there was a general and increasing sense of unease in the country that Richard had done little to dispel by failing to refer in any sense to the existence or whereabouts of his nephews. The void that royal silence created was filled by men's own conclusions as to the fate of the royal princes. Richard's silence did little to counter the accusations of usurpation and tyranny that his government had to contend with; nor did it defuse the threat of invasion from abroad.

Securing the ports with Lovell's men

Richard's government began to institute its own security measures. Even before the Collingbourne plot came to light, trusted men were put in place to secure the principal ports of England. These new men were now all trusted officers appointed by Francis Lovell who, in his capacity as Chief Butler of England, appointed deputies as customs officials to oversee the trade of these ports; each deputy reported directly to him. The first of these appointments was Lovell's trusted follower, Geoffrey Frank, who was appointed a deputy of the Chief Butler and therefore responsible for overseeing the collection of the appropriate customs and tonnage and poundage at the port of Newcastle-upon-Tyne and other ports in the north east.[3] This was followed by the appointment of Richard Rugge of Staffordshire as deputy for the port of Southampton.[4] Richard Nichol was appointed deputy for the ports of London and Sandwich; and, on 5 March 1484, Richard Cromer was appointed deputy for the port of Tynemouth.[5] On 8 March, Morgan of Kidwelly, the Attorney-General, was appointed the deputy for Poole and the other Dorset ports.[6] On 11 March, Henry Davey was appointed for Ipswich and Chichester. Davey's appointment is particularly interesting, in that he came from a mercantile background and was the tailor for the Great Wardrobe; with his familiarity with fine fabrics, he was an ideal choice for the control of the mercantile activity of these ports. He was also a dyed-in-the-wool Ricardian and a follower of Francis Lovell; a man who would rise in rebellion in 1487 for Lambert Simnel and who would be hung for his traitorous activities in 1489. Francis also appointed James Walton to deputize at the ports of Lynn and Boston. Finally, on 26 October, Philip Ricart was appointed deputy for Bristol and Bridgewater.

Between the end of December 1483 and October 1484, these new deputies, dependent for their office on the person of Francis Lovell, were appointed to all the strategic ports of England, from Newcastle in the north-east to Bristol in the west. The ports of the east and south were in the hands of men upon whom the regime could rely and whose loyalty was unquestioned. They, in turn, would have had a staff consisting of two collectors and a controller for the wool customs and the petty customs of tonnage and poundage under them. These would have been joined by a surveyor, a searcher and a tronager as well as clerks and servants. In London, for instance, in 1490 there were forty-two officials in all who were waged from between £10 to £40 per year.

All these men can be seen to be part of Francis Lovell's own connection; men who were directly dependent on him as Chief Butler of England and who, therefore, acted as his deputies in a very real sense. Even Morgan of Kidwelly, who was the king's Attorney-General, was still a lawyer who, in this hierarchical society, needed the patronage of a court noble to support him, especially in the new estates he had acquired in the autumn of 1483. Lovell's support in Dorset was crucial to the advancement of Morgan's authority in a county that, as his name implies, was alien to him. The promotion of Geoffrey Frank, a Yorkshireman from a family with close links with Lovell, best exemplifies the personal nature of the men promoted by Lovell in these deputy positions. Almost all can be seen to have some prior relationship with Francis Lovell or the household of Richard III.

The appointment of these deputies gave Lovell dependants on a national scale and cemented his place within the role of government itself. It is also evidence of the large reservoir of patronage and influence that he now controlled. The Butler's deputies acted in conjunction with prominent burgesses in the local mercantile community and had a hand in the appointment of the port's officers, reeve, collectors, surveyors and searchers. Whilst not all ports employed anywhere near as many personnel as that of London, there was still a number of significant jobs dependent upon the goodwill of the Chief Butler's deputy. Some included the wine merchants whose contribution to tonnage, poundage and petty customs were directly collected by the deputy. The importation of wines was an extremely large and lucrative business involving wines from as far afield as Gascony, Cyprus and the new wines that came from the recently discovered Madeira. The nobility and those aspiring to the gentry all drank wine rather than ale. This consumption was added to by the continual demands of the Church, which required wine for its many liturgical functions.

Discouraging traitors

The placing of reliable men to cover the ports was one part of the regime's security measures. Such a guard could help to deter and prevent the contagion of sedition arriving from abroad, but it could do little to deal with domestic dissent. Internal sedition was dealt with by the meting out of exemplary punishments on those deemed to be traitors. The punishment meted out to William Collingbourne was an example of this and one that was meant to discourage others. Whilst Collingbourne's piece of doggerel regarding the cat, the rat and the hog has given him a posthumous fame that was not what truly concerned the authorities. The pinning of the verse to the doors of St Paul's had no doubt caused amusement amongst those who understood its ribald egalitarianism, but it was his action prior to this that caused the government greater alarm. On 10 July, Collingbourne had given £8 to a man called Thomas Yates, to deliver a letter to Henry Tudor in Brittany. In this letter, Collingbourne offered to recruit and raise the county of Dorset on Henry's behalf and to offer to him the use of the port of Poole and other Dorset harbours. He also promised that if Henry invaded that he and his associates 'would cause the people to raise in arms and to wage war against king Richard'.[7] Collingbourne also advised Henry Tudor to inform the French king, or at least his council, that Richard III was deliberately prevaricating over a truce planned for the coming winter because the king hoped in the spring to 'invade that realm with all pursuance'.[8] Collingbourne encouraged Henry Tudor 'by this means to persuade the French king to aid the Earl of Richmond and his partakers in their quarrel against king Richard'.[9]

The letter and its contents clearly constituted treason, involving as it did the offer of aid to a proclaimed rebel to invade England and advice on English policy to a foreign monarch. On both counts Collingbourne was clearly guilty. Promising to keep one of the kingdom's most important ports, Poole, as a gateway for foreign invasion was treasonous in itself; that this should be compounded by the offer of direct assistance by Collingbourne and others was fatal. There could be no doubt of the verdict since the conspirators had been caught red-handed and were damned by their own correspondence. Once the jury's guilty verdict was given, Collingbourne's fate was sealed: he was to be executed under the full and dire penalties allowed by the 1349 Treason Act, and this punishment was to be as public as possible. Collingbourne, bound by ropes, was dragged behind a cart from Westminster to Tower Hill, so that as many of the capital's citizens as possible could witness his degradation. Dragged past St Paul's, he could look only fleetingly at the cathedral that symbolized the redemption that an imminent afterlife would offer him. Bareheaded, he stood upon a raised dais in full view of the crowd beneath the gallows as the executioner enumerated his crimes. Placing his head in the noose, he was then hung by the neck. But, before breathing his last, he was cut down and thrown onto a table 'where he was straight cut down and ripped from chest to groin and his innards thrown into a brazier of hot coals'.[10] He was then castrated so that his tainted blood would not be perpetuated into the next generation. At this point, the executioner proceeded to thrust his hand into Collingbourne's chest cavity to pluck out his heart and, as he did so, Collingbourne was heard to utter 'Jesus, Jesus yet more trouble' in what must have been one of the greatest understatements of all time. That said, Collingbourne, brave though he was, was not executed for a piece of insulting doggerel, but for treason – a crime of which he was manifestly guilty and one that the authorities could not allow to become contagious.

Networks of influence

There is evidence that Collingbourne's plot was much broader and more deeply embedded then has previously been recognized. Whilst attention has focused on the piece of doggerel he is purported to have written, little attention has been paid to his many connections. As a South Wiltshire man, Collingbourne had links with Margaret Beaufort and the Beaufort affinity in that area and also with John Morton, Bishop of Ely, a man who also had strong local links. As late as 29 November, a commission of Oyer and Terminer was issued to Francis Lovell to investigate 'treasons and offences committed by William Collingbourne late of Lydiard co Wilts Esquire and John Turburoyle late of Fyremayne, Co Dorset'.[11] Interestingly, the commission is for the counties of Norfolk and Suffolk, representing the broad extension of Francis Lovell's authority. This follows a pattern where his authority increases during 1484 and he becomes an increasingly important and integral member of Richard III's government, acting much more as a national figure rather than just a regional magnate.

It is highly unlikely that Lovell was appointed to this commission in any form of irony by Richard III or for any aspect of personal revenge on Lovell's part for Collingbourne's diatribe. Thus, it raises a number of questions as to why Lovell should have been appointed to a commission in an area where he had previously exerted no authority. It would have been far easier for Richard III to have appointed John, Duke of Norfolk, to a commission that operated in his own home county, since not only did Norfolk have the local standing to carry out such a commission (being a justice of the peace and a local landowner), he would also have had the ties to local society that would ensure their cooperation – certainly more than an outsider such as Lovell would have had. Similarly, we can speculate as to why the Duke of Suffolk or any of his officers were not used or appointed. That neither were used suggests that the plot that Collingbourne was involved in was of greater seriousness and complexity than was first thought. Lovell's appointment points to serious concerns regarding the renewed threat posed by Henry Tudor after the escape of John de Vere, sometime Earl of Oxford, from Hammes Castle, in the Marches of Calais. De Vere had escaped from this grim fortress with the aid of James Blount after Richard III had determined to have him brought back to England and closer confinement on 28 October. A free de Vere, now in league with Henry Tudor, raised the spectre of a descent on the east coast where the de Vere family had long enjoyed strong support, especially on their ancestral lands, which straddled the Suffolk/Essex border.[12] In addition to this, there was the slippery eminence of John Morton, Bishop of Ely and conspirator supreme, who, being in exile in Flanders, was ideally placed to stir up trouble in East Anglia. The sending of the King's Chamberlain to the region indicated the importance Richard III placed upon rooting out those engaged in treason in this crucial area, it would also ensure that whatever was discovered would be reported back directly to him.

During the previous summer, as part of the king's progress, Lovell had been personally rewarded by the king. Lovell was also able to use his own influence to secure an income for the wives of two relatives who had been convicted and attainted during Buckingham's rebellion. In August 1484, Lovell was able, by royal grant, to obtain pensions of £40 and £24 respectively for his cousins-by-marriage, Margaret Harcourt and Anne Stonor.[13] This was an astute political act, demonstrating to local society his influence with the king, and also an act of chivalry in seeking to provide for two defenceless women, irrespective of the crimes of their husbands. This form of good lordship and chivalric largesse would have impressed the gentry of Oxfordshire and Berkshire, making it clear who had influence at court.

Francis Lovell was not the only member of his family to gain that summer: on the same day, Lovell's sister, Frideswide, received an annuity of 100 marks from the honour of Wallingford, which, of course, was administered by her brother.[14] This was a most generous and unusual act by the king for it gave Frideswide a guaranteed personal income for life, allowing her some measure of independence. This unusual grant also represented an act of considerable affection by the king since rewards of this nature would not normally given to young women and were rarely enrolled as royal patents. Clearly, Richard must have held Frideswide, and the Lovell family as a whole, in some great regard to reward them like this.

Defusing a threat from the north

The plotting of Collingbourne and potentially others was not, however, the sole issue to consume Richard III during the summer of 1484. In July, he issued new regulations for the government of the north and a new regulatory basis for the Council of the North now that he was no longer at its helm. The same month, Richard III promoted his nephew John, Earl of Lincoln, as Lord of the North. At this time, Lincoln was in his early twenties and this was to be his first significant appointment. Clearly, since he had few estates in the north, he enjoyed the king's confidence and was being groomed for high office. Though Lincoln was young, contemporary chronicles speak highly of his ability and in the place of Richard's dead son, he represented royal authority in the north. Under Lincoln, the council was to meet quarterly at York 'to hear, examine all bills of complaint, authority to act over riots, forcible entries and disputes ... against our laws and peace', with the council commanded to take action against 'any assemblies or gatherings contrary to our laws and peace (and the subjects in the north parts be at all times obedient to our council in our name)'.[15]

The appointment of John, Earl of Lincoln, as president of the Council of the North was part of a broader policy of pacification that Richard III was now pursuing in that region and on the Scottish border. In February 1484, Richard was preparing to lead an army personally against James III of Scotland,[16] but by July that policy had softened and James III wrote to Richard offering to open negotiations and to resolve any outstanding issues on the border. Richard responded to these overtures on 7 August 1484 positively: 'your loving disposition is to us right agreeable'.[17] Negotiations for a truce now carried on apace well into September when Richard considered the proposals brought by Archibald Whitelaw, the secretary of James III. It is clear that from the summer of 1484 onwards Richard III was doing all he could to defuse any potential threat on the northern frontier to focus on his own preparations to pursue his policy of active intervention on behalf of his sister, Margaret of Burgundy, and the Archduke Maximillian.

A boost for Henry Tudor

In the midst of these diplomatic preparations, Richard III had to face more misfortune closer to home. During September observers noted that he had begun to shun the bed of his wife Anne, who was beginning to show signs of a disease that was probably tuberculosis. His physician's advice was that her husband should now sleep in separate rooms from his wife. Such a change in sleeping arrangements did not imply any lack of affection on Richard's part, but rather the taking of sensible precautions against a highly contagious illness. This diagnosis had political as well as personal implications: first, it created a further impediment to re-establishing the dynasty as hopes for a son and heir receded further and further into the background; secondly, it potentially weakened Richard's relationship with his northern connection, which was the central pillar of his rule. These and other looming difficulties moved into focus during the autumn of 1484.

Richard's response to these looming problems was to initiate his own intelligence network, directing spies to France and Brittany to glean all he could about Henry Tudor's plans. This became all the more necessary when the French king, Charles VIII, deliberately and erroneously recognized Henry Tudor as the younger son of Henry VI; this was disingenuous, but it was preferable to the truth, which was, as Molinet, stated, that Henry was 'quite far removed from the crown of England regarding bloodline'.[18] This move on behalf of the French government was clearly intended to justify its sponsorship of Henry Tudor. Henry, however, was so buoyed by this recognition and by the defection of the Earl of Oxford and the majority of the Hammes garrison, that in his letters he now styled himself 'H.R.' and now wrote of his 'rightful claim due and lineal inheritance of the crown'.[19] It was no doubt in recognition of the potential threat posed by a renascent Henry that Richard III now invited Elizabeth of York to court.

A prize worth guarding

Elizabeth of York was the eldest of Edward IV's children and now an attractive nineteen-year-old woman of marriageable age. From almost everyone's perspective, Henry Tudor's claim to the throne, apart from some seriously diehard Lancastrians, was tenuous in the extreme and only acquired serious legitimacy by his promise to marry Elizabeth of York. Despite the declaration of her illegitimacy by her uncle, Elizabeth remained in many peoples' eyes the legitimate heir of her father Edward IV, especially as no sightings of her brothers had been made for well over twelve months. Whilst the legitimacy of this Yorkist princess was denied by Richard's government, to many others the girl had a greater claim to the throne than either Richard or Henry Tudor. Elizabeth was, therefore, a prize worth guarding and for as long as she was at Richard's court, she could be closely watched.

Richard's military preparations continue

As Elizabeth was brought to court and steps taken to ensure that she would remain under close supervision, military preparations were underway to guard against any invasion of England that Henry Tudor might be planning. From Westminster, commissions went out to the coastal counties of the south and east of England and for the

Warden of the Cinque Ports to mobilize a squadron of ships for service in the Channel. Furthermore, on 8 December 1484, Francis Lovell received a new Commission of Array for Buckinghamshire, Oxfordshire, Berkshire and Northamptonshire.[20] Lovell was the senior peer on each of these commissions and now clearly dominated the political life of these counties, holding as he did both judicial and military authority. He was also quite clearly trusted by the king to muster and array the military capabilities of these populous counties and bring them again to the king's chosen muster point. Evidently, the king was expecting some imminent invasion to coincide with the Earl of Oxford's joining with Henry Tudor and the announcement of the support of the king of France. This fear was, in reality, irrational given the lateness of the season and the stormy conditions that would have been prevalent in the English Channel in December. Also, the mobilization of the county array of so many inland counties rather than coastal ones points more to fear and suspicion, to jumping at shadows than a serious appraisal of the likelihood of invasion. In fact, during the Christmas period, Richard's spies were able to deduce that no invasion was likely before the summer. The Crowland Chronicle states that the news delighted Richard when he stated that 'Victory would put an end to all his doubts and misfortunes.'[21] This fits in with what we know of Richard, the man of action, desperate to cut through the miasma of suspicion that now seemed to shroud his court, and echoes the sentiments he expressed to the diplomatic emissary, Nicholas von Poppelau, the previous spring. Having this knowledge, though, did not mean that the Commissions of Array stood down; on the contrary, they remained in force into the New Year and Sunday practices in arms were maintained throughout the winter months. The maintenance of the Commissions of Array and the ships in the Channel inevitably absorbed a measure of royal expenditure. During the winter this was not a serious burden, but continuation of these costs was to have serious implications later the following year.

Christmas at court

The Christmas of 1484 was a busy period for Francis Lovell. In his military role, he had to oversee the commissions of array for the Thames Valley. At the same time, he had to supervise the Christmas festivities for the court and organize the provision of the victuals for the twelve days of royal celebrations. Despite the deteriorating condition of the queen, Richard's Christmas celebrations were both elaborate and splendid, as befitted one of the great courts of Europe. Christmas at Westminster was a magnificent round of feasts and religious services with the king at the centre, dancing and engaging with the entertainments with gusto. Attendance at court by the leading magnates of the realm was not only a requirement, but also a demonstration of the strength of the monarch in the face of an external threat. The celebrations were designed to overawe by their extravagance and their conspicuous display, both of which were expected by the king's subjects. By such means, Richard and his nobles also demonstrated that in a truly Christian court they not only acknowledged an important religious festival, but they knew how to keep the spirit of Christmas appropriately.

Christmas at court was not only a time for men to show off; the women of the court also stood out in their new finery, which had been commissioned specially for the festivities. This year, though, heads were turned and tongues wagged over the appearance of Queen Anne and Elizabeth of York. Anne and Elizabeth were dressed similarly, making a mockery of the disparity in rank between the two ladies, and also effectively diminishing the charge of Elizabeth's illegitimacy. This shocked most people, as recorded in the Crowland Chronicle: 'The people spoke against this and the magnates and prelates were greatly astounded.'[22] Many within the court felt that this was a disparagement of the queen who, it was felt, had been humiliated by the attempt of anyone, let alone Elizabeth, to even approach her dignity. What also struck contemporaries was the obvious contrast between the young and healthy Elizabeth of York and the sickly queen, who was herself only approaching thirty, but was clearly by now ravaged by the effects of her illness. The inevitable comparison between the two was seen as insulting to the queen and demeaning to both her status and rank, fuelling suspicions that, as the Crowland Chronicle puts it: 'the king was applying his mind in every way to contracting a marriage either after the death of the Queen or by means of a divorce'.[23] The marriage of Elizabeth of York was clearly seen as a means of politically neutralizing the marital and, therefore, dynastic ambitions of Henry Tudor, but to suggest that Richard planned to marry his own niece seems most bizarre, bordering on the irrational. The fact that this rumour persisted raised serious questions about how others viewed Richard's judgement and his character. As the new year dawned, Richard must have mused upon the precarious and woeful situation in which he now found himself. As his son had been taken away from him and his wife withered before his eyes, Richard's haunted face turned towards the continent and a now resurgent Henry Tudor.

Henry Tudor's growing confidence

Richard's personal and political woes gave Henry Tudor's pretensions a validity that his lineage did not warrant. There were others with a better claim to the throne and who were closer to the royal family than Henry, but no one else was in the position to fulfil the role of a royal alternative to a king whom it would appear the gods had already condemned. In an age when the writings of the classical tragedians were becoming fashionable once more, the parallels were too obvious to ignore. Henry Tudor now offered a viable alternative, his promise to marry Elizabeth of York confirming to most people what they had long suspected – that the two princes in the Tower were already dead. A successful invasion by Henry Tudor would replace the usurper and return to the throne the legitimate line of succession whilst uniting the houses of Lancaster and York. As Richard's family's fortunes diminished, so Henry's credibility grew. On top of this, as Richard began to move closer and closer to Burgundy, and as Archduke Maximillian began to assert his control over the Netherlands on behalf of his son, Philip, a pre-emptive strike against England became more and more attractive from the perspective of French policy. It did not much matter to France whether or not Henry Tudor replaced Richard on the throne, but an invasion of England by another claimant to the crown would destabilize English politics and prevent Richard's government from playing a more active role on the continent (a course on which it seemed set).

The death of Anne, Richard's queen

As winter turned to spring, at Westminster, Queen Anne's condition grew increasingly worse. Despite the attention of the royal physicians, her lungs continued to fill with fluid and her handkerchief became increasingly and ominously flecked with blood and a pink, foaming mucus. Richard now maintained some distance from his wife, whom he still called 'his dearest consort'. Typically, as the queen's demise inevitably drew closer, he threw himself into outdoor pursuits such as hunting and hawking. The end came at 9 o'clock on the evening of Wednesday 16 March. Queen Anne was buried with full honours as soon as her embalmed body was ready, adding to the gloom that now seemed to surround the court. The pall of suspicion, inference and innuendo grew even worse in the fortnight after the queen's death and it was now rumoured that the king had poisoned his wife, having, it was said, complained of his wife's unfruitfulness 'for that she brought him no children'.[24] The rumour that he had poisoned his wife quickly began to gain credence, leading Richard into conflict with his trusted councillors, Richard Ratcliffe and William Catesby. Ratcliffe, a Durham man, and Catesby exhorted the king to move quickly to quash the rumours, claiming that if he did not, northerners would 'impute to him the death of the Queen, the daughter and the heir of the Earl of Warwick through whom he had first gained his present high position'.[25] The use of Warwick's name – a man who had been dead for fourteen years – leads to the assumption that the rumours probably started amongst the older members of the Nevill connection, who now, on the death of Anne, had lost the last surviving link with the great earl himself. Recognizing this, Ratcliffe and Catesby:

> told the king to his face that if he did not deny any such purpose and did not counter it by public declaration before the mayor and the commonality of the city of London, that the Northerners in whom he placed his greatest trust would rise against him.[26]

Richard was aware of the danger inherent in the loss of his northern support and now moved quickly to deny the rumours that he had murdered his wife or that he planned to marry his niece. He agreed to refute these rumours before the mayor and

Francis Lovell's family coat of arms showing the quarterings of the baronies of Lovell, Deincourt, Holland and Grey of Rotherfield, with an escutcheon for the barony of Burrell.

Minster Lovell as it appears today.

Richard III, Francis Lovell's friend and sovereign. An early sixteenth-century portrait by an unknown artist. This intriguing portrait seems to capture some of Richard's character traits: the outward appearance of an open face is belied by the nervous tension revealed in the self-conscious fidgeting with his rings. The portrait seems to convey the anxieties that beset Richard when he assumed the crown.

A nineteenth-century stained-glass representation of Jasper Tudor, half-brother of Henry VI, uncle of Henry VII and inveterate enemy of the House of York. Cardiff Castle.

Contemporary picture of German *Landschnechts*.

A contemporary image of Margaret, Dowager Duchess of Burgundy, implacable enemy of Henry VII and the woman who contracted Martin Schwartz to Lovell's invasion of England.

The gateway to Abingdon Abbey, a view with which Lovell and John Sante would have been very familiar. Sadly, very little else remains of the mediaeval abbey but the gateway stands as testimony to its previous grandeur and importance.

Coat of arms of John, Earl of Oxford, Henry VII's commander at both Bosworth and Stoke Field.

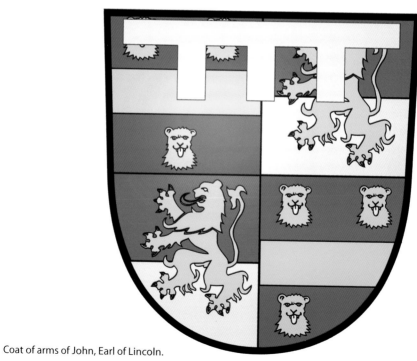

Coat of arms of John, Earl of Lincoln.

corporation of London, who were to be accompanied by twelve doctors of theology. The meeting took place on 30 March at the Priory of St John, Clerkenwell, and gave Richard the opportunity to deny that he had ever intended to marry his niece, publicly stating that 'no such thing had entered his mind'. The Crowland Chronicle, perhaps cynically, wrote that: 'there were some at the council that knew well that the contrary was true.'[27] The twelve doctors of theology, acting like a Greek chorus in support, 'asserted that the Pope had no power of dispensation over that degree of consanguinity',[28] reinforcing Richard's point that such a marriage was theologically and legally impossible. The episode has all the hallmarks of political theatre to enable Richard to be able to lance the boil of suspicion and innuendo that had dogged him since Christmas. The whole occasion was a highly staged means of both quashing a potentially damaging rumour and having the king address his subjects' concerns in the most public way possible.

The producer of this piece of political theatre was probably Francis Lovell, who, as the King's Chamberlain, would have been responsible for ensuring that the royal point of view – the message, as it were – was got out. Lovell's role in organizing this piece of public theatre would explain his absence from the main stage. As the director, he would have had an important backstage function, which might explain why he does not feature in the Crowland Chronicle's account of this event. That such an orchestrated denial was necessary can be deduced from a letter Richard wrote, or at least signed, on 4 April to the mayor and corporation of York, to be publicly read out at the Guildhall in York. In the letter, Richard complains of 'seditious and evil persons … [who] sow the Seeds of noise and slander … [by] false and abominable language and lies'.[29] Richard then empowered the mayor to take action against those caught spreading such sedition, but the very fact that the king had to personally admonish the mayor to take action against the rumour-mongers demonstrates how widespread and credible these rumours must have appeared outside the capital; it also demonstrates that Richard and his government were aware of the dangers presented by the unrebutted sedition and that they were prepared to counter and supress such propaganda as they came upon it.

Richard's marriage plans for Elizabeth of York

Whilst these public denials may have had some effect, it did not alter the more fundamental and deep-rooted problem of political trust – or rather the lack of it. That people found it at all credible that the king could murder his sick wife and would be then capable of slaking his lust on his young niece emphasized how low Richard's reputation had sunk in public perception. By 1485 the political capital that Richard had possessed in 1483 had been demolished so spectacularly that nothing was now regarded as being beneath a man whom many thought had displaced his two nephews and then had them murdered. All the theatrics that Lovell and the court could concoct and all the public denials could not materially alter public opinion and people's perception regarding the altogether untrustworthy character of the king, despite the probability of his innocence in this instance.

That Richard had no real intention of marrying his niece was supported by the fact that on 22 March 1485, only nine days after the death of his wife, he and his council instructed Sir Edward Brampton, a converted Portuguese Jew,[30] whose baptismal father in Christ had been Edward IV himself, to sail to Lisbon. There, Brampton was to offer Elizabeth of York as a match for Manuel, Duke of Beja, and Richard as a suitable husband for King John II's sister, the Infanta Joanna. Brampton's mission reflected the real thrust of Richard's diplomacy: by marrying into the house of Avis, the king would not only be removing a troublesome Yorkist ghost, but he himself would be marrying the senior Lancastrian claimants to the throne of England, as the Infanta was descended from Henry IV's sister Philippa. The Portuguese Council recognized this and stated that Richard's marriage to the Infanta would unite 'as one the party of Lancaster and York which are the two parties of that kingdom out of which the divisions and evils over the succession are born'.[31] This double marriage would deny Henry Tudor the legitimacy of either party and would place Elizabeth of York permanently beyond his grasp. No wonder Richard III wanted the marriage to take place straight away. Such a marriage would also be more than acceptable at the Burgundian Court since the mother of Charles the Bold (the husband of Richard's sister, Margaret) had also been the Portuguese Princess Isabella of the House of Avis.

Henry Tudor, waiting in the spring of 1485, was only too aware of how the proposed dual marriage seriously jeopardized his plans. If Henry could not marry Elizabeth of York (and he could not consider marriage to one of her younger sisters for reasons of precedence and prestige), he recognized that those of his supporters who had come to him after Buckingham's rebellion intent on re-establishing the line of Edward IV, would abandon him, leaving his sole support a rump of the old Lancastrian party – and that would only endure until a legitimate Lancastrian prince was born to the Infanta Joanna, who would then represent the senior and legitimate Lancastrian line, not that of the illegitimate Beauforts. No wonder Henry watched with frustration the agonisingly slow build-up of his forces at Harfleur whilst observing events across the Channel with increasing trepidation.

13 BOSWORTH

Foreign politics

IT HAS OFTEN BEEN argued that if Richard III's foreign policy had been more conciliatory towards France, the French government would have had little incentive to support Henry Tudor. However, a rapprochement with France was unlikely for two reasons. First, Richard's character and political make-up were acutely focused towards restoring England's position on the continent and to revive its reputation after the political collapse of Edward IV's policy in 1482. Secondly, Richard would have been driven by a chivalric impulse to accede to the request for aid from his sister Margaret, Dowager Duchess of Burgundy. With these imperatives, it can be argued that all Richard did was to resume England's traditional policy of friendship with Burgundy, and its alliances with the other semi-independent French lordships, such as Brittany.

However, to view France's actions purely through the prism of English policy is equally misleading. In the case of French foreign policy, the prime mover was the Marshal of France, Philip de Crevecoeur,[1] a man who saw his mission as one of expanding France's vulnerable north and eastern frontier into the Burgundian provinces of Artois and Flanders. He is reputed to have said that he would gladly live seven years in Hell if he could capture the English enclave of Calais. In 1485, de Crevecoeur was the commander of the Pont de l'Arche military base on the Seine, to the south of Rouen. To achieve his goal of French expansion to the north-west, he had to look to uncouple English support for Margaret and the Archduke Maximillian, and to do this he had the prime weapon in Henry Tudor. Henry was brought to Pont de L'Arche, where de Crevecoeur mustered 3,000–4,000 men for *Le Voyage de l'Angleterre* in support of Henry Tudor. The camp at Pont de L'Arche consisted of professional soldiers, archers du camp, professional archers and crossbow men, ablaters, halberdiers, voulgiers and pikemen, all of whom were waged professional soldiers and not, as Comynes describes them, 'the worst that could be found'.[2] This core of French professionals was joined by a contingent of Scots troops and 'beggerly Bretons', plus around 300 to 500 English exiles. All were to be commanded by a Savoyard, Philibert de Chandee, who was a personal friend of Henry Tudor and who referred to him as 'our dear kinsman in spirit and blood'.[3] Henry's preparations were impossible to hide and inevitably drew the attention of Richard's agents, who soon got wind of the build-up of forces across the Channel. Richard had known for some time that Henry Tudor was likely to descend upon his kingdom, but Henry and Charles VIII's concentration of military resources in Normandy made clear that this was now imminent; possibly as soon as late spring, but certainly by summer.

The cost of defending the realm

Richard's defences had been in place since his general commission of array of the previous November and December. East Anglia, the Humber and the south coast had all been put on a war-footing. On 8 December 1484, for instance, a letter was sent to the commissioners of array for Gloucestershire, which required each commissioner upon receipt 'to be armed and arrayed and to come before you all and defensible and able bodied men of the said County array and arm them accordingly to their grades and ranks'.[4]

The maintenance of defences for such a long period of time had inevitably put a great strain on the finances of the government, and this had not been helped by Richard's politically expedient decision not to raise taxes during his first parliament. The financial situation had been ameliorated initially by the confiscations and fines which had been imposed after the failure of Buckingham's rebellion, but after the awards to Richard's supporters had been made, little was left with which to finance long-term military expenditure. To revive the royal finances without resorting to taxation, the king and his council decided to revert to the policy of Edward IV and request a benevolence (or a forced loan). On 25 February 1485, a letter was sent to Francis Lovell containing instructions to be issued to 'those appointed and ordained for the counties of Oxford, Berkshire and Buckingham'. This was a covering letter meant to be duplicated and sent to 'such personnes within our said counties by your discretion'.[5] The letter requested a loan of a specified amount, to be determined by the appointed county commissioners, 'to be employed for the defence and suritie of his royal person and the weal of the realm'.[6] The letter suggests that all true Englishmen should want to support and aid the king in the defence of the realm. One of those from whom aid was confidently expected was Francis Lovell's clerical acquaintance, John Sante, Abbot of nearby Abingdon, who was assessed for and required to loan the king the sum of 200 marks (roughly £136). Unfortunately for Richard, the benevolence and its collection was a failure, unsurprisingly producing a yield far below what had been expected.

Gathering against Richard

Soon after Easter, Richard, having spent the previous six months at Westminster, set out from Windsor to Kenilworth where he spent Whitsuntide. From here he set off on the road north east to Nottingham Castle, where he took up residence in the royal apartments he had recently built. Whilst Richard referred to Nottingham as his 'castle of care', it made strategic sense to place himself at the very centre of the realm. From here he could watch the east or west coast and be one day's march away from the muster points of his northern and East Anglian supporters. Also, in the bountiful Midlands at harvest time he would be able to retain and feed the royal household through the summer months.

However, this strategic move did not mean that the king neglected the periphery; on the contrary, his nephew, John, Earl of Lincoln, had been appointed Justice of the Peace in the East and North Riding of Yorkshire and, as Lieutenant of the North, was charged with acting as leader of the commission of array for those parts. To the far north, the Earl of Northumberland would act for the king in Northumberland and Durham. In both regions royal power also rested on the many members of the royal household who were resident there and awaited the royal summons. From Nottingham, the king and his household could also supervise the suspect loyalties of the Stanleys in the north west, particularly Lancashire and Cheshire. Whilst William and Thomas Stanley had been absolved of any blame or treachery in the rebellion of 1483, they still had to be treated with circumspection. Not only was Lord Stanley the stepfather of Henry Tudor, but the Stanleys had been enemies of Richard and his friends, the Harringtons, since 1467, so whilst professing their loyalty, Stanley power had to be watched and supervised.

Jasper Tudor's long-standing influence in west Wales meant that this also was an area of concern for the government. Jasper had been deprived of his earldom of Pembroke in 1461, and again in 1471, but this had not stopped his ability to tap into the latent Welsh loyalty that had survived through the many vicissitudes and travails of his career. Many Welshmen felt an enormous element of pride, not only in Jasper's ancestry, but also in the fact that he and his brother Edmund had been the first Welshmen to sit in the House of Lords. As well as these loyalties, Jasper could count on a number of Welsh families who had suffered on his behalf, such as those of Rhys ap Thomas of Carmarthenshire and the Mansels of Gower, whose place in local affairs under the Yorkist kings had been taken by the likes of the Donnes of Kidwelly.

Although in the far west many men still thought wistfully of Jasper Tudor, there were still those further east who remained loyal to Richard and who thought equally wistfully of the days of William Herbert, Edward IV's master-lock of Wales. William Herbert, first Earl of Pembroke (1467–69), had occupied his Welsh earldom until his death at the battle of Edgecote. Between 1471 and 1478, his son, William Herbert, had occupied his father's lands, titles and offices, offering further opportunities for native Welsh advancement. After the death of his Woodville wife, Mary, in 1478, William had effectively been demoted by Edward IV and forced to exchange his earldom of Pembroke for that of Huntingdon and to surrender his lands and offices in Wales to Edward's eldest son. William had re-emerged in 1484 and married Richard III's illegitimate daughter, Lady Katherine Plantagenet, and had been amply rewarded for his support during Buckingham's rebellion. William Herbert was now charged with the defence of south Wales by the king. In this, he was firmly supported by the

Vaughan family of Tretower, who had had a blood-feud with Jasper Tudor since the 1470s, if not the 1450s.[7] The Herberts, alongside their relatives, the Vaughans and the Devereux, were long-time Yorkist retainers with little love for the Tudor uncle and nephew. Together, the Herbert, Vaughan and Devereux families controlled south-east Wales, the present-day counties of Glamorgan, Brecon and Monmouth. In addition, they were supported by the connection forged by Richard III's trusted henchman, Sir James Tyrrell, who held substantial property in Glamorgan and was Constable of Cardiff and Caerphilly castles. Sir James himself was also Constable of Guines castle at Calais and after the escape of de Vere his presence was needed there. Therefore, his supporters were instructed to place themselves at the disposal of William Herbert, Earl of Huntingdon. All in all, this Ricardian bloc made south-east Wales inhospitable territory for the Tudors.

Keeping 'a faithful watch on all the ports ...'

The most important defensive element of the realm in the face of a seaborne invasion was the English Channel and those ships that could operate on it. Richard III obviously recognized this, having already had fleets at sea in 1483 against the French and the Bretons and, in 1484, against the Scots. He also had experienced commanders in John Masefield and Thomas Everingham.[8] It is likely that Richard maintained Edward IV's small professional fleet, which was augmented by impressed merchant ships as the need arose. The control of the Channel and denying Henry Tudor use of the ports of the south coast, particularly those where the Beaufort influence had traditionally been strong, was a strategic imperative.[9]

Richard and Francis Lovell were still at Kenilworth at Whitsun 1485 where, on 25 May, a commission of Oyer and Terminer was issued to Lovell, Sir William Stanley and others, including William Catesby and Morgan of Kidwelly, to investigate 'counterfittings, sweatings and falsification of coin and money'[10] for Warwickshire and other Midland counties. The commission clearly denotes that the everyday procedures of government continued with routine efforts to maintain the integrity of the realm's coinage. This was very soon supplanted by more urgent business that required immediate and serious attention. The Crowland Chronicle is quite specific that soon after Whitsun 1485 Richard III left Kenilworth to go north to Nottingham to assume a watch over the centre of the kingdom. The chronicle recorded that: 'Lord Lovell, his Chamberlain, was left near Southampton there to deploy [Richard's] fleet.'[11] The Crowland Chronicle specifies that Lovell was to take command 'of the united forces of the whole neighbourhood so as to keep a faithful watch on all the ports of those parts'.[12] Nothing perhaps demonstrates the lack of capable personnel available to Richard III at the highest level of government more than Lovell's appointment to command the fleet at Southampton. Lovell, by this time as King's Chamberlain and Butler, already held two of the great offices of state; he had also been active investigating sedition and conspiracy across southern England for the previous two years. Now, in addition to these duties, Lovell was expected to be the realm's first line of defence against foreign invasion at sea.

The popular view at the time was that the Tudor invasion was heading towards the small port of Milford on Southampton Water rather than Henry and Jasper Tudor's true intended destination of Milford Haven in west Wales. Indeed, the Crowland Chronicle repeats the supposed commonly held belief at the time, based on the insight of 'some people, gifted with the Spirit of Prophecy, [who] foretold that these men would land at the port of Milford.' Taking this to mean the port of Milford on the south coast of England, Lovell spent his time securing the wrong port in the wrong part of the country.

Preparing to stop Henry Tudor at sea

The government of Richard III was neither complacent nor so naïve as to trust in those 'gifted with the spirit of prophecy', however, and it seems that Richard's espionage network on the continent was at least partially successful. At some point near Whitsun 1485, whilst the court was at Kenilworth undertaking the routine business of government, news came to the king that Henry Tudor's expedition was close to sailing. The fact that Lovell was preparing to intercept Henry's fleet at the wrong Milford was a perfectly rational decision. Milford in Hampshire was as likely a destination as Milford Haven; it was close to the ports of Christchurch and Lymington and near the area from which Collingbourne had promised a warm welcome to Henry Tudor, not only from himself but also from his friends. It was also close to the Beaufort recruiting grounds, where loyalty to the family had proved remarkably resilient as the support for Margaret of Anjou and the Duke of Somerset had proved in 1471. Of course, Jasper Tudor's previous connections had been exclusively in west Wales and especially Pembrokeshire in which Milford Haven lay. Still, Richard could not take the risk of ignoring the possibility of the use of a port appreciably closer to London. Francis Lovell had also some experience in the area of Southampton and to a certain degree with nautical matters, as was proved by his overseeing of Lord Powys's departure with 1,000 archers from Southampton for Brittany the previous June. Lovell had also led the investigation into the full extent of Collingbourne's conspiracy and connections the previous autumn and, therefore, had probably a greater understanding of the extent of dissent and unrest on the south coast than anyone else. As a prominent southern magnate and the man who held the king's ear, Lovell was the obvious choice to send to the region.

Lovell was at Woburn, on 20 June, with Lord Scrope of Bolton, Sir Richard Ratcliffe, William Catesby, Sir Thomas Mauleverer and his associate Edward Frank, Sheriff of Oxfordshire. Soon after, Lovell travelled through the southern Midlands towards Southampton, a distance of approximately 110 miles, probably passing through his own estates as he did so and quite possibly staying at Minster Lovell as he headed south toward Southampton. At that time, Southampton was the principal port of the south coast, a centre of shipbuilding and the staple port for the great Genoese trading carracks that brought the luxury goods of the Far East and the Mediterranean to England. From Southampton, Lovell could intercept Henry Tudor towards the east or the west of the Isle of Wight. Lovell was, no doubt, also in close contact with his associate on the council, Morgan of Kidwelly, who was his appointee as Butler's deputy for the adjacent port of Poole. Further to the east, the Earl of Arundel, as Warden of the Cinque Ports, could patrol the Sussex and Kent coasts covering the English Channel up to the Thames estuary. It is likely that Lovell was in place sometime after 25 June and had mobilized the resources of the Crown and the port of Southampton soon thereafter.

We do not know how many ships Lovell had at his command at Southampton, there are sufficient references to royal ships during the reign of Richard III to suggest that he maintained a small professional royal fleet and that this was augmented by royal purchases and impressments. Lovell certainly had the fleet to sea patrolling the Channel during the early summer of 1485. From across the Channel, he maintained a closer watch on French activity at the mouth of the Seine, particularly the traffic of the great northern port of Harfleur where Lovell must have known that Henry Tudor was mustering his forces. However, no matter how diligent the patrols were or how good a seaman Lovell was, fifteenth-century ships were not designed to stay at sea indefinitely; they had to return to port periodically to replenish provisions and to repair and re-fit rigging and undertake general maintenance. Neither did fifteenth-century ships have the capacity to tack against the prevailing wind, particularly the Westerlies that blew up the Channel from the Atlantic. To maintain and supply a fleet at sea was enormously expensive, and there is some evidence that by the end of July, Richard was having difficulty paying for his fleet. Indeed, it may well have returned to port because of Richard's financial difficulties. For these or other reasons, the fleet under Lovell's command failed to intercept Henry Tudor's fleet.

Henry Tudor makes landfall

On or about 1 August – a date possibly chosen when Lovell's fleet was in port – Henry's fleet, under the command of Guillaume de Casenove (nicknamed *Coulon*), in his flagship, the *Poulain de Dieppe*, set sail from Harfleur. Henry's expedition comprised of at least thirty ships with approximately 4,000 professional French soldiers. It seems that the fleet hugged the French Coast as far as Brittany and then sailed north around Land's End into the first inlet within Milford Haven, near the beach and village of Dale. Arriving on dry land unchallenged was doubtless a relief for Henry. The French chronicler Robert Fabian has him fall to his knees and recite the 43rd psalm, 'Judge me, oh God, and distinguish my cause.'[13] Having disembarked his men, which must have been a slow and ponderous process undertaken with a nervous watchfulness, the Earl of Oxford, Jasper Tudor and other military professionals would have been only too conscious of their little force's vulnerability. By Monday 8 August,

Henry was at the local town of Haverfordwest where his army was received with the 'utmost good will of all', but no significant recruits to his cause, despite the assurances of the renegade Welshman Arnold Butler. Henry left Haverfordwest that afternoon as a rumour gripped his camp that the Earl of Huntingdon's brother, Sir Walter Herbert, was 'at Carmarthen with a huge band of armed men'.[14] It was a nervous and watchful force that crested the Preseli Mountains, marching northwards towards Cardigan.

Richard's response to the news from Milford Haven

Richard's agent in Pembrokeshire, in the south of the Haven, Richard Williams, Constable of Pembroke Castle, had spotted the rebel fleet[15] and immediately sent messages to the king, some 200 miles away at Buckwood Lodge in Nottinghamshire. These messages arrived four days later on 11 August. Immediately, Richard sent out couriers with urgent summonses to sheriffs and commissioners to now enact the procedures that had been in place since the previous winter. As promised, the Duke of Norfolk promptly organized an array of a thousand men at Bury St Edmunds on 16 August. He instructed John Paston to meet him there with 'such a company of tall men as you can easily make up at my expense'.[16] At Nottingham, on 5 August, Richard III was in the company of the Earl of Lincoln, Lord Scrope and Lord Strange, with Strange almost certainly being there as a hostage for the good behaviour of his father, Lord Stanley. Other members of the nobility and gentry had also received their summonses, the most prominent being the Earl of Northumberland and Lord Stanley, who were to bring with them the levies of the north and Lancashire and Cheshire. The *Ballad of Bosworth Field* has the earls of Northumberland and Westmorland coming to join the king alongside the Earl of Lincoln. With them stood the lords Zouche, Maltravers, Welles, Grey of Codnor, Ferrers of Chartley, Audley, Fitzhugh, Scrope of Masham, Scrope of Bolton, Dacre, Ogle and Lumley. With the exception of Lord Maltravers (the son of the Earl of Arundel), all were lords of the north or the Midlands, indicating from where Richard was drawing his principal support.[17]

Whilst many of these lords are named in the poem, it is unlikely that all of them were present at the battle and later records do not specify those who were in attendance upon Richard on that day. The *Ballad of Bosworth Field* states that Francis Lovell was present; this indicates that Lovell was recalled from Southampton sometime after Richard became aware that Henry Tudor had landed in Pembrokeshire. Lovell would have had approximately 175 miles to march (at roughly 20 miles a day) to reach Richard at Nottingham in good time. It is likely that he rode north through Winchester, crossing the Thames at Abingdon and from there on to Oxford. Whilst this route brought him into his home county, it is unlikely that he had time to recruit a substantial following from his own estates. It is far more likely that he was only able to mobilize the core of his retinue, especially those higher-ranking members of his connection and some gentry supporters, rather than a large rank-and-file company of foot soldiers.

Henry Tudor's march through Wales

Henry Tudor, meanwhile was marching purposefully through Wales, advancing through the relatively inhospitable countryside of the far west Welsh coast. Having left Haverfordwest, he was at Cardigan on 9 August, where he found that the bridge over the river Teifi was undefended and the garrison of the castle, such as it was, unprepared to resist him. Marching on, he reached Aberystwyth on 12 August and crossed the Cambrian Mountains towards Welshpool by 16 August. Outside the town stretched the old Roman road leading to Shrewsbury and on then to Watling Street. As Henry stood here, looking for the first time towards England, he was joined by his most important Welsh supporter, Rhys ap Thomas of Llandeilo in Carmarthenshire, whose family were Lancastrian adherents who, in 1461, had held out against Edward IV in the mountain castle of Carreg Cennen. That loyalty to the House of Lancaster had brought destruction on the castle and a generation of political eclipse for Rhys and his family as their traditional influence in their home county was supplanted by the Donnes.

Tracking Henry northward, Rhys ap Thomas had with him the men of Kidwelly, Carnwyllion and Iscennen, together with others from northern Carmarthenshire. These men had been recruited under Richard's warrant and marched north under Rhys, unsure of their role in the coming campaign, but implicitly trusting in the leadership of a member of the native *Uchelwyr* ('high born'), whose *bonedd* ('lineage') accorded him the right to command. If Rhys' men were unsure of his intentions so far, more worryingly, so was Henry Tudor. Henry had sent messages requesting the support of Rhys, but had received vague or ambivalent replies. It must have been a great relief when Rhys arrived at Mynydd Digoll above Welshpool and declared his support for Henry; even more welcome was the fact that he brought with him around 1,500 men, who considerably swelled Henry's forces. Rhys' support was vital to Henry for, although Henry had thus far crossed Wales unopposed and was displaying the banner of the Red Dragon of Cadwallader, he had actually attracted only scant support until this point. The adherence of one of the most important Welsh chieftains was a fillip for Henry and his small army.

Henry Tudor advances on to the heart of England

Richard III could have expected Henry perhaps to have been stopped in Wales. He certainly expected him to be stopped at Shrewsbury whose town bailiff, Thomas Mitton, Richard felt sure he could rely on.[18] Shrewsbury commanded one of the strategic bridges over the Severn and, if closed, would have locked Henry Tudor in Wales as had happened to Buckingham in 1483. Mitton held out over the night of 17 August, during which he was advised by Sir Richard Corbet, Lord Stanley's son-in-law and Christopher Urswick, that Henry Tudor possessed a number of secret friends and that Richard's position was not as secure as he had presumed. In light of this, on 18 August the gates of Shrewsbury were thrown open and Henry Tudor and his forces marched through and continued on across the Severn towards the heart of England. At Nottingham, when he heard the news, Richard, recognizing the scope of the treachery, 'began to burn with chagrin' and promised revenge on all the knights from Lancaster to Shrewsbury. Richard now began to suspect that the Stanleys – Sir Thomas and Sir William – who held the castle of Holt, only thirty miles north of Shrewsbury, had clearly failed to exert any pressure on Shrewsbury's mayor and council to close the city against his stepson, Henry.

Richard's mood would not have been lifted when he learned that Sir Gilbert Talbot, uncle of the young Earl of Shrewsbury, had brought 500 mounted men of the Talbot retinue to join with Henry Tudor at Newport. The stain and the stench of treachery was already beginning to infect Richard's camp at Nottingham. This would become even more galling to Richard as he impatiently awaited the arrival of what were rumoured to be two 'great companies' – those of the Earl of Northumberland and those of Lord Stanley, who were both frustratingly dilatory in joining the king, despite having had ample warning of where and when to rendezvous. Surprisingly, Henry Tudor did not take Watling Street, the old Roman road south from Chester to London, in an attempt to capture the great prize of London, but instead moved eastwards towards Richard. Whilst many men were gathering to join the king, particularly northern loyalists, Richard and his high command began to wonder if they would arrive in time. Henry Tudor's forced march eastwards from Newport in Cheshire on 18 August brought him closer and closer to Richard and his army at Nottingham, stealing the initiative of time and space. Richard also knew that to continue to await events at Nottingham would inevitably mean surrendering the political initiative and, possibly with it, his crown, Therefore, he believed that although his army was not yet fully assembled, it was imperative that he acted as a king and did not allow Henry Tudor to march any further into the centre of his kingdom unopposed. For this reason, it is unlikely that all of the lords recorded in *The Ballad of Bosworth Field* were actually with him as part of his army when he departed Nottingham for Leicester on Saturday 20 August.

Richard makes his move

The king's forces moved out of Nottingham in the traditional array of three divisions surrounded by the full panoply of chivalry. He was accompanied by the Duke of Norfolk, his son, the Earl of Surrey, and the Earl of Northumberland who had brought south the Yorkshire and northern levies. At the centre was the king, accompanied by the chief personnel of Ricardian government, Francis Lovell and John, Earl of Lincoln, who, although Lieutenant of the North, seems to have remained with the king and delegated the recruitment of the northern counties to the Earl of Northumberland. Lovell would have had a small retinue with him, alongside personal servants, rather than a large contingent of troops from southern England. With the king would have been his household knights and the officers of court such as his secretary John Kendall, Richard Ratcliffe, William Catesby, Robert Percy, Robert Harrington and Robert Brackenbury. With them would have been the Midlands retinues of Lords Devereux and Zouche, plus the specialist gunners that the king would have brought with him. King Richard III and his closest confidantes would have been concerned, since despite the size of the royal army that surrounded them, politically the situation was far more volatile than any of them would have liked. An impecunious exile who had not set foot in England in fourteen years and who should have been a political footnote on the aspirations of the House of Lancaster, had been able to land a fleet and bring a foreign army into the heart of England with seemingly little or no opposition. A largely French army had crossed through the mountains of Wales, marched through the old middle March of Wales and on into the plains of Cheshire and Staffordshire. Whilst the small Welsh towns of Haverfordwest and Cardigan had, it would appear, little choice in opening their gates to the invader, the same could not be said of the town of Shrewsbury, guardian of the Severn and strategically important. The capitulation of Shrewsbury had demonstrated a wider political apathy, or even antipathy towards the king and his government, despite all their efforts to besmirch the name of Henry Tudor and his foreign army, described in a letter sent out from Nottingham Castle as 'rebels and traitors associated with our ancient enemies of France and other strangers'.[19] In spite of these castigations, the rebels had successfully passed through the county town of Stafford, the cathedral city of Lichfield and on to Tamworth, all the time getting closer to Ermine Street and the direct route to Leicester.

Although Richard and his advisors were no doubt aware of the ambivalence of the Stanleys, they would have taken note of and comfort in the fact that they had not actually joined forces with the rebels. Equally, the king, from what we know of his personality, would probably have welcomed at last the opportunity to take direct action to secure his crown, fighting his enemies face-to-face rather than the furtive and evasive war of nerves and propaganda that he had endured in the preceding months. Richard had confidence in himself as a commander, having been present on the field of battle since the age of eighteen at Barnet and Tewkesbury and then at the expedition to France aged twenty-three – and this besides leading the defence of the north and a campaign into Scotland. His adversary Henry, now twenty-eight, had no corresponding martial experience and whilst the Earl of Oxford was an experienced commander, Richard III had been part of the army that had bested him at Barnet in 1471. Equally, the other experienced commander in Henry's army, his uncle Jasper, had yet to be on the winning side in any battle; brave, tenacious, fiercely loyal and elusive he may have been, but militarily lucky he was not. As the royal army of approximately 15,000 set up camp in the neighbourhood of Sutton Cheney on the night of 21 August, Richard should have felt some confidence in himself as a commander, his large army and a sense of relief that all the suspicion, rumours, innuendos and conspiracies would be brought to an end by the God of battles in whom he so fervently believed.

Despite these encouraging thoughts, Richard III spent a bad night prior to the battle. According to the Crowland Chronicle, he had 'a terrible dream, a multitude of demons apparently surrounding him … and his countenance [which] was always drawn [was] even more pale and deathly'.[20] The king's temper can hardly have been improved when an anonymous note was found pinned to the Duke of Norfolk's tent reading 'Jack of Norfolk be not too bold, for Dicken thy master is bought and sold'.

The morning of the battle

Daybreak came at 5.15am on 22 August 1485. Richard asked for mass to be said before him as his army stirred and soldiers began to steel themselves for action as the night-watchers stood down. There was an element of confusion amongst the king's large and possibly unwieldy forces as they saw that the rebel army was not only awake, but its formations already alert and in position. Seeing Oxford's men already arrayed and ready for battle, the king's commanders began to rouse the commonality, who were expected to undertake most of the fighting. The majority of these would have been country levies summoned to fight by their local superiors, but men all from the same village and county, who felt a certain cohesion and bonding, fighting with those they had always known. According to the Italian diplomat, Dominic Mancini, all of Richard's men possessed helmets, bows and arrows, a sword, and carried a small iron shield, a buckler. Whilst a few wore an iron breastplate for protection, most wore a linen and 'more comfortable tunics that reached down below the loins and … stuffed with tow or some soft material'.[21] Those who were not archers were equipped with billhooks or pole arms with which the English were known to be particularly adept.

Richard's desire to celebrate mass was hindered by his chaplain's inability to get together all the requirements for the liturgy so that when the priests were ready, no wine could be found, or when the wine was found, no bread was available. Equally remiss in their preparations were the army's cooks, making Richard depressed to find that 'nor was there any breakfast ready to revive [his] flagging spirit.'[22] To make matters worse for Richard, he found his army under attack from the Earl of Oxford's men. Consequently, Richard and his army went into battle unshriven and unfed that fateful morning.

Battle commences

Despite the smaller size of Oxford's forces and its disadvantages in topography – being encamped at the bottom of the rise occupied by Richard – Oxford had formed up his men into a broad wedge formation and, close to daybreak, had begun to lead them on against the larger royal army. The bulk of Henry Tudor's forces had taken their place in this formation, which now advanced as a 'forward'. The forces under Oxford's direct command contained as much as two-thirds to three-quarters of Henry's available force. Oxford's plan was to commit his more disciplined men to the battle before the much larger royal army was properly assembled and suitably disposed. It was also probably a stratagem to encourage or force the Stanleys to commit, as Lord Stanley had sent a message to Henry Tudor 'that he would lead his men into the line but only when Henry was there with his army drawn up'.[23] For Henry and Oxford, now was the testing time. For Richard, it was an unwelcome surprise: holding the high ground as he did, he thought that he had the advantage. Now wrong-footed, it was he who would have to respond to the Earl of Oxford's tactics.

Archaeological evidence has suggested that another reason for Oxford to advance against superior numbers was to reduce the effect of the king's gunners. Richard, like his brother Edward, took a great pride in his firearms and had thought to use the higher ground to good effect by positioning his firearm troops before his front line. Oxford's advance certainly reduced the range, but it also ensured that his men did not become a static target. Oxford's men in their wedge formation had a crust of professional French troops at their head and along the sides. These men, hardened in the Burgundian War, were professional troops who knew and trusted their officers. They were also well-versed in the modern military tactics of current European warfare and, therefore, more responsive to command and control procedures and drill than their English adversaries.

In response to Oxford's advance, the Duke of Norfolk, backed by his son, the Earl of Surrey, advanced down the hill to meet Oxford's onslaught. At the first impact of battle, Oxford's professional soldiers were knocked back by the greater number of Norfolk's men and their downhill momentum. The French, while giving ground were desperately trying to retain their cohesion, conscious that, should their formation be broken, the melee that would follow would soon become a rout as they retreated in the face of superior forces. Oxford had no love for Norfolk, his rival for primacy in East Anglia and a man who held a large portion of Oxford's erstwhile estates and patrimony. Oxford now planted his standard firmly in the ground and ordered his men to disengage from Norfolk's superior numbers. Orders were passed to Oxford's professional troops to give ground while they gave themselves the space to redress their ranks and to square off into a tighter formation. Only professional troops, able to respond to sequenced commands endlessly rehearsed, would have been able to redress their ranks thus in the presence of an enemy of such superior numbers. For Norfolk's men, who thought that their initial onslaught had been a success, there must have been surprise and consternation that the enemy, only recently having been forced back, had now disengaged and coolly reformed in a tighter formation, and renewed their advance.

This renewed advanced hit Norfolk's East Anglian irregulars at a time when they had thought the battle was almost won and when they had stopped to rest, having fought the rebels to a standstill. The renewed rebel attack knocked the wind out of their sails and forced them to give ground as they were slowly pushed back up the hill, fighting to the front, but walking backwards. At the same time, Henry Tudor's 'prickers' – light cavalry under John Savage and Gilbert Talbot – began to jab at and run down any stragglers, or any unlucky enough to be separated from Norfolk's main body. Norfolk's levies fought well for him and probably had faith in him as one of their own. But that faith and confidence was not given to other of Richard's commanders, such as Sir Robert Brackenbury or Sir John Huddleston, who were relative strangers to them. As the pressure of Oxford's attack began to tell, so Norfolk's force not only began to give ground, but also to disintegrate as men's spirits began to dip. At some point during Oxford's sustained and by now relentless attack, Norfolk himself was killed, probably as the commons he commanded began to lay down their arms and run from the field, bemused and frightened in a fight that had never been theirs. As his force disintegrated and the bonds of loyalty snapped, Norfolk and his captains had been left more and more exposed to be cut down by the relentlessly advancing professionals Oxford commanded.

A critical moment for Richard

As an experienced commander, Richard III and his advisors were well aware that a critical moment had been reached in the battle; the crumbling of Norfolk's forward line in front of the rest of the army had had a dispiriting effect. Although the centre and the rear had yet to be committed, the men within them had seen the defeat and eventual disintegration of the forward and began to reach their own conclusions on whether they could defeat Oxford's troops. The very size of the royal army, which some thought was arrayed for display, now stood in the way of its effective deployment. In addition to the stench of betrayal, treachery and treason began to affect royal morale as more and more men began to question whether they could depend on those they had been arraigned with. Men now began to desert the field, they 'fled even before coming to blows to the enemy, others abstained from fighting and slipped secretly away'.[24] Others amongst Richard's command recognized the collapsing morale of the royal forces. Richard's captain, the experienced Spaniard Juan de Salazar, advised the king to flee, look towards rebuilding another army and retreating back to London. Richard realized that this was politically unfeasible and understood that Henry Tudor had to be despatched that day or he would only get stronger. To bolster morale and reverse the defections, Richard determined that he had to be 'his own champion',[25] and to this end Richard had spotted an opportunity.

Since Henry Tudor had committed a large proportion of his forces to Oxford's vanguard, which was now fully committed to the attack on Richard's line, Henry himself had only a small company about him for his own protection and as a tactical reserve. Richard, with the advantage of height, which gave him a better view of the battlefield, now determined on a course of action that would eliminate his chief rival, revive the morale and commitment of his own troops, and ensure his reputation as a warrior king. To this end, he summoned to him his own household. Sir William Harrington tried to persuade Richard to retire, pleading that 'another day may your worship win, and reign with royalty and wear your crown and be our king'.[26] Richard rejected this advice and donned his helmet crested with a circlet of gold and mounted his horse. With him were Robert Percy, Controller of the Household, Sir Percival Thirlwall, his standard bearer, and knights of the body such as Sir Richard Ratcliffe, Sir Ralph Ashton, Lovell's brother-in-law, Sir Marmaduke Constable, Sir John Nevill, Sir Thomas Broughton, Sir John Gray, Sir Thomas Pilkington and Sir Thomas Markenfield. These were the most intimate of the king's familiars – northerners almost to a man – who had known the king for nigh on twenty years. These men would form the king's strike force, which would ride right into the heart of Henry Tudor's banners, the Cross of St George, the Red Dragon of Wales and the Dunn Cow of Richmond. These men came together for what would be the death-ride of Ricardian chivalry.

One last, desperate attempt to turn the tide of the battle

One close companion one might have expected to find in this group of knight was Francis Lovell. After all, as King's Chamberlain, he had led and regulated these men and, like Richard, grown up with them. However, for Richard's plan to work someone had to hold together the royal centre and pin down Oxford's forces, still engaged on the hill, for if Oxford's forces were in any way free to redeploy, they would be able to prevent Richard getting anywhere near Henry Tudor. To this end, Richard needed a committed supporter with the rank and stature to hold the royal centre together and continue to contain and occupy Oxford's battalions. Not only did Francis Lovell fit that role, but as a southern noble he was far more likely to hold together and shore up what was left of Norfolk's levies and to lead them forward when the time came. Lovell's association with the de la Poles gave him as much an acquaintance with the men of Suffolk and Norfolk as he had with the men of the north. Equally, in the face of Northumberland's inactivity (which some men now saw as deliberate), Lovell found himself the most senior noble with military experience, especially now that Norfolk's son, the Earl of Surrey, had been wounded. No doubt John, Earl of Lincoln, would have been by Lovell's side but, despite his high birth, this was his first taste of battle, leaving Lovell in reality to hold the line. At this point also, there had been no movement by the forces under the command of the Stanley brothers.

As Lovell and the Earl of Lincoln steadied the royal line and tried to restore some semblance of order to Norfolk's brigades in the face of Oxford's continuing onslaught, Richard III, prominent upon his royal charger and with the royal circlet surmounting his helmet, formed up the royal household of no more than 200 men. Assembling behind the main battle, engaged in brutal hand-to-hand fighting, under the royal standard of England and his own personal standard of the white boar, Richard III led his men in a sweeping manoeuvre down the hill. Skirting the marsh at its foot, the royal squadron picked up speed and charged directly towards Henry Tudor's banners. Henry Tudor was on foot in the centre of a group of dismounted men since, as described by a French archer, 'he wanted to be on foot in the midst of us.'[27] Henry also had with him a squadron of cavalry, later assessed as between thirty to thirty-five men, but an indeterminate number at this time. Richard's household men smashed into Henry Tudor's small group, with Richard himself skewering with his lance Sir John Cheney at the first contact.[28] Richard then hacked down Henry Tudor's standard bearer, apparently cleaving apart the man's head with one blow of his battle-axe. However, despite giving some ground, Henry and his men stood firm. Henry impressed his men by keeping his nerve and joining in with the attempt to repel Richard's onslaught. Alas, the Shakespearean notion of Henry and Richard indulging in single hand-to-hand combat is a sixteenth-century dramatic embellishment by the likes of Holinshed; no contemporary mentions such an encounter. It is more likely that Henry's men formed a tight knot around their leader, determined after Richard's initial success to ensure Henry's safety. Henry was in serious difficulties, for whilst the initial impetus of Richard's charge had been held back with difficulty, Richard was whittling down Henry's immediate bodyguard. It was at this time, whether responding to a request from Henry or on his own initiative, that Sir William Stanley led his men into the fray – on behalf of Henry Tudor.

The deciding factor

Throughout the battle, Thomas, Lord Stanley, had remained motionless, either awaiting an appropriate time to intervene or constrained by the knowledge that his son, Lord Strange, was a hostage for his good behaviour in the royal camp. It was Sir William Stanley who now brought the Stanley forces – men from Lancashire, Cheshire and North Wales – onto the field. Numbering up to 3,000 strong, these men now swamped Richard's men, turning the course of the battle. Hemmed in by the Stanley tide, the king's men began to succumb one by one to the inevitability of numbers. Men such as Sir Richard Ratcliffe, Sir Robert Brackenbury, Sir Robert Percy and others met their end here, fighting with their king to the last. Pushed back by sheer weight of numbers and with his household falling around him, eventually the king's horse became mired in the marsh at the bottom of the hill. With his horse probably unable to move in the saturated ground, Richard III was either dragged from it or chose to face his attackers on foot.

The recent discovery of Richard's remains allows for some reconstruction of his final fate. The chin strap of his helmet was cut away and his helmet wrenched from his head. Two sword blows were inflicted on his head and a dagger thrust to the face. The final blow was a halberd to the back of the head, which is just as Molinet recorded – that Richard had been killed by a 'welsh halberd'.[29] This accords with a traditional Welsh praise poem by the Welsh poet Guto'r Glyn, who states that it was Rhys ap Thomas who 'killed the boar destroying his head'.[30] However, other than Guto'r Glyn, no other contemporary source names the man who delivered the fatal blow. In medieval society, it took a special form of courage to slay the Lord's anointed, an act that carried a weight of sacrilegious implications and, once done, it is hardly surprising that men would think twice about boasting of such a deed. This would also explain the subsequent desecration of Richard's corpse as men thought to belittle his regal status and to destroy what remained of his aura of kingship. Another theory is that Richard was surrounded and hacked to pieces by men of North Wales under Sir William Stanley's command and that, as Welsh speakers, they would not have understood Richard's desperate cries declaring that he was the king.

On the crest of Ambion Hill, Francis Lovell could only watch helplessly as Richard's small force was overwhelmed by the red and white Stanley tide. Recognizing the inevitable as Sir Percy Thirlwell fell, having both his legs stricken from beneath him, and the king's banner went down for the last time, Lovell and what remained of Richard III's commanders tried in vain to rally what was left of the royal army. Yet even he and Lincoln must have realised this was a forlorn hope. The morale of the royal army had not been high before Richard III had undertaken his final gamble in leading the charge down the hill. With his death, no matter how brave and noble, morale was shattered. Molinet recorded that 'the rear guard seeing king Richard dead, turned to flight'.[31] The Crowland Chronicle also recorded 'those in the field threw down their arms and willingly surrendered in to Henry's power.'[32] In the face of Oxford's continued assaults, the royal line disintegrated and men began to meekly lay down their arms or to turn and run. There can be no doubt that Francis Lovell and what remained of Richard's command must have been stunned; only two hours earlier they had been part of a well-placed royal army that outnumbered Henry Tudor's largely foreign forces by perhaps two to one. Since then, the incredible had happened. Not only had they been defeated but for the first time since 1066 a reigning king of England, the Lord's anointed, had been killed on the field, a truly unthinkable outcome. The death of the king brought an end to the battle, but not to the lives of Lovell and other prominent Ricardians. Whether Lovell had remained on horseback throughout the battle, commanding the cavalry reserve as some have suggested, or fought on foot, we have no way of knowing. Unlike the Duke of Norfolk, Lord Ferrers, and others he knew well, he was not dead upon the field; neither, like the wounded earls of Surrey and Lincoln and William Catesby, did he become a prisoner of the new Tudor king. At some point on the late morning of August 22, Francis Lovell rode from the debacle of Bosworth Field into the shadows of history.

14 'LOYALTEE ME LIE'

In search of sanctuary

IN THE IMMEDIATE AFTERMATH of the battle, Francis Lovell had to come to terms with a world turned upside down. As the day had dawned, he had been the King's Chamberlain and Butler; by noon, he had become a hunted fugitive whose 'death' would soon be announced by the new king. The man whose friendship he had enjoyed for over twenty years was dead and the greater family in which he had been brought up was in disarray. Lovell's departure from the battlefield is something of a mystery. He would have begun the battle fully equipped for war in expensive armour and resplendent with the heraldic badges and coats of arms of his family, all of which denoted who he was, his heritage, his lineage, his chivalric identity – all of this would now have to be discarded and replaced with drab anonymity. For now, it was imperative for Lovell and what remained of his retinue to find some place of safety.

Leading a small body of men, which included Humphrey and Thomas Stafford of Worcestershire, he headed away from Henry Tudor's army. But in what direction? He could head south towards Minster Lovell and his own estates in Oxfordshire, but that would be a risky proposition for the new king would probably anticipate such a move and send men in pursuit to arrest him. Besides, a return to Oxfordshire would mean having to face the Stonors and Harcourts and all those other exiles returning with the victorious Tudors – men who would now be seeking revenge for nigh on two years of exile. Also, Oxfordshire was a long way from any ports and the opportunity to escape to the continent. As Lovell's party rode away, all of these factors must have weighed heavily on his mind.

In the end, the choice was made to ride to Colchester, some 200 miles from Bosworth. Colchester was chosen presumably for its close connections to Flanders and Burgundy. In the fifteenth century the town was one of the twelve richest boroughs in England and had a thriving cloth trade, exporting its russet cloth throughout north-western Europe. The estuary of the river Colne also offered a direct route towards the continent with ample shipping. The first thoughts of Lovell would have been to use his contacts as the King's Butler to enable passage to Burgundy where he must have felt he would be offered not just asylum but a welcome by the dead king's sister, Dowager Duchess Margaret.

At some point the plan to go to Burgundy changed, and Lovell decided to remain in England for the immediate future. When and how this plan changed cannot now be known, but it must have been relatively soon after Bosworth since Polydor Vergil states:

Two days after, at Leicester William Catesby lawyer with a few that were his fellows were executed. And of those who took to their feet Francis Lovell, Humphrey Stafford, with his brother Thomas and much company fled into the sanctuary of St John which is at Colchester a town by the seaside in Essex.[1]

Vergil's writings make it quite clear that Lovell still had a considerable following with him when he arrived at Colchester, meaning that he still retained some measure of authority. It may have been the difficulty of obtaining shipping for a large body of men that delayed their departure, or more likely the realization that they were not in any immediate danger. Henry Tudor, now King Henry VII, had stayed at Leicester immediately after the battle of Bosworth. In Leicester he had given thanks for his victory and had interred the mutilated corpse of Richard III in the Franciscan priory in the town. It had then taken him a further two weeks to arrive at Westminster. During this time his government had issued a proclamation stating that John, Duke of Norfolk, Thomas, Earl of Surrey, John, Earl of Lincoln and Francis, Viscount Lovell were all dead. This was a piece of political expediency that allowed the new king's government to give the impression that the main pillars of the Ricardian regime had all died on the field so that any opposition had no real figure of substance to rally to. Of course, the statement was only true in the case of Norfolk and whilst his son, the Earl of Surrey, had been wounded, he was now in the new king's custody, as was the Earl of Lincoln. Francis Lovell, however, was both very much alive and at large. The government's proclamation may well have done Lovell a favour in that very few would look for a man who had been proclaimed dead. At Colchester, Lovell and his companions sought sanctuary at the Benedictine abbey of St John the Baptist, a foundation with strong links to the Howard family and especially with John, Duke of Norfolk, who had influenced the election of the abbot of St John's since the mid-1460s. The current abbot (no doubt a Yorkist), Walter Stansted, was likely to have been well briefed about Lovell's intentions, yet he must have been extremely anxious at having the most wanted fugitive in the country ride through the abbey's elaborate gate seeking sanctuary for himself and his companions. The rules of sanctuary allowed Lovell's party to spend the next forty days within the abbey confines; in fact, they stayed at the abbey for substantially longer. They could do so because, contrary to popular opinion, Henry VII was more interested in reconciliation than revenge. After Bosworth, there were only twenty-eight attainders, a tiny number compared with those of Edward IV's reign. Some of those attainted (such as Norfolk, Lord Ferrers and Richard Ratcliffe) were already dead; fifteen of those attainted were below knightly rank and relatively unimportant. There was no great desire by Henry VII to create more bloodshed; in fact, he wanted to avoid this at all costs if he were to obtain any political gain from marrying Elizabeth of York. Obvious Lancastrian supporters of long-standing such as Jasper Tudor and John de Vere, Earl of Oxford, were restored to their dignities and estates, as were Lord Clifford and the Butlers. However, there was no purge of the Yorkist nobility. Henry recognized that to govern, he would need these men, who had been participants in Richard's government, alongside those returning exiles who had supported his own cause. Thus, on 25 September, Francis Lovell's own brother-in-law, Richard, Lord Fitzhugh, was appointed to major offices in Richmondshire and the Constableship of Barnard Castle.[2] Clearly, Fitzhugh felt no especial animus existed against him or his family. Immediately after Bosworth, Henry did send Robert Willoughby to Sheriff Hutton in Yorkshire to take possession of Clarence's young son Edward, Earl of Warwick. This was a security measure, 'lest if the boy should escape and given any alteration in circumstances, he might stir up civil discord'.[3] With Warwick in Henry's possession and the majority of Ricardian leaders dead or imprisoned, Henry felt that he could now put away the stick and instead rely on the carrot.

This desire for reconciliation is reflected in the contemporary evidence of Sir Hugh Conway, who, having told Henry VII that Lovell was about to break sanctuary and foment further trouble, stated that the king did not believe it and told him: '… that hyt would not be so and reasoned with me to the contrary'.[4] Prior to his execution, William Catesby had said as much and had hoped that Lovell would make his peace with Henry VII and that when he did so he would pray for Catesby's soul.[5] Both sources seem to suggest that Henry VII believed that it was only logical that Lovell would sooner or later beg for and receive Henry's clemency. After all, with Richard dead, what did Lovell have to fight for any more? Yes, Lovell had been declared dead; yes, Lovell had subsequently been attainted and his lands, estate and offices confiscated. Even so, these were not insurmountable barriers to a return to royal favour, as shown by the example of the Earl of Surrey. This surely was the logical course of action, especially since Henry had already agreed to marry Elizabeth of York. In this, as in so many other aspects of Henry VII's dealings with Francis Lovell, Henry had seriously misread the man he was dealing with.

A chance to re-group

For Francis Lovell, now in sanctuary in Colchester, Henry VII was not a legitimate king. Richard III's proclamations earlier in the year had been correct to describe Henry as illegitimate on both his mother's and his father's side. Henry was nothing more than a penniless Welsh adventurer with no knowledge of either England or the English – someone who had been placed on the throne by England's traditional enemy, France. His supporters were convicted traitors and conspirators who had rebelled against their true king. For Lovell, it was impossible to effectively renounce all that he had stood for over the previous three years, to turn his back on those pronouncements he had made regarding Henry Tudor. How could he, Francis Lovell, be reconciled with the man who had brought about the defeat and death of his friend and king, Richard III? How could he bend the knee to the man who had taken from him his birthright, his titles, his offices and his lands? How could he beg for clemency from a man who claimed that his crimes were so heinous that his blood was tainted? He must also have reflected that scant mercy had been shown to the others mentioned in Collingbourne's piece of doggerel: with 'the catte' (Catesby) executed and 'the ratte' (Ratcliffe) dead, only he ('the dogge') now remained to exact any form of vengeance. Added to this, Lovell must have seen Henry's victory as depriving him on a very personal level of friends and comrades and breaking apart the extended family with whom he had grown up.

From his sanctuary in Colchester, Francis Lovell now began to get in touch with other Ricardian loyalists who also inhabited the world of misplaced men whose future, like his, had been cut short. These were men who also retained a residual personal loyalty to Richard III that made them intransigent towards the new regime. They too hoped that the game was not over. As Henry VII waited for Lovell to recognize him as king, Lovell began to plot revenge. It was this thirst to strike back at Henry VII that shaped the events of the early months of 1486 as Lovell and others rejected the idea of escaping overseas and instead sought to exact vengeance on the foreign adventurer who had stolen their future.

Lovell the leader

It is at this time that Lovell shouldered the leadership of what was left of the Ricardian party and assumed the direction of the opposition to Henry VII. For this he was ideally placed, having an extensive network of influence throughout England from his position as the King's Chamberlain. In that role, he had become familiar with the members of the royal household and the court and also with influential members of parliament. In the role of the King's Butler, Lovell had officers in all the key ports in the country, and through this and the provisioning of the king and his household he had developed many links with England's mercantile community. As a major magnate in his own right, Lovell had strong connections in the Thames Valley, Northamptonshire, Shropshire and Yorkshire. In Yorkshire he was known as a man who had been brought up in the Earl of Warwick's household and whose wife, a Nevill, was one of their own. He could also count on the tacit support of the de La Pole family with whom he had had strong links going back to 1471. True, John, Duke of Suffolk, may well have been ambivalent over the change of dynasty, especially as his eldest son John, Earl of Lincoln, appeared to be honoured by Henry VII. But Suffolk and his wife, Elizabeth, could only look on with apprehension at the future as their own proximity to the throne and their own precedence in rank receded more and more as the new dynasty established itself. Equally, it is questionable how accepting of a king who had killed her brother, Duchess Elizabeth really was. Whilst Lincoln had been released soon after Bosworth and his presence at court honoured as a close relative of the new queen, he had been deprived of his offices and was under constant watch. In these circumstances, de la Pole support was tacit rather than overt. Lovell could also look to the support of other Ricardian malcontents who had survived Bosworth but who had found no place in the new Tudor regime.

What now for England and Francis Lovell?

Henry VII's first parliament of November 1487 formally attainted Francis Lovell, degrading him from his rank of viscount and depriving him of his lands and estates, which were now handed out to others such as the king's uncle, Jasper Tudor. One view is that the battle of Bosworth was decisive in bringing the Wars of the Roses to an end. Another view is that somehow men woke up on 23 August 1485 and realized that they had left behind the Middle Ages and entered the Tudor Age. For those who lived in 1485, nothing could be less obvious. True, an unpopular king had been overthrown and astonishingly had died in battle in the very heart of his kingdom. Yes, he had been replaced by someone whose claim to the throne was tenuous at best and who most of the kingdom had not heard of until that summer. Moreover, he was a man who had been placed on the throne of England by an army largely composed of foreigners: French, Scots and Welsh – peoples the English usually viewed with suspicion and disdain. Throughout England there were men who were uncertain in their loyalties and confused as to who the rightful king should be. Equally, there were men who were very certain of their loyalties and were sure that those loyalties were not owed to an obscure quarter-Welsh exile. For men who had been 'true men' to Richard III, there were princes of the House of York who had a far better claim to the throne than this Tudor upstart. Indeed, there were others for whom Richard's death was a disaster and for whom the triumph of Henry Tudor brought only eclipse and exclusion from office and their former areas of influence.

A bleak future

One such family was the Harringtons of Hornby Castle in the north of Lancashire. For the previous twenty years, the Harringtons had been in dispute with the Stanleys over possession of the bulk of the family estates, in a quarrel between the heirs general and the heirs male. Richard III, as Duke of Gloucester, had stood by the Harringtons as his clients since 1467, and prevented Stanley power from encroaching into the area. With the death of their patron and the elevation of Lord Stanley to the earldom of Derby, the Harringtons expected little of the new king. Certainly he would not rein in Stanley pretensions in the locality; nor could much be expected through the law courts. The Harringtons simmered with fear and resentment as they looked to the future.

In Devon and Cornwall, the return of the Courtenays, long-time earls of Devon and ardent Lancastrians, represented the eclipse of prominent Ricardians such as Sir Henry Bodrugan. Sir Henry had been a venal and corrupt bully who had terrorized his neighbours, but had been tolerated by Richard's government because he kept a remote and traditionally fractious part of the realm quiescent. However, Sir Henry's authority could not challenge that of a Courtenay once more resident at Tiverton, who held not just the king's commission in the duchy of Cornwall but also the king's ear.

In Worcestershire, the Stafford brothers, Humphrey and Thomas, who had held the Severn bridges against Buckingham could look forward to bleak futures as those who were exiled for their participation in Buckingham's failed rebellion returned and sought recompense for their loyalty.

In south-east Wales, the Vaughans of Tretower and other members of their extended family could only look on in apprehension at the Tudor triumph. The Vaughans were a family that had been Yorkists for generations. As such, they had earned the enmity of the Tudors. The Vaughans had been present at the humiliating imprisonment of Henry VII's father, Edmund Tudor, in the dungeons of his own castle at Carmarthen in 1456, an episode that had led to his early death. They had been in the field at Mortimer's Cross (1461) fighting against Edmund's brother, Jasper, and had been part of the victorious Yorkist party that had beheaded Jasper's father, Owain, in the marketplace of Hereford after the battle. In revenge for this, Jasper had executed members of the Vaughan family at Chepstow after the battle of Tewkesbury in 1471. In 1483, at the instigation of Richard III, the Vaughans had captured and ransacked Buckingham's castle at Brecon, ensuring that he had no secure base to retire to once he failed to cross the Severn. The Vaughans could only look on in trepidation as their old enemy Jasper Tudor was now one of the great men in the kingdom. Not only was he the king's uncle, he was now Duke of Bedford and their immediate and overweening neighbour. Jasper now held the earldom of Pembroke and also the lordships of Glamorgan and Brecon, from which he would be able to dominate the Vaughans' home of Tretower and the surrounding locality.[6] Little wonder the Vaughans were worried.

Even in Ireland, far from the battlefield of Bosworth, the Earl of Kildare ('the great Kildare') could only be discomforted by the return of his family's traditional rivals, the Butlers, to the earldom of Ormond. The Butlers had been restored to their Irish estates by Edward IV in 1475, but in 1485, John, the 5th Earl of Ormond, was returned to his English lands. As a die-hard Lancastrian who had fought at Tewkesbury and a man of unimpeachable loyalty, he was now warmly welcomed at court and his family restored to their traditional 'supremacy' over the counties of Kilkenny and Tipperary. For the Earl of Kildare and his Geraldine relative, the Earl of Desmond, such developments could not bode well for his and his family's domination of Irish affairs.

An unstable realm

There were two other aspects of the Tudor triumph that should have possibly concerned Henry VII. His victory inevitably brought back to England the men who had risen in rebellion with the Duke of Buckingham and who now expected to receive their reward and at the very least the return of their patrimony. That inevitably meant that a large number of Ricardian lords would lose the gains they had made in 1483. For some, such as Sir Richard Ratcliffe, it did not matter as his death and attainder at Bosworth allowed for the Courtenay estate to be returned to the Earl of Devon without any difficulties. For others, such as the Earl of Westmorland, it meant the loss of lucrative southern estates and offices, which could be guaranteed to create some element of resentment. These actions may have been just and inevitable, but they would not help Henry win hearts and minds for the new regime.

Equally, many men who had been used to having a place in the world through their Nevill connections now found themselves excluded from national and local affairs. The livery badge of the 'ragged staff', which had given them a place in society and a sense of pride and authority, now counted for very little; it was the portcullis and the green dragon badges of the Beauforts that now counted for far more in local and national affairs. The usual paths of preferment and promotion were now closed to the men of Richmondshire, North Yorkshire and the West Midlands and their rightful lord, Edward, Earl of Warwick, partially rehabilitated under Richard III, remained a virtual prisoner and was powerless in the clutches of the new king, his Yorkist blood making him too dangerous to be left at large. Whilst apparently not a very prepossessing young man himself, his bloodline commanded loyalty.

All of these groups, disparate as they were, proved receptive to the approaches of Francis Lovell, the only Ricardian now at liberty with leadership potential. As autumn turned to winter, there was plenty of evidence that unrest existed within the realm. More than a whiff of conspiracy can be found in a letter, dated 13 December 1485, written from London to Sir Robert Plumpton: 'there was speculation in London of another upheaval, involving northerners, Welshmen and even members of the royal household'. The correspondent also noted that there was 'much running among the Lords but no man knows what it is: it is said it is not well amongst them'.[7]

As the winter nights drew in, Francis Lovell and his followers were about to break sanctuary.

15 THE ASSASSIN

Taking control

THAT HENRY VII FELT some unease in the winter of 1485 is hardly surprising. Such unease would have stemmed from two reasons: firstly, Henry's failure to marry Elizabeth of York immediately after his victory at Bosworth, which caused some mutterings at court, and, secondly, Henry's own concern about the extent of Ricardian plotting post-Bosworth.

In Rennes Cathedral on Christmas Day in 1483, Henry Tudor had vowed to marry Elizabeth of York. But now that he was in a position to fulfil that promise, it seemed to committed Yorkists that Henry was doing whatever he could to delay the marriage. It could even be argued that he had gone out of his way to avoid any such promise by having himself crowned alone on 30 October 1485 in Westminster Abbey. At his first parliament one month later, Henry issued the *de facto* statute, which, ignoring factors such as birthright and claim by conquest, established Henry as sovereign, making no reference to Elizabeth of York or to his earlier promises. For Yorkists who had supported Henry, this caused some disquiet as it now looked as if their support had been used to place a Lancastrian claimant on the throne. Henry's delay could be explained by the fact that the realm needed a monarch crowned and consecrated to summon a parliament into existence; with no monarch, constitutionally parliament could not be summoned and, therefore, could not meet. Parliament had to meet to repeal Richard's *Titulus Regius*. The repeal of this act would not only condemn Richard III's claim to the throne, but would also provide the legal basis for legitimizing Elizabeth of York and her sisters. It was necessary to legitimize Elizabeth before any petitions could be made to the pope requesting that the appropriate banns be made available allowing Henry and Elizabeth to marry, since they were both related in the proscribed degrees of consanguinity. These legal processes took time. However, as time passed, it became quite obvious to people, particularly to the Woodville faction, that there would be no swift return to their previous position of pre-eminence in the land. Indeed, it was quite clear that Henry's closest domestic political advisor was to be his mother, Margaret Beaufort, now Countess of Derby.

In a sense this was inevitable since Henry and his closest male relative, Jasper Tudor, now Duke of Bedford,[1] had been in exile for the last fourteen years, so their knowledge of English affairs was, at best, second-hand. Nevertheless, Margaret had been an active participant in the governance and rule of England since the late 1450s. She also knew most of the key players on the English political scene and was related to many of them to a greater or lesser degree. Margaret's knowledge, judgement and commitment were three qualities upon which Henry would come to rely. Thus, Margaret Beaufort became her son's chief adviser. This in itself was sufficient to consign Elizabeth Woodville, Dowager Queen of England, to a secondary role – one that was not very influential. Without the crowning and acknowledgement of her daughter as queen, Elizabeth Woodville existed in a form of limbo, unable to regain the rank, privileges and power she felt were her due. This left her unable to offer the good lordship and rewards that many of her connection had revolted against Richard III to obtain. Coupled with this was the suspicion that had hung over her eldest son, Thomas Grey, Marquis of Dorset, since he had tried to defect from Henry Tudor in France early in 1485. For Elizabeth Woodville and her family, Tudor ingratitude and Henry's seeming indifference to honour the pledges he had made were causes for murmurs and disenchantment which, if not yet complaints writ large, were already showing some vestiges of disillusion.

As for Henry's concern about the extent of Ricardian plotting post-Bosworth, perhaps this is not surprising. The victory Henry had enjoyed at Bosworth had been unprecedented save for William the Conqueror's victory at Hastings 400 years earlier. The death of Richard in battle had been a huge bonus and an immensely lucky outcome for Henry for it had immediately deprived Richard's supporters of their leader and their cohesion. Their subsequent weakness had been reflected in the surprisingly small number of attainders after the battle. This did not mean that all men accepted the new order; although many saw it as a fait accompli, others were not so accepting. Even if they retained their positions, it was not so easy to forgo loyalties that had been built up over many years. Henry VII was not deaf to these subterranean whispers of sedition and ambivalent loyalties; having experienced adversity and exile in his youth, he was, more than most monarchs born to the role, attuned to undercurrents of treachery and conspiracy. As someone who had had to trust in his instincts and his own guile to survive as the 'guest' of a foreign power, Henry could sense something was afoot. However, what that 'something' was exactly, eluded him.

Escaping sanctuary

At some point during the winter of 1485/86, Francis Lovell slipped out of sanctuary and disappeared into the wider realm. We are unsure as to his whereabouts, as were his contemporaries, such is the nature of conspiracy. It is more than likely that he headed north to meet with other Ricardian malcontents such as Sir Thomas Broughton in north Lancashire on the shores of Morecombe Bay. This was a dangerous undertaking – traversing the length of the country without being recognized and detained by the forces of a king who must, by now, have realized that Francis Lovell would not be making his peace with the new regime. It also pointed to what must have been a renewal of confidence on the part of Lovell. No longer the last remaining significant supporter of Richard III, with no realistic options other than to surrender, Lovell was now the leader of a party that could offer something more than just truculent defiance. During his period in sanctuary it appears that Lovell had used his time well and had established contact with a network of Ricardian loyalists throughout the country, loyalists who were no longer prepared to accept the verdict of the battle of Bosworth. These were misplaced men whose fortune and future had been snatched away. Ill-prepared to meekly acquiesce to their fate, they looked for some manner of restoration and revenge. Their palpable sense of grievance mirrored Lovell's own and allowed him to use the connections he had made in Richard III's service to organize and plan a reaction against what has been called the Tudor interlude.[2] Plumpton's correspondent's reference to 'the running amongst the lords' was the incipient conspiracy that Lovell was hoping to orchestrate.

Christmas in the Tudor court

That year, Henry VII celebrated Christmas at Westminster, indulging in the regular round of festive activities. This was his first Christmas as king, and his first in England since 1470. Indeed, it was probably the first Christmas Henry had truly enjoyed since he was a child. Having celebrated the full twelve days of festivities, Henry now prepared for his wedding with Elizabeth of York. The ceremony would take place on 18 January 1486, after the arrival of the papal legate Giacomo Pasarella, Bishop of Imola, with the appropriate dispensation. The wedding appears to have been a relatively low-key ceremony and one for which no contemporary record survives. Emissaries were sent to Dublin to inform the king's subjects in Ireland that the king had been married and in recognition of this, on 2 February the Earl of Kildare organized a celebratory mass.

The marriage of York and Lancaster

The marriage of Henry VII and Elizabeth of York went a long way to achieving the union of the Houses of York and Lancaster, becoming for many the physical embodiment of the Tudor rose. It laid to rest the suspicion that Henry would renege on his vow made in Rennes Cathedral. For supporters of the Woodville family and followers of Edward V and the House of York, here was a return of the true bloodline to the throne after an illegal act of usurpation had been rectified. For most Yorkists, Henry VII was a means by which the rightful heirs of Edward IV were restored to the throne. True, it had required a compromise with a Lancastrian claimant, but it would have been unthinkable at that time for a woman to wear the crown. For large elements of the political nation the royal couple were strangers; people whom they neither knew, nor who commanded their loyalty other than in the abstract. It was therefore incumbent upon the royal couple to show themselves to the wider realm and to earn that loyalty and affection for the monarchy, which had become tarnished and diminished in the preceding three years.

For Francis Lovell and others the royal marriage represented none of this. It was not the return of the true royal bloodline of York, but the marriage of a foreign usurper to the bastard line of an illegitimate prince. Titulus Regius had clearly stated that Richard III was a legitimate sovereign and had demonstrated that Elizabeth of York, like her brothers and her sisters, was illegitimate by Edward IV's pre-contract with Eleanor Butler. The papal dispensation and the royal marriage changed very little as far as they were concerned. Equally, for many men, the realities of politics meant that if they were to regain their previous positions and resume their standing in society then the current regime had to be overthrown and replaced with one that recognized a Ricardian, not Yorkist, past. The task became more urgent once it was announced that the queen was pregnant, founding not only a new monarchy but a new dynasty. This increased the pressure on Lovell and those who were opposed to Henry Tudor. If they did not act soon, they could see their current parlous situation extending further and further into the future.

Henry Tudor in the north of England

After the conclusion of the Christmas festivities and his subsequent marriage, Henry VII began to look towards showing himself to the realm. In particular, he looked to head north to the most troubled and recalcitrant part of the kingdom. A letter sent from London in February stated that Henry intended to go 'northward hastily after the Parliament to do execution quickly there on those who have offended against him'.[3] It was, however, no coincidence that at this time Henry and his council began to hear rumours that Lovell had escaped from sanctuary and was plotting with other Ricardian malcontents. Initially, Henry refused to believe these rumours because he could see no logic in Lovell's continued opposition, particularly since Henry had now married the Yorkist princess. In the rather dry calculation of Henry's mind, there was no longer any logical reason for Lovell's continued opposition.

In fact, Lovell had already begun to plot for the day that Henry made his appearance in the north, and he and his co-conspirators were waiting until Henry had left the relatively safe precincts of London. Probably based in the north Lancashire fells, which would offer a haven for opponents of the Tudors for the next two years, Lovell began to conceive of a plan to take personal and political revenge on the king who had deprived him of his future and that of his friends.

Francis Lovell's conspiracy of the spring of 1486, known as 'Lovell's rebellion' is usually dismissed as a damp squib, but this was not how it appeared to contemporaries, especially not to Henry. As Henry set out for the north, his uncle Jasper, now Duke of Bedford, set out for his new satrapy of Wales to view the vast new estates his nephew had conferred on him. Prior to heading north, Henry travelled to East

Anglia from the beginning of March, and on 9 March was at Waltham Cross in Essex. From there he travelled to Cambridge and went on to celebrate Easter with Bishop John Russell at his episcopal palace at Lincoln. Bishop Russell had obviously put the past behind him and evidently stood high in Henry VII's favour, having a personal visit from the new king so early in the reign. For Henry's part, he bore no rancour for the man who had been Richard III's chancellor and who had preached the homily at Richard's coronation. On Maundy Thursday, Henry washed the feet of twenty-eight poor men (one for every year of his life), following which he heard mass in the cathedral on Good Friday. After Easter, the king moved on to Nottingham, which must have brought to mind Richard's mournful presence there scarcely one year earlier. As Henry wished to present himself to the north as a king, not a conqueror, he had with him a royal retinue that comprised of the royal household and the necessary officers of state whose purpose was to exhibit splendour and display, not military might. Henry was not accompanied by the other two pillars of the Tudor regime, John, Earl of Oxford, and Thomas Stanley, newly promoted Earl of Derby. Oxford, Henry's foremost military commander, was allowed to remain in Essex and East Anglia looking after his estates, which were back in his possession after fifteen years of being in the hands of others. Similarly, Henry's stepfather, Thomas Stanley, had been given permission to look towards his own affairs in Lancashire. This may well have been a tactical decision since Henry's intelligence system may have picked up on the comings and goings in the north Lancashire fells and the low whispers of sedition emanating from the vicinity of Hornby Castle, home of the Harrington family. When Henry left Nottingham behind and crossed the Trent into the north, he did so without any of the military capability that had placed him on the throne. At Barnsdale, he was met by the Earl of Northumberland and a company of Yorkshire knights, some of whom had fought for Richard III at Bosworth.[4] Other northern knights joined the king at this time, including Sir James Harrington, Geoffrey Frank and Sir William Eure, who was also retained by Richard III. Henry was also joined by the prominent Nevill retainer Sir Richard Conyers of South Cowton, a clear sign that some of the old Nevill connection were able to accept the new king. If Henry had looked more closely at Northumberland's company, heartening as it was, he might have pondered the whereabouts of Sir Edward Frank of Knighton. Sir Edward was a prominent Yorkshire knight who had been sheriff of Oxfordshire and a close associate and long-time adherent of Francis Lovell; Frank's absence and that of other northern gentlemen should have given Henry a cause for concern.

The king's 'great fear'

By the middle of April 1486, Henry VII had progressed through Doncaster and Pontefract on his way to York. It was here that Henry was struck by 'a great fear'[5] on one of only two occasions noted by Polydor Vergil (the other occasion being during Richard III's attack at Bosworth). Henry's fear was occasioned by the news that Francis Lovell had risen in revolt in Yorkshire, as had the Stafford brothers in Worcestershire and so later would the Vaughan family in Wales. In a cleverly thought-out plot, Lovell and the Stafford brothers had looked to the old centres of the Nevill connection of Richmondshire and the West Midlands to raise rebellion. Lovell had planned the revolt well. As the king came northwards, the Stafford brothers would raise the West Midlands, effectively cutting the king off from London and leaving him and his retinue exposed in the north. Lovell himself would simultaneously raise the standard of revolt in Wensleydale and Richmondshire where he hoped to mobilize residual Ricardian loyalty and at York to trap the king in a north that had returned to its true allegiance. During this time the Vaughans would attack Brecon Castle, thereby holding down Jasper Tudor and Henry's Welsh supporter Sir Rhys ap Thomas and again blocking the road between Wales and the Gloucester bridges over the Severn.

Faced with rebellion in what he suspected may be hostile territory and without any appreciable body of soldiers with him, it is no wonder that Henry VII experienced 'a great fear'. However Henry kept his head and from Doncaster he sent most of the armed men of his retinue under Sir Richard Edgecombe, the Controller of the Household, accompanied by a local knight, Sir William Tyler, northwards ahead of the main royal cavalcade.[6] Edgecombe was told to make a show of force, which is probably all he could offer just then, but more importantly and diplomatically, to offer pardons and promises to receive the rebels back into the king's grace. These royal blandishments were sufficient to make men question their involvement in the rising and stall the momentum of the rebellion. Memories of past risings and older loyalties were no longer enough to hold men together in the face of a king in full royal majesty who was getting closer and closer every day. As his support melted away, Francis Lovell, elusive as ever, disappeared, presumably returning to the Lancashire fells, that remote corner of the Pennines where Lancashire, Yorkshire and Westmorland meet. Henry VII moved on to a triumphal entry into York on 20 April when he was met at the gates by the mayor and aldermen and by the assembled citizenry who apparently cried out 'king Henry king Henry our lord preserve that sweet and well favoured face'.[7] Looking around him in this, his first visit to the northern capital, Henry VII had a great deal to be thankful for: he had travelled to the most troublesome part of the realm where loyalty to the previous king had been strongest and his memory most cherished. Not only had Henry faced down and resolved a rebellion, but he had been dutifully received in the largest city in the north and tumultuously greeted by the commonality. Henry could be well pleased with how events had played out; equally, he could take pleasure in the fact that the one prominent Ricardian die-hard, Francis Lovell, had raised a rebellion that had palpably failed. Surely now Lovell would surrender to the king's grace and accept the fate that had been waiting for him since August 1485? The collapse of Lovell's rebellion and the fact that the old names of Robin of Redesdale and Jack Amendall (names last heard in Warwick's revolt against Edward IV in 1469) were aliases that no longer carried the same resonance in 1486 as in previous times must have pleased a relieved Henry VII. Equally, Henry could take comfort in the fact that no prominent member of the nobility or the gentry had joined the rebellion and, in this respect, Henry's hold on the north seemed now to be unchallenged. It would appear that Polodore Vergil's description of Lovell as 'an irresolute fellow' was correct. Yet, in reality, nothing could be further from the truth.

An attempt on the king's life

On 23 April – St George's Day – Henry VII chose York as the place in which to celebrate the Garter Feast coupled with a crown-wearing ceremony. For this Henry was joined by an array of his nobility, including the earls of Oxford, Lincoln, Northumberland, Shrewsbury, Rivers and Wiltshire and the northern barons, Scrope of Bolton, Scrope of Masham and Lord Fitzhugh, together with the staunchly Lancastrian lord Clifford, now sitting down with the very men who had enjoyed his possessions and lands for the previous twenty-four years.[8] After the Garter Feast, Henry and his entourage entered York Minster where mass was heard to celebrate the patron saint's day of the Order of the Garter. Afterwards, the crown-wearing ceremony took place at the Archbishop's Hall alongside a chapter meeting of the Order of the Garter and a feast to celebrate St George's Day. At some point during the feast, Henry was assailed by at least one attacker who tried to stab him. The man was cut down on the spot by the Earl of Northumberland who, it was said, rounded up the accomplices of the would-be assassin and had them hung immediately.[9] The act is obscure and deliberately so, because then, as now, no government would wish to be seen to be weak and lax on issues of security. The attempt on Henry VII's life was, however, more than just embarrassing, it was deeply worrying, for here at one of the great showpiece events of the royal calendar, amongst the highest in the land, at a meeting of the Knights of the Garter and at an event of European significance, the king had been shown to be extremely vulnerable. It was exceptionally rare for a king to be physically threatened in medieval England; for an attempt on a king's life to take place during such a prominent and public event was unprecedented. For the perpetrators to be able to orchestrate such an attack – one that would be able to penetrate the inevitable security surrounding both the event and the person of the king, in particular – inevitably required planning and influence at the very highest level and also a knowledge of royal procedures and protocols. The person who possessed both the influence and the knowledge to organize such a plot was that 'irresolute fellow' Francis Lovell who, as Richard III's butler, would have been familiar with the staff of the royal kitchens and the household, men who had been in position under Richard III (and probably Edward IV) and retained their positions under Henry VII. These would be men whom Lovell would have appointed, controlled and paid and whom, if not still loyal to him, could be suborned into acting in his interest.

From the scant evidence we have it does not seem that the men who tried to strike the blow were themselves members of the royal household, but it must certainly have been with the connivance of some of its members that these men were able even to get close to the king. It is intriguing to speculate on Northumberland's peremptory action. Was his swift response evidence of unqualified loyalty to his king, or did he act quickly to silence those he was familiar with and whom he did not want questioned too closely? That the attempt on the king's life took place on such a public stage indicates a high level of personal animus and a clear attempt to publicly debase the king's regality and to demonstrate the reach of those who opposed him. Although a shaking Henry stated after the event that the rising was 'but a rag or remnant of Bosworth Field, and had nothing in it of the main party of the House of York',[10] he was being disingenuous and knew that he had nothing to fear from the senior branch of the House of York who looked upon an already pregnant Elizabeth of York as the restoration of the line of Edward IV. What Henry had to fear was the sharp enmity of those who saw Elizabeth of York as illegitimate and Henry as a usurper; for those who rejected the senior line of the House of York as one born in adultery, other candidates were now beginning to be tentatively offered. Lovell, having made two attempts to topple and then eliminate Henry VII, now once again receded into the shadows, this time to produce a plan that offered an alternative Yorkist successor rather than to slake his personal revenge.

As part of Lovell's plans other Ricardian loyalists also rose in rebellion against the new king. To tie down Jasper Tudor in Wales and prevent Welsh reinforcements coming to help Henry VII, Sir Thomas Vaughan of Tretower raised rebellion in Brecon and Hay and besieged Sir Rhys ap Thomas and his garrison of 140 men inside Brecon Castle for seven weeks during the crucial weeks of April and May, belying the notion that Wales was solidly behind the Tudors.[11] The actions of the Vaughans demonstrated that Henry VII faced a coordinated and widespread revolt that was more than just a revolt of a small number of northern malcontents.

The rebellion of the Staffords

What proved this beyond all doubt was the coordinated action to the east of Brecon, in the heart of Warwick the kingmaker's old area of influence. Here in Worcestershire, Sir Humphrey Stafford and his brother Thomas raised the city in revolt – initially, it was later stated, in King Henry's name.[12] Calling in support from friends and retainers, especially from Kidderminster and other towns in the West Midlands, the Staffords assembled a force of several hundred men and soon occupied the episcopal city of Worcester with its strategically important bridges over the Severn. The rebellion soon spread to Warwick and Birmingham where they proclaimed that Henry VII had been captured or killed by Francis Lovell in the north, thereby revealing Lovell's centrality to the conspiracy. Whilst the king's death was quickly disproved by royal agents, more worryingly for Henry, the crowds that surged through Birmingham, Warwick and Worcester raised the old cry 'a Warwick, a Warwick' demonstrating their support, not only for the grandson of the kingmaker, but also for an impeccably legitimate male Yorkist prince. The young Edward, Earl of Warwick, the son of George, Duke of Clarence, had resided at Sheriff Hutton castle in Yorkshire since the accession of Richard III, where his title and estates had been used to boost the prestige of the Council of the North.[13] Immediately after Bosworth, Henry VII sent Robert Willoughby to take possession of Warwick and his sister Margaret, who were now 'guests' in the household of Henry's mother Margaret Beaufort. These were the first cries for a living Yorkist claimant to the throne that Henry Tudor now occupied.

In all the accounts of Lovell's revolt no mention is made during the northern rising or, for that matter, by the Vaughans in Wales, of the Yorkist alternative to Henry VII. Lovell's rebellion is a rebellion against Henry VII based on loyalty to Richard III: it was in some ways a revolt into the past, a wish to restore a Ricardian regime without Richard himself. As such, it had collapsed because it did not offer a credible alternative; neither was a Yorkist claimant available as a focus for Lovell's revolt. Of the two most credible Yorkist princes, John, Earl of Lincoln, was a member of Henry VII's retinue and no doubt closely watched, whilst Edward, Earl of Warwick, was safely under lock and key and soon to be in comfortable isolation within the Tower of London. Ricardian loyalists saw Edward IV's daughters as illegitimate and barred from the throne by Titulus Regius; as a result, the men of Richmondshire and Yorkshire were not offered a genuine Yorkist alternative to support. That alternative was now emerging from the mouths of the men of Warwick and Birmingham, whose traditional loyalties to the Earl of Warwick now formed the genesis of the Lambert Simnel conspiracy.

Help for the rebels

The failure of Lovell's rising in the north and the clear evidence that Henry VII still lived brought about the collapse of the Worcestershire rising and the abandonment of the Stafford brothers by the crowds who had previously voiced their support. The Staffords initially fled to woodlands near the old Yorkist Town of Bewdley. Then, with the help of their neighbours, to the village of Culham in Berkshire.[14] Initially, Culham seems a strange choice – an obscure village two miles from Abingdon – however, the manor and the church of St Paul was a grange of Abingdon Abbey and under the authority of its abbot, John Sante. The Staffords were no doubt offered sanctuary by Sante, who had held the favour of Lovell and seems to have been a committed (financially, at least) Ricardian prepared to defend the brothers and his abbey's privileges. When two days later Sir John Savage arrived with sixty men to remove the brothers from sanctuary, Sante protested, arguing that the abbey had rights of sanctuary from time immemorial. Sir John demurred in the face of this legal argument. The issue of sanctuary went to the court of the King's Bench where the Staffords' case and the privileges of sanctuary were pleaded by Sante using charter evidence supposedly going back to the eighth century, during which, Sante claimed, sanctuary rights had been bestowed on the church of St Paul. The judges ruled that sanctuary could not be pleaded in cases of high treason and Sir Humphrey Stafford was hung, drawn and quartered with the full weight of the law, whilst his brother was pardoned on the grounds that he was acting under the influence of the elder Stafford. A further proclamation was then issued excluding five people from any hope of pardon: Geoffrey Frank, Edward Frank, John Ward, Thomas Oter and Richard Middleton – all were Lovell's adherents.[15] The proclamation is interesting in that it reveals that Lovell still exercised some influence in Oxfordshire, as presumably did Edward Frank, sheriff of that county under Richard III. The proclamation also reveals the government's suspicion that the revolts of the spring of 1486 were related and coordinated. Lovell is not named here because it was legally unnecessary as he had already been attainted by act of parliament. Whilst the Staffords and others involved in the rebellion in Worcestershire had been captured, the same could not be said of its principal organizer. Despite extensive searches and what must have been the offer of a huge reward, Lovell had not been found.

After the failure of the assassination attempt on Henry VII in York, Lovell again disappeared from view. Francis Bacon has him lurking with Sir Thomas Broughton in north Lancashire, as does Polydore Vergil, but this is speculation. Far more likely is that, with Henry's agents searching for him, Lovell decided to try to escape to the continent and beg help from Margaret, Dowager Duchess of Burgundy. This is far more probable since on 19 May Lovell was reported as being on the Isle of Ely, amongst the fens of eastern England. In a letter to John Paston, recently appointed Sheriff of Norfolk and Suffolk, the Countess of Oxford wrote that Paston should:

> ... endevore that suche wetche [watch] or other means be used and hadde in the ports and creks [creeks] ... and to use all the waies ye can ...to the taking of the same lord Lovell.[16]

The nature of the letter makes it clear that the countess thought that the presence of Lovell on the Isle of Ely indicated that the authorities believed he was travelling eastwards and looking for some means of travelling to the continent. It is likely that Lovell's party was too well known to use Hull or the ports of the Humber, and instead had chosen to head south-east to the many creeks, estuaries and rivers of the Suffolk and Essex coasts, where the ports and anchorages would have been less well watched and spied upon than their larger neighbours, and where a captain and his crew were more likely to ask no questions if the rewards were great enough. This was also the territory where the estates and the influence of the Duke and Duchess of Suffolk were at their greatest. For the second time in his life, Francis Lovell was to seek the support and protection of the de la Pole family.

16 A LAD NAMED JOHN

A lost cause?

DURING THE SUMMER OF 1486, well hidden amongst the de la Pole properties in East Anglia, Francis Lovell would have been forced to confront failure once more and to contemplate his next move. No doubt he would have mused long and hard on the fact that loyalty alone was not enough to motivate men to join with him in overthrowing Henry VII and it appeared that a desire for vengeance was an insufficient incentive to divert men from political realities. Men like Sir Ralph Bigod of Settrington, previously a staunch Ricardian, now had a position in Margaret Beaufort's household and had recently been appointed Constable of Sheriff Hutton castle. Men such as Sir Ralph now had too much to lose and no wish to look backwards. For rebellion to succeed, Lovell and what remained of his co-conspirators had to look forward and persuade men that they, not Henry, could offer a better tomorrow.

A true figurehead for Ricardians

It is no coincidence that after Lovell's disappearance sometime after 19 May and midsummer, rumours started to circulate that Clarence's son, Edward, Earl of Warwick, now eleven, had escaped the close supervision in which he had been held and was now at large. Edward of Warwick had been born at Warwick Castle on 25 February 1475, but had only known any real security for the first two years of his life, the death of his mother and the attainder and death of his father in January 1478 having placed his young life in the hands of others. He had been the ward of the Marquis of Dorset, who also had control of his marriage during the reign of Edward IV. However, that arrangement had ended on the accession of Richard III and the publication of Titulus Regius, after which Edward of Warwick's position became both more prominent and more precarious. The disappearance of his two cousins – Edward V and his brother, Richard, Duke of York – made him one of the most prominent male members of the House of York and one with a better claim to the throne than Richard III himself, descended as he was from Richard's elder brother, George, Duke of Clarence. Whilst Titulus Regius presumed to debar Edward from the throne on the grounds of his father's attainder, it had not stopped him acquiring and holding one of his father's titles as Earl of Warwick. This recognition muddied the waters regarding any claim to the throne whilst at the same time recognizing his proximity in blood. Legally, if his father's treason did not debar him when old enough from sitting in the House of Lords, it is difficult to see how it could exclude him from the throne. Kept in the north during Richard's reign, he had been brought south by Henry VII who had been only too aware of the danger posed by this boy during the recent troubles. The recent public acclamation and pronouncements in towns in the West Midlands were unlikely to encourage Henry to loosen the reins upon Warwick anytime soon.

For Lovell and the other Ricardian malcontents, Edward of Warwick represented the ideal figurehead around which all 'true men' could unite: he was an impeccable Yorkist prince of unquestioned lineage and one who did not raise all of the complications and ambiguities that a member of Edward IV's family might. Authentically Yorkist, Warwick was also young enough to be moulded and led, at least for the foreseeable future. Support for Warwick would also effectively raise the banner of opposition to Henry VII whilst at the same time side-stepping the issue of the two lost Yorkist princes – the Princes in the Tower. The major hurdles to be overcome in securing Warwick the throne were that Lovell was a hunted fugitive and Warwick a closely guarded guest in Margaret Beaufort's household. Unable to get his hands on the real Warwick, Lovell and his supporters – and he must still have had many – determined to create their own Earl of Warwick to be played by a 'feign boy' called, if not actually named, Lambert Simnel.

Who was Lambert Simnel?

At the centre of the Lambert Simnel mystery is a boy who the earliest sources refer to simply as 'John'. According to *The Herald's Memoir* ' … there was taken the lad that his rebels called king Edward (whose name was indeed John).'[1] The 'lad' would not be officially recognised as Lambert Simnel until the act of attainder in October 1487, even though this is the name by which the whole conspiracy is known. The name 'John' fits much better into the world of medieval England than does the more exotic Lambert, or indeed Simnel. Michael Bennet[2] is more than likely correct in stating that the name Lambert Simnel was an invention: 'the name makes most sense as a pseudonym under which the boy travelled and by which he was introduced.'[3] The later government accounts regarding the boy are contradictory, implying initially that he was the son of an organ maker from Oxford or that his father was a carpenter, or, indeed, that he was illegitimate. In some senses this reveals the difficulty in trying to glean information on the genesis of any conspiracy which, by its very nature, is necessarily elusive. For Henry VII's government, the facts were to remain tantalisingly out of reach for most of 1486 and the early part of 1487. In truth, the antecedents of the boy called Lambert Simnel are unimportant; it is quite possible that his father could have been an organ maker or indeed a carpenter, since both were trades required in the construction of organs for churches and colleges. The low birth of the lad John or Lambert Simnel would have been a positive advantage since, if the rebellion succeeded and the real Earl of Warwick liberated, he would have been more easily disposable.

An audacious plan

Much of the information that we have about the Lambert Simnel conspiracy comes from information Henry's government released after the interrogation of one of its main participants, a young priest called Simonds, in February 1487. This testimony states quite clearly that both the conspiracy and Lambert Simnel himself originated in Oxford. Oxford was England's oldest university town and, whilst it had a reputation for intellectual attainment, it was not necessarily for this reason that it attracted the majority of its students. In the fifteenth century, the colleges of Oxford contained over 1,000 students who studied theology, grammar and philosophy in addition to foreign languages, deportment and some estate management. The colleges of Oxford offered routes to advancement in the church and noble and royal governance; the bishops and royal officials were mostly Oxford men who in turn offered the benefit of patronage to their old colleges and their students. These men ensured that it was Oxford men who dominated at the higher levels of church and state. As now, in the fifteenth century, education was viewed as a path to advancement and in this sense there was a climate of striving and ambition that permeated the town as a variety of independent scholars sought students to coach to attain places at the prestigious colleges. Indeed, Oxford was a university town with learning at its core, but it was also an extremely competitive place where scholars jostled with one another to use education as one of the principal means of rising in the world.

One such scholar was Richard – or William – Simonds, a twenty-eight-year-old priest and possibly one of a pair of brothers (the evidence is confusing). According to Polydore Vergil, Simonds was disinclined to take the slow and steady path to ecclesiastical advancement for which his education would have prepared him. Vergil states that Simonds concocted the idea that he would obtain a young lad who he could then mould into one of the young princes of the House of York. At first, under interrogation, Simonds said that he had planned to pass the boy off as one of the Princes in the Tower, either Edward V or his younger brother, but decided instead to train the lad as Edward of Warwick who, when he ascended the throne, would then reward Simonds by making him a royal chaplain or even awarding him a bishopric. With this in mind, Simonds had searched Oxford for a boy of a suitable age with the innate abilities, wit and looks to undertake the role. If the boy were illegitimate – a boy of no family, as the government later asserted – so much the better. The details of the plot came to light after Simonds was captured in February 1487 or after the battle of Stoke; governmental evidence is contradictory in this respect, giving two names to the priest and two occasions on which he was captured and interrogated. Some clarity can be obtained from the evidence of a meeting of the convocation of the archdiocese of Canterbury in February 1487, which mentions that 'a priest name Simonds was brought forth to identify the Earl of Warwick, at that time in Dublin, as the son of an Oxford tradesman named Simnel.'[4]

This is information that the government of Henry VII wished to make public and, whilst it contains certain elements of what later can be discerned as fact, it also raises some very real questions regarding the veracity of the tale. First, it is beyond credibility that a lowly priest could hope on his own to instil in his protege all the attributes of an aristocratic personality and to fool the higher echelons of the aristocracy. It is inconceivable that a simple priest would have known anything of the true *gentilesse*, the essence of nobility, deportment, speech, grace and ease of carriage that a true prince would possess. Nor would such a priest have had access to information about family, cousins, etiquette, personal relationships – the whole back story necessary to successfully impersonate a young prince. This would have been necessary before the boy began acquiring knowledge of the classics, of Latin, French, hunting, hunting texts and history – all of which would have been the basic education of any noble boy, let alone a prince. These components were considered to be the building blocks of a noble personality, allowing him to be able to exhibit 'quiet assurance in his part to proclaim his identity, not by laboured words, but by his very demeanour.'[5] All of this required an input by someone with knowledge of the nuances of royalty and the intricacies of courtly life and who would have shared a close and personal relationship with the Earl of Warwick. These requirements would far outstrip the knowledge and experience of a simple priest, no matter how well educated.

Secondly, it is even more intriguing that, according to the statement, Simonds had initially thought to pass the boy off as one of the Princes in the Tower, then changed his mind and chose, instead, to pass the boy off as the Duke of Clarence's son. This is surprising because one might have thought that it would have been far easier to concoct an identity for a prince nobody had seen since August 1483, rather than one whose existence, if not identity, was well known and whose presence at the Tower of London was widely known. Also, the successful impersonation of one of the Princes in the Tower would have created a far greater problem for Henry VII and Elizabeth of York than Edward, Earl of Warwick, was proving. An acknowledged resurrection of either Edward V or his brother Richard, Duke of York would have trumped the claim of Henry VII and his queen. It is curious that Simonds discarded what could be seen as the easier option and opted instead to mould the boy, Lambert Simnel, as a direct competitor to a prince who already existed, requiring, as it did, a much greater attention to detail and a far more rigorous back story than that for a prince no one had seen for the best part of three years. The answer to this conundrum is, of course, that the choice was not actually his to make.

The most important and unchallenged fact that emerged from Simonds' confession is that the deception took place at Oxford and this is of the greatest significance. Oxford stood at the confluence of a number of intersecting Yorkist influences and was a city and a county that held no discernible Tudor loyalties. Oxford was not far from Minster Lovell, in a county that Lovell had dominated in the preceding three to five years – a county in which his family had wielded influence for centuries. Up until the Reformation, Magdalene College was the site of the Lovell family chapel where priests prayed for the souls and repose of the family. The appointment of these priests and the upkeep of the chapel were funded by the Lovells. Equally prominent and still influential in the Thames Valley were the Duke and Duchess of Suffolk. They were ostensibly loyal and at peace with the new regime, but they could hardly forget their Yorkist blood and their previous higher standing under both Edward IV and Richard III. Whilst their eldest son, John, Earl of Lincoln, had been in constant attendance at the royal court since the aftermath of Bosworth, another son, Edward de la Pole, was a cleric and a Don at Oxford. Also, Oxford was only eight miles from Abingdon, where Abbot John Sante, who had already come into conflict with Henry VII over the Stafford brothers, had ruled over the abbey and was himself an Oxford theologian. Also resident in Oxford was Bishop John Stillington of Bath and Wells, a man who had been a high-ranking civil servant of Edward IV and a long-time adherent of the Duke of Clarence. Despite having participated in the crowning of Henry VII, as Archbishop Bourchier was too infirm, Stillington was out of favour with the new regime as the man who had proclaimed the illegitimacy of Edward IV's children and had questioned the canonical legality of Edward and Elizabeth's marriage. As a composer of Titulus Regius, he was under some suspicion and had retired to his old college at Oxford. These were all men who had reason to provide the knowledge, the money and the protection that Simonds required to work on his protege.

It was these men who determined who that protege should impersonate and which direction the conspiracy should take. The decision to impersonate Edward of Warwick indicates that those who backed Simonds and Lambert Simnel were Ricardian loyalists rather than Yorkists and who saw Edward of Warwick as a legitimate heir to Richard III. It was not a revival of the Yorkist party that these men sought, but a return to the dynasty and chosen succession of Richard III. Those members of the Yorkist establishment who had been supporters of Lord Hastings and Elizabeth Woodville, and who had risen in rebellion alongside Buckingham, now stood behind Henry Tudor and Elizabeth of York. The Tudor monarchy of Henry VII represented these men who had previously held faith with the House of York. For those who found it impossible to offer their loyalty to the new regime, the only legitimate prince was Edward of Warwick, whose accession offered them a return to the power and positions they had enjoyed under Richard III. The subject of Lambert Simnel's impersonation would be Warwick because its principal architect, Francis Lovell, had decided that it would be so. Who better than the previous king's chamberlain to provide Simonds with information and the details required to successfully impersonate a prince? Who better to know and understand the workings of the court than the man who had previously regulated it? Who better to provide the details of the personal interactions and interplay of the wider Yorkist royal family than someone who had lived amongst them for most of his life?

Was Elizabeth Woodville behind the Lambert Simnel conspiracy?

It would appear that between the sighting of Lovell on 19 May 1486 in the East Anglian fenlands and his departure for Burgundy in January 1487, Lovell's whereabouts are a mystery. There is no evidence that he spent any of this time abroad as his presence is not recorded at any European court. This would suggest that he remained in hiding in England, protected by those closet Ricardians who were still at liberty. Later events would suggest it was during this time that Lovell formulated and directed at one step removed the beginnings of the Lambert Simnel conspiracy, and used his influence to draw into that conspiracy the disparate strands of Ricardian loyalists. It has been suggested that others could have been behind the creation of Lambert Simnel: Elizabeth Woodville or her son, the Marquis of Dorset, who had been Warwick's guardian, or, indeed, John, Earl of Lincoln.

Elizabeth Woodville is extremely unlikely to have conspired to have replaced her daughter as queen with the tenuous benefits likely to have arisen from placing Clarence's son on the throne. Even if she had been jealous of the influence that Margaret Beaufort exerted over her son-in-law, it is inconceivable that she would have wished to have displaced both her daughter and the potential grandson her daughter was carrying. Likewise, her son Dorset seems to have been a relatively insubstantial figure and one whose actions to date ensured that he commanded the political loyalties of none. John, Earl of Lincoln, was by all contemporary accounts an attractive figure and one whose subsequent actions demonstrated that he possessed no love for either Henry Tudor or the Tudor regime. It is a myth much repeated to say that Richard III recognized Lincoln as his successor: he did not. By 1486 Lincoln was a young man of much promise who, although respected, had yet to hold high office or to exercise genuine authority. Likewise, since his release after Bosworth he had been in almost constant attendance upon Henry VII at court and seems to have been held in gilded chains. None of the above would seem to possess either the motivation or the opportunity that Lovell and his coterie at Oxford did. The lack of any references to Lovell suggests that the Tudor authorities had no inkling as to his whereabouts. The requirements of the plot to recreate Edward of Warwick and the subsequent complexities of the Lambert Simnel conspiracy suggest that Lovell was in full and constant contact with his co-conspirators and, therefore, likely to have been in the vicinity of Oxford. The training and equipping of Lambert Simnel as Edward of Warwick seems to have been initially the undertaking of Lovell with the priest Simonds conducting the day-to-day transformation under the auspices, and possibly the protection, of John Sante, who was certainly involved in the plot by Christmas 1486, and probably under the supervision of Edward de la Pole or Robert Stillington.

Rumours of conspiracy

The first manifestations of the conspiracy occurred in the summer of 1486 when rumours began to circulate that Edward of Warwick was at large, having escaped the Tower of London, and was now resident in the Channel Islands, specifically in Guernsey. These rumours were deliberately designed to confuse and muddy the waters and to raise the question of whether the real Edward of Warwick was now at liberty. This campaign was the first stage in providing the disparate groups of Yorkist die-hards in Cornwall, the north, the Channel Islands, Ireland and northern Lancashire a sense of coherence and providing a Ricardian candidate for the throne around who they could rally. These rumours were designed to undermine the government's statements that the real Edward of Warwick remained in London, for what the plotters intended the question was enough.

By autumn the rumour had gained such potency that the old Yorkist captain of Mount Orgueil castle in Jersey, Richard Harlston, previously a prominent Ricardian, who came under suspicion by association, found it wise to sue for a pardon.[6] Harlston had been Edward IV's governor of Guernsey and had been resident in the Channel Islands for over twenty years, having married a local woman, but now found himself replaced. Hence, Harslton had little love for the Tudors or their new supporters. The rumour that placed Edward of Warwick in the Channel Islands was not arrived at by chance, but had been deliberately and cleverly chosen. The islands were close to France, yet were still English territory. From here, one could use the Channel to sail to Burgundy and its many ports, west to Ireland, or towards St George's Channel and the western coast of England. They were also sufficiently remote from mainland Britain so that the normal rigours of royal government did not necessarily apply there, leaving them as areas suitable for speculation. The suggestion that 'Edward Earl of Warwick' was at liberty in the Channel Islands gave the initiative to the plotters who were able to use the freedom of the sea lanes to confuse the government.

The rumours had some success and spread rapidly throughout England. On 29 November 1486, Thomas Betanson wrote from London to Sir Robert Plumpton that 'here is but little speech of the Earl of Warwick now, but after Christmas they say, there will be more speech of him'.[7] Betanson's comments indicate that in London at least, men were fully aware that Edward of Warwick was likely to be much more prominent in the New Year and this would suggest that the conspiracy was beginning to gain momentum and that further trouble was brewing.

The Irish connection

In what must have seemed ominous and puzzling for Henry VII, rumours also began to circulate placing Warwick in Ireland where he had been greeted and given an enthusiastic reception by the king's governor, Garret Fitzgerald, Earl of Kildare. The earls of Kildare had been staunch supporters of the House of York since the 1450s, supporting the lieutenancy of Richard, Duke of York, and subsequently of the Earl of Warwick's father in the 1470s. This support was not entirely altruistic; it was based on Edward IV's support for the Fitzgeralds in their conflict with their Lancastrian rivals, the Butler earls of Ormonde. The victory of Henry Tudor at Bosworth had brought about a return of the Ormondes to court favour and to power in Ireland, challenging the supremacy of Kildare. The rumoured presence of Warwick in Ireland was another strand of the process of disinformation and placed him in another part of the realm's more vulnerable extremities. Whilst it is highly likely that the conspirators had made overtures for Irish support and emissaries had been in touch with various Anglo-Irish nobles, it is actually unlikely that Lambert Simnel was present in Ireland at this time. The rumours are more likely to reflect the approaches made to capitalize on Ireland's perceived affection for the House of York. From Garret Fitzgerald's point of view these approaches had to be weighed carefully, whilst his power had been curtailed by the return of the Butler family, they had done little to dislodge his ascendancy over the native aristocracy. Still, the revival of the Butler 'supremacy' in the centre of Ireland challenged Fitzgerald's dominance over the Pale and the Irish parliament in Dublin. Of great concern for the English government was that Ireland offered a secure and welcoming bridgehead from which to invade England and easier access to the less well defended coasts of the north and west. Furthermore, Ireland offered an additional and welcome source of manpower if the conspirators could mobilize the kerns and gallowglasses of the native nobility.

Lovell in the north of England

A more compelling reason why Warwick or Simnel was unlikely to have been in Ireland at this point can be gleaned from the later evidence of the priest Simonds himself. When questioned, no doubt after an intense interrogation, by the council in February 1487, Simonds stated that he had been in the north with 'Lord Lovell in Lancashire' sometime during November and December.[8] This would indicate two things, firstly that not only was Francis Lovell in the country, he was able to move relatively freely around, since the two acknowledged sightings of him in the Fens in May and northern Lancashire in December are about as far apart as is possible in England, over 250 miles. It seems that Lovell was not only able to disguise himself and clearly avoid recognition, but also must have had a substantial network of agents and access to safe houses, which enabled him to move around the country undetected. This implies that Lovell must have inspired intense and genuine loyalty in those that knew him and served him. A cursory look at his career after Bosworth in which he travelled from Leicestershire to Colchester, from Colchester to Lancashire into Yorkshire and from Yorkshire to the Fen country and thence back to Lancashire, reveals an incredible perambulation that must have made him beholden to many people. Yet at no time was he betrayed; in fact, over a fifteen-month period, he seems to have criss-crossed the country with impunity. He was never betrayed, which compares particularly well with the fate of the Duke of Buckingham in 1483. Both men were the most wanted men in the country and very high rewards were offered for their capture. The reward for Buckingham's capture was £1,000, or a manor with an annual income of £120 – a reward that would transform an ordinary man into a member of the gentry at one stroke. It is likely that similar rewards were offered for the capture of Lovell, but frustratingly, documents do not survive specifying these. What we do know is that rewards for Lovell's capture were regularly issued up until 1495. This also belies the idea that Lovell was a man of little resolution; on the contrary, he appears to have been a man of great application, for even under the strain of being hunted across the country Lovell persisted in planning the demise of Henry VII and the vindication of Richard III. This was done from within the heart of England rather than from a safe haven abroad.

Simond's confession that he had accompanied Lovell to Lancashire, probably bringing Simnel along with them, has the ring of truth and logic about it. The north of Lancashire and in particular Lancashire beyond the Sands which abutted Cumbria, were dominated by a number of disaffected families such as Sir Thomas Broughton and his brother John and their neighbours the Huddlestones of Millom who were die-hard Ricardians. These were backed up by the Harrington family of Hornby Castle just east of Lancaster who, whilst supporters of Richard III, were more motivated by a long-standing hostility to the Stanleys in a prolonged feud of a family property. With the Harringtons came the Middletons and others who had formed part of Richard III's connection as Duke of Gloucester and Lord Palatine of Cumberland and Westmorland. This connection with its strong roots in the preceding Nevill dominance of the West March had been effectively both leaderless and rudderless since Bosworth. This was especially true with the encroachment of Stanley power into northern Lancashire which was now unchallengeable since Thomas Stanley was not only Earl of Derby but the king's stepfather. In addition, the baronies of Westmorland and Craven were now once again dominated by the Clifford Family, strong Lancastrians led by the shepherd-lord Clifford, who from his castles of Brough and Appleby now dominated eastern Westmorland and whose castle of Skipton again controlled the Pennine passes from Lancashire into Yorkshire.

For these men, Lovell's visit would have been a welcome reminder that their current position was not irrevocable and must have given them some sort of hope for the future. The timing of Lovell's visit would also have been crucial for these men: the birth of a son, Arthur, on19 September 1486 to Henry VII and Elizabeth of York meant the founding of a dynasty and for these men the prospect of any form of restitution receding further and further over the horizon. The birth of a Tudor prince made any plot to alter the current situation more imperative. Yet these men were already hardened to the consequences of fifteenth-century politics and probably had no wish to repeat the fiasco of Lovell's abortive rising of the previous spring; they would have demanded greater guarantees for toying with treason this time. This is probably why, in the depths of winter when travelling was at its most awkward and unpleasant, Lovell took the long trek north. Here, in one of the remotest parts of the kingdom, Lovell and Simonds met with the Ricardian recalcitrants of Lancashire and presumably presented the new 'Earl of Warwick' to them, offering them a Yorkist prince to rouse old loyalties anew. It may well be that on this journey or at these meetings the boy was announced as Lambert Simnel, possibly with a knowing wink. What was important was that Lovell obtained the commitment and support of these men, an agreement that they would be prepared to exert themselves in the task to come. Lovell probably at this point assured these men that the plan in hand not only had a creditable figurehead, as they could presumably see or at least be informed of by Simonds, but he could promise the backing of some extremely influential supporters both in England and abroad. In this, Lovell would have alluded to the very thing that Henry VII feared most: hidden, highly placed traitors in England acting in conjunction with foreign powers. Whether Lovell mentioned the Earl of Lincoln at this time is a matter of fruitless speculation since at this point Richard III's closest male relative, along with his family, appeared to be reconciled with the Tudor regime. It is almost certain, though, that Lovell would have revealed to these men that he had the support of Richard III's redoubtable sister Margaret, Duchess of Burgundy.

Lovell on the road

Francis Lovell spent Christmas 1486, presumably on the road between Lancashire and the east coast. We know this because early in January 1487 John Paston, Sheriff of Norfolk and Suffolk, wrote to his patron, John, Earl of Oxford, that Lovell had slipped away across the sea with some of his followers. Oxford replied chillingly that he was already aware of this, and that this was, in fact, old news and that Lovell had departed 'with XIIII [14] persons and no more'.[9] This reveals that Oxford had precise information about Lovell's point of departure since he is quite specific as to the size of his following. That Lovell could move around with fourteen people and evade capture speaks volumes for the efficiency of Lovell's security procedures and his ability to plan ahead and to retain the loyalty of his men. At the beginning of January 1487, Lovell set sail from East Anglia to cross the perilously stormy North Sea to the Netherlands to bring into the conspiracy – if she were not already – the most powerful of Richard III's relatives and the aunt of Edward of Warwick. The timing of Lovell's point of departure seems to have been well planned because John Sante, Abbott of Abingdon Abbey, sent funds overseas with a courier on 1 January 1487. This has usually been attributed to forward planning by the Earl of Lincoln but Lincoln did not leave England, and then quite suddenly, until the middle of February 1487. It is much more likely that John Sante, a staunch Ricardian, who would not be finally unmasked until 1491, was already acting in conjunction with Lovell during the autumn of 1486. The sending of money abroad, particularly to

Burgundy coincides far more with Lovell's plans rather than Lincoln's. Early in January, Lovell set foot in Burgundy and made his way to Margaret's court at her dower property of Malines. Here he was assured a warm welcome, not only as her late brother's closest friend, but as a man who could bring up-to-date news from England and could reassure Margaret that, like her, there were still Englishmen opposed to Henry Tudor.

17 THE DIABOLICAL DUCHESS

Richard III's loyal sister

MARGARET, DUCHESS OF BURGUNDY, was born in 1446, the youngest daughter of Richard, Duke of York, and Cecily Nevill. Younger than her brother Edward, she had grown up particularly close to her brothers, George, Duke of Clarence, and Richard, Duke of Gloucester, with, it is said, Clarence being her favourite. In 1467, as part of Edward IV's foreign policy, Margaret was married to Charles the Bold, Duke of Burgundy, ruler of a band of duchies and counties that straddled the frontier between France and the Holy Roman Empire. Although the dukes of Burgundy were French princes of the House of Valois, the economic interests of the lands and territories, particularly the cloth industry of Flanders, meant that economically they enjoyed a close relationship with England. The sheer extent and wealth of the 'Grand Dukes of the West' (as the dukes of Burgundy were known) allowed them to adopt an independent political line, making them in practice subservient neither to the kings of France nor to the Holy Roman Emperor, both of whom were their feudal superiors. Charles the Bold's father, Philip the Good, had emerged from the Hundred Years War, having conveniently changed sides, with his lands and wealth considerably enhanced. His son Charles had continued his policy of expanding his realm into Lorraine, Switzerland and Guelderland. What Charles most hoped to gain was a crown and acknowledgement that he was an equal with his rivals in the west, the kings of England and France. To this end, he relentlessly pressured his German overlord, Emperor Frederick III, to bestow on him the royal dignity.

By 1467, Charles sought to enter an alliance with Edward IV to revive the threat to France and to put pressure on his cousin and erstwhile overlord the French king Louis XI. To this end, Charles proposed marriage to Margaret as means of cementing his alliance with England. The French spread spurious rumours regarding Margaret's morality that owed more to her brother Edward's activities than her own, but which received an extra fillip when the bed broke during the wedding night and the bed-chamber caught fire. The marriage was deemed by both parties to be a success with Charles feeling respect and affection for his duchess even though they had no children and Charles' sole heir was his daughter Mary from a previous marriage. From 1475 onwards, Charles was almost constantly on campaign, either on the Rhine or in present-day Switzerland, and during this Margaret had been an efficient and effective regent, managing the estates and legislative assemblies of the Burgundian lords in her husband's absence. This was no mean feat since the demands of the ducal government and Charles' armies were rapacious and constant. Unfortunately, despite his impressive library of classical military treatises, the impressive military resources of the Burgundian state were badly led by Charles. In 1476 he led his armies into the Black Forest region of Germany to extend his dominance in that area and to punish the Swiss cantons who had allied with his enemies, but his armies were roundly defeated at the battles of Morat and Grandson and Burgundian military power was shattered.

Disaster for Burgundy

Taking advantage of the situation, the young Duke of Lorraine, Rene II returned to the duchy from which Charles had expelled him in 1475 and reclaimed his capital, Nancy. Charles, who now faced being cut off in southern Germany, away from the most important part of his dominions (the Netherlands), led what was left of his armies north to confront Rene and his allies. It was a disastrous mistake; outnumbered and without allies the Grand Duke of the West led his small army against the Lorrainers, fighting outside the capital of Nancy, and was totally defeated. In the aftermath of the battle of Nancy, men searched for two days for Charles' corpse, which could only be identified by his valet by a birthmark on his body as his face, having been split in half by a Swiss halberd, had been gnawed on by hungry wolves as it lay stripped of its wealth on the snow-covered battlefield.

The dowager duchesss

In Brussels, Margaret as regent, comforted her young stepdaughter, as both faced a very uncertain future. Charles' cousin and bitter rival, the French king Louis XI immediately invaded the duchy of Burgundy itself and the county of Artois to the north near Flanders.[1] The French invasion left the Burgundian government reeling and desperately searching for allies and soldiers as Charles' many enemies now took advantage of his death and the disarray in which he had left his daughter's inheritance. Margaret proved her worth by holding Mary's inheritance together and doing her best to resist the French onslaught. Margaret had to cope also with some high-level Burgundian defections such as Duke Charles' illegitimate half-brother, Anton the Grand Bastard, and the former minister and chronicler Philip de Comynes. Despite this and a lack of troops, Margaret and the new Duchess of Burgundy, Mary, were able to stem the French advance in the north, though they had to acquiesce to the loss of the Duchy of Burgundy in the south.

Margaret and the Burgundian government desperately looked for a potential husband for Mary who could offer some form of protection from French aggression. Margaret's suggestion of her recently widowed brother, George, Duke of Clarence, does not seem to have been seriously entertained by Edward IV or by the Burgundian estates. Instead, they looked to the son of the Holy Roman Emperor, Maximillian. It was felt that, whilst Frederick's personal possessions only amounted to the Alpine duchies that today comprise the modern country of Austria, as overlord of the Holy Roman Empire and, in particular, the Netherlands, he would be best placed to mobilize the resources of the empire to defend its western frontier. Maximillian had a reputation of being something of a gallant knight errant who could not resist the idea of riding to the rescue of a noble lady in distress; nor, it must be said, of marrying the greatest and richest heiress of her day. In 1477, the eighteen-year-old Maximillian was married to the nineteen-year-old Mary in an effort to bring stability to a land ravished by war and civil unrest, for not only had the French invaded, but the communes of powerful towns such as Ghent and Ypres, now free of Charles' yoke, sought to extend their urban privileges at the expense of ducal power. Margaret stood staunchly behind the young couple in the face of all these threats and was not just a trusted confidante of Mary, but enjoyed a very good relationship with Maximillian. In 1478 Mary and Maximillian gave birth to an heir, Philip, known to history as Philip the Handsome, and it was hoped that the French could be held at bay so that the boy had an inheritance worthy of the name. Margaret tried in vain to bring her brother Edward IV into a formal alliance with Burgundy between 1478 and 1482, but it was said that Edward IV preferred to retain his pension from Louis XI and so remained on the sidelines.

Margaret as regent

In 1482 Mary died in a riding accident leaving Maximillian regent for their young son Philip, but with a strong place in the government for Duchess Margaret. That year, Maximillian, on behalf of his son, had to sign the Treaty of Arras and formally acknowledge the loss of Picardy, the county of Artois and the duchy of Burgundy – such was the price of peace. Maximillian also had to contend with the continued civil unrest of the cloth towns that were rejecting his authority and insisting, in their own interests, on offering their obedience to the infant Duke Philip. To this end, when Richard III became king, both Maximillian and Margaret looked to him and hoped that England would become more bellicose on Burgundy's behalf. Richard III was perceived as being far more warlike and aggressive towards France than his brother Edward IV and he gave Maximillian and Margaret the licence to recruit 6,000 archers in England in 1484 and again early in 1485. This rapprochement with Burgundy was one of the reasons that the French government was prepared to back Henry Tudor and adopt a forward policy of destabilizing England. This French support for Henry Tudor was duly noted with concern in Burgundian circles.

Margaret loyal to the House of York

However, Margaret, at her dower property of Malines, had been stunned by Richard's defeat and death at the battle of Bosworth. 'Once more the House of York had been left wretched and deserted by good fortune',[2] wrote the Burgundian chronicler Molinet. It would appear that Margaret viewed her brother's defeat by Henry VII initially as one more blow that Fate had dealt the House of York. In this respect, her view would have fitted in with the profound contemplative piety associated with both Margaret and her mother, Cecily Nevill. In this sense it would have been one more event in a litany of misfortune that had afflicted the House of York since 1460, when her father and brother Edmund had died outside Sandal Castle in Yorkshire at the battle of Wakefield. Edward IV's success had only heaped more fratricidal misery on the House of York, with Clarence's trial and murder, then her nephews' deposition by her brother. By 1486 the only male representatives of the House of York were Edward of Warwick, the son of her favourite brother, and her sister's sons, the de la Poles. Few would criticize the childless Margaret for taking a close and attentive interest in her nephews, particularly the motherless Edward of Warwick to whom she felt a dynastic obligation. This familial obligation is best demonstrated by her enthusiastic support of Perkin Warbeck,[3] a later pretender of the 1490s: Margaret felt compelled to write to a variety of European rulers extolling both her pleasure and her faith in providence and God, which she maintained had restored her young nephew, 'Richard, Duke of York', to her. From Margaret's perspective it would appear that having her nephew, Edward of Warwick – a true son of York – on the throne was preferable to her niece, Elizabeth of York, married as she was to a Tudor and presiding over a court where the king's greatest confidante was his mother, the Lancastrian Margaret Beaufort.

Much has been made of Margaret of Burgundy's loss of valuable trading licences, which had allowed her to trade with England, particularly in wool, without paying the relevant taxes and customs dues. These terms had been granted by Edward IV and renewed by Richard III. Henry VII had not renewed these licences and this was clearly a bone of contention with Margaret who, as late as 1494, would insist on their reinstatement as part of her protocols of agreement with Perkin Warbeck. These trading privileges were, however, small beer in comparison with the extensive dower income Margaret enjoyed in the Netherlands and were unlikely to be the determining reason for Margaret's support for a Ricardian plot centred on the Earl of Warwick. It was much more a case of family honour and of striking a blow at fate itself, to restore both her nephew and her family to what she regarded as their proper place. No doubt familiar with the metaphor of the wheel of fortune so popular at that time, she would recall her brother Edward's situation in 1470/71, when he had been ejected from England ignominiously, but had triumphantly returned victorious from exile in the Netherlands to regain his throne. For Margaret, a burning dynastic pride and an affection for her brothers formed the driving force behind her welcome for Lovell. For her stepson-in-law Maximillian, the motives for supporting Lovell and his plans were different, but no less compelling.

The motives of Archduke Maximillian

Forced by the Treaty of Arras in 1482 to cede territory to France over which he was the governor on behalf of his son Philip, Maximillian had been thought of as irrelevant in the diplomacy of north-western Europe ever since. Perpetually short of money and men, he was an archduke of compromised circumstances. Since 1482 Maximillian had been confronted by a series of rebellions by the Burgundian estates and had spent his time trying to restore both order and his own authority in the Netherlands. The situation had been exacerbated by the fact that he was only the regent for his young son Philip. Also Maximillian's father, the Emperor Frederick III who, as Phillip's overlord and grandfather, should have come to his aid, had his own problems with his capital Vienna being occupied by the Hungarians. Maximillian had doggedly overcome these problems – sometimes brutally – and had brought the Netherlands, with Margaret's help, to heel. At the diet of Frankfurt in 1486, Maximillian's personal prestige had soared when he had been made King of the Romans and was designated as his father's co-ruler and accepted successor. Maximillian was now not just open to advances from English rebels, but actively considering how to reverse what he saw as a great victory for French foreign policy. For Maximillian, Henry Tudor's success at Bosworth was not a purely domestic event; rather it was all part of a much wider picture, which encompassed the interrelationships of the states of north-western Europe from Brittany to Frisia. To Maximillian's mind, Henry Tudor, sponsored by the government of France, represented a victory for French diplomacy under which France's traditional enemy (and the traditional ally of Burgundy and Flanders) had been neutralized. This had allowed France to focus on her war with Burgundy and to continually push back its vulnerable north-eastern frontier as far from Paris as possible. An indication of the continuation of this policy had been the French invasion of the county of Hainault in 1486. Now in relatively complete charge of his son's patrimony and backed by the prestige of the Holy Roman Empire, Maximillian welcomed these English dissidents as a means of reversing the French triumph of 1485 and placing his own proteges in charge of English policy.

The scheming sisters of York

There is some evidence that Margaret of Burgundy had been aware of plots in England from the middle of 1486. On 1 July, at her chief residence of Malines, locals celebrated the Feast of St Romboult, the town's patron saint, a celebration in which Margaret always participated or allowed her governor to oversee on her behalf. In that year's records for the *Ommegang*, the parade of the saint's image and celebration, a gift of eight flagons of wine were given to '*the Sone van Claretie uit inglant*' ('the son of Clarence of England').[4] Whilst there is no record of Edward of Warwick ever visiting the Netherlands, the records perhaps collude with the notion that Warwick was free, and possibly in the Channel Islands. The gift would seem to be a wish to curry favour with Margaret by offering wine either for a close relative or for someone who was already being mentioned for a future campaign. This makes it clear that the son of Clarence was already known in the Netherlands by July 1486. Also, between early 1486 and 1487, the town of Malines gave Margaret a grant of 750 livres for 'her reyse to England'.[5] In this case, a 'reyse' may mean a journey or a venture: it is in the latter case that the grant would fit in with Margaret's plans. It is intriguing that both of these events occur in 1486 when Maximillian was absent with his father, firstly in Austria and then at the Diet of Frankfurt. Maximillian left the affairs of the Netherlands in the hands of a ducal council, which consisted of four great magnates who had shown conspicuous loyalty both to the Burgundian state and to Margaret herself. It seems that during this period when Maximillian was concentrating on the affairs of the empire, Margaret was formulating her own plans and gathering together the resources to implement them.

Despite the evidence from the Netherlands that demonstrated Margaret's support for and complicity in the conspiracy, it is hard to believe that she was the originator of the enterprise, as some have suggested. However, as a senior member of the House of York and one who enjoyed both freedom of movement and control of large resources, Margaret's participation in the plot was clearly desirable. Equally, her prestige and standing would bring much needed credibility to the 'earl of Warwick' once the plotters landed in England. Margaret's recognition of 'Warwick' would carry the authenticity of a close family member and that of a ruler of a friendly foreign state, and so Margaret's acquiescence was crucial. It would, however, appear that Margaret's participation in the plot went much further than this: indeed, she gathered together money and resources to support the venture in the autumn of 1486. This would infer that Margaret was part of the plot before Lovell arrived in the Netherlands early in January 1487. It is possible that Margaret was kept in touch with events in England by persons such as Sir Edward Brampton,[6] a converted Portuguese Jew who had had Edward IV as his godparent when he had been christened in 1475, and who, as a merchant and a diplomat, had served with Edward IV and Richard III. Ever since Bosworth, Brampton had been resident in the Netherlands looking to aid the restoration of his Yorkist masters. It is equally possible that Margaret learned of the conspiracy from her sister. Elizabeth, Duchess of Suffolk, is one of the great forgotten figures of the early Tudor period of whom little is known, and while her husband, John de la Pole, has been categorized as a nonentity, we should perhaps resist applying the same epithet to his wife who was, after all, a Plantagenet. Elizabeth, Duchess of Suffolk, enjoyed high standing at court, but had also had Francis Lovell as her ward from 1471 to 1478, and is as likely to have acted as a conduit for the conspirators such as Brampton.

The arrival of Francis Lovell

At some point in early January 1487 Francis Lovell arrived in the Netherlands, probably at one of the ports of Flanders. Lovell's presence at Margaret's court at Malines was crucial: as Richard III's closest friend, he brought with him a genuine link with Margaret's last surviving brother; he would also have brought an up-to-date picture of the political situation in England, along with some understanding of the politics of the realm, including news of the quality and true extent of the conspiracy's supporters in England – those 'good men and true' who were likely to support a Ricardian restoration. Unlike others, Lovell had moved and operated at the highest level of politics and government and, therefore, was able to give an accurate picture of what was happening on a national level and of the plotters' progress and their readiness to take action. Lovell's presence now allowed him to coordinate both wings of the conspiracy and to assure Margaret and other supporters that 'Warwick' (Lambert Simnel) was prepared and probably actually on his way to Ireland where he would be harboured by Kildare and his associates until the time was ready. Also, in place after Lovell's time in Lancashire, was the support of those dissidents in England who were ready to greet Lambert Simnel's invasion and were then prepared to show their true colours. No doubt Francis Lovell and those who had travelled with him were curious as to how Margaret's preparations were progressing.

Martin Schwartz

In this they were not to be disappointed for Margaret's preparations had also come to fruition. Either late in 1486 or early in 1487 (and it makes more sense for the latter), Margaret entered into a contract with Martin Schwartz, one of Archduke Maximillian's most trusted military captains. Martin Schwartz was, by 1487, a man in his forties and an experienced military entrepreneur. He had been born in Augsburg where, tradition has it, his father had been a shoemaker. Since his youth he had been part of the Burgundian forces, under Charles the Bold, who had deployed him in the Siege of Neuss (1475). He had steadily progressed, rising in Burgundian and Imperial service ever since. Heavily involved in suppressing the Burgundian rebellion between 1477 and 1486, Schwartz and his men had achieved a reputation for ferocity and violence, while Schwartz himself had an unenviable reputation for arrogance. In 1485, Schwartz and his company had to be persuaded from sacking the city of Ghent and had to be bought off by Maximillian. They were, however, excellent soldiers and the most modern and professional infantrymen in Europe, called the famous *landsknechts* (literally 'lowland soldier'), to distinguish them from the highland or Swiss soldiers and alluding to their Swabian origins. These *landsknechts* were trained to fight in formation with a long 18ft pike and supporting arms such as the halberd and other pole weapons. Most famously, some of the *landsknechts* were armed with a great two-handed sword, up to 6ft long, which was used to break up enemy formations. Whilst noted for the colourful extravagance of their clothing (not uniforms) and their insolent pride, they were also some of the best infantry in Europe and always in great demand. Schwartz and his men would bring a steely discipline and a militarily advanced formation into the service of Lovell and his associates. With the pacification of the Netherlands after the surrender to ducal authority of Ghent and Bruges, Schwartz and his company were awaiting redeployment and their inactivity was an expensive luxury in the war-torn Netherlands, now temporarily at peace. Maximillian gave his assent for Schwartz and his company to enter Margaret's service, no doubt to the relief of the citizens of the Netherlands. The contracts were probably signed in early 1487 for a company of roughly 2,000 men, along with baggage and the inevitable camp followers, to be engaged for an invasion of England.

There can be little doubt that Francis Lovell and his companions would have been filled with confidence when reviewing these men, for here were 2,000 of the most redoubtable infantry in Europe. These formidable soldiers would form the core of the forces that would rise up and sweep Henry Tudor from his throne. Dowager Duchess Margaret had also contracted the relevant shipping and supplies to ferry these men to their intended destination. The Germans were to be augmented by Englishmen who had deserted the Calais garrison, led by Thomas David – men who had been ejected from Calais for their Yorkist sympathies and who had now entered service with Margaret and the conspirators.[7] At the same time, John Colet, a Calais merchant, and others came forward to offer support with money, shipping and supplies. These recruits would have boosted both Lovell's and Margaret's confidence in their enterprise, particularly since Lovell would have been aware just how many more men were committed to joining the rebellion once they landed in England.

Spying on Burgundy

News of the plot was impossible to conceal as Henry VII's agents were active on the continent seeking out information on possible conspiracies. There had been a number of attempts by Henry's men to try to infiltrate Margaret's household, but all had failed to date. On 2 February 1487, at a meeting of the Privy Council in the palace of Sheen, Henry announced to his councillors that a plot had been discovered involving secret conspirators and some of the highest in the land, yet the king named no names nor did he surrender any further information. This implies that either Henry's evidence was vague or that he was attempting to flush out those who sympathized with the conspiracy by indicating that he knew more than he actually did. It is probable that the preparations in Burgundy had not gone unnoticed and Lovell's mere presence in the Netherlands would have been sufficient evidence of a threat for Henry VII, whose senses had been heightened by the various plots and vicissitudes he had experienced during his lifetime. Henry's suspicions would have gone into overdrive if he had obtained any information on the engagement of Martin Schwartz and his men. A further cause for concern would have been the news that the 'earl of Warwick' had travelled to Ireland either in late 1486 or early 1487. Henry's information could also have been obtained from Simonds, the priest who had been arrested in Oxford and interrogated in February 1487. From Simonds' evidence, it seems that he was with Lovell in Lancashire in the late autumn of 1486, but he mentions neither Burgundy nor Ireland. These omissions may indicate that Lovell's departure for Burgundy, and Simnel's for Ireland, occurred after Simonds was dispensed with. According to Simonds' confession, Simonds' role was to train Simnel into a facsimile of Edward of Warwick; after that had been accomplished, Simonds had either been paid off or discarded, his earlier episcopal ambitions unfulfilled.

It is more likely that it was a combination of all these sources that gave Henry VII the first inklings that he faced a serious conspiracy that constituted a real threat to his throne. By 8 February 1487, Henry's security apparatus had moved into gear, issuing warrants for the arrest of 'Henry Bodrugan, knight and John Beaumont and others who [had] withdrawn themselves into private places in these counties and stir up sedition and rebellion'.[8] Sir Richard Edgcombe, Sheriff of Devon, scoured the county for the two men, but was unable to find any trace of them. Clearly, it was not only Henry VII's agents who were moving into action; so too were the conspirators. Ideally placed in the West Country, Bodrugan and Beaumont had already sailed for Ireland, either to be in attendance upon Lambert Simnel or to prepare for the arrival of Francis Lovell and Martin Schwartz and their forces.

The Privy Council at Sheen Palace

Sitting calmly throughout the Privy Council meeting at Sheen was John de la Pole, Earl of Lincoln. Lincoln had gone from being the nephew of King Richard and possibly his heir to being merely a first cousin to the queen with whom he shared Plantagenet blood. After the battle of Bosworth, when it was proclaimed that Lincoln was dead, the Earl had rehabilitated himself in Henry VII's eyes. He had not joined the rebels in 1486 but, at the king's behest, sat in judgment on them. Throughout 1486 he had been present at court and, indeed, had been present at the christening of Prince Arthur in September 1486. Although he had been deprived of the great offices of state that he had enjoyed under Richard III and was no longer the king's Lieutenant in the North, nor the Lord Lieutenant of Ireland, for someone who had been regarded as a possible future king, he seemed to have reconciled himself to the realities of the new regime. At least, that is how it appeared to Henry. But in Lincoln's case, appearances were deceptive. The Crowland Chronicle states specifically that Edward IV's sister Elizabeth, Duchess of Suffolk, Lincoln's mother, longed for the overthrow of Henry VII.[9] This latent hostility towards Henry VII must have festered at their residences at Wingfield and Ewelme and may even have split the family, especially since Henry VII had ordered that nothing was to be done to diminish the dignity of John de la Pole, Lincoln's father.

The Earl of Lincoln's role in the Lambert Simnel conspiracy

It is worth here reconsidering the traditional view that John, Earl of Lincoln, was behind the Lambert Simnel conspiracy or that he immediately became its leader on joining it. There is no evidence to link Lincoln with the initial stages of the conspiracy, or to suggest that he had a role in it during the autumn of 1486. Rather, his association with the conspiracy occurs after it is fully formed, just prior to the conspirators putting their plans into action. Whilst the Earl of Lincoln was highly thought of by contemporaries, he was still relatively young and his elevation to high office under Richard III was still very recent. Lincoln did not become a justice of the peace until January 1485 and so was rather inexperienced – indeed, he had merely held, rather than exercised, high office. It would appear from the timings involved that Lincoln was reminded of his true allegiance by both his mother and Francis Lovell. Lovell's role was central to the conspiracy, for not only had Lovell and Lincoln been colleagues in the government of Richard III, they had also grown up together when Lovell had been the ward of Lincoln's family, the de la Poles. Inevitably, Lincoln would have looked up to Lovell, who was some eight to ten years older than him. We cannot be sure whether the conspirators made any overtures towards Lincoln prior to February 1487, but it is unlikely that Lincoln would have been completely ignorant of either the plot or the conspirators' intentions. Henry VII's announcement regarding a conspiracy involving the highest in the land may well have been a veiled reference to Lincoln. Equally, it is likely that Lincoln felt the pressure grow in early 1487, for, as the conspiracy became more and more a reality, it inevitably increased Henry's suspicions. Stuck between the two, by February 1487, Lincoln would have had to choose which side he was on.

What would have ratcheted up the pressure on Lincoln and others were Henry VII's actions during February 1487 when Robert Stillington, Bishop of Bath and Wells, was summoned from the University of Oxford to answer charges regarding 'damnable conjurations and conspiracies'.[10] The university protected Stillington, protesting that such a summons broke the privileges of the university. Stillington had a long history of association with the House of York and the Duke of Clarence. After Bosworth, he had been placed in confinement at York, but was then pardoned on account of 'his great age, long infirmity and feebleness'.[11] Whilst this may have been true, it had not stopped the prelate from being 'sore crazed' by these indignities. The university protested on his behalf throughout the month of March before surrendering him into the arms of royal authority for interrogation at Windsor. In answer to the 'damnable conjurations and conspiracies', particularly the pernicious rumour that the real Earl of Warwick was at liberty in Ireland (demonstrating that perhaps Lambert Simnel was already there), Henry VII ordered the Earl of Derby to take the real Earl of Warwick from the Tower of London and parade him through the streets of London, bringing him to St Paul's. Here the boy was presented to a large assembly that included the Chancellor, Archbishop Morton and the convocation of Canterbury, alongside the mayor and the corporation of London. All attested to the fact that he was truly the Earl of Warwick and the son of George, Duke of Clarence. After a night at Lambeth Palace, the real Earl of Warwick spent some time at Sheen Palace where he was regularly visited by his cousin, John, Earl of Lincoln, who, no doubt, was a sympathetic voice. After this, Warwick was taken back to his apartments at the Tower, which he was never again to leave until his execution in 1499. Lincoln was present at the next meeting of the Privy Council, which again met at Sheen. At the conclusion of the meeting, he informed other members that he was going to Suffolk to visit his father's estates. However, once in Suffolk, he immediately took a ship to Flanders to join his aunt and Francis Lovell. Ultimately, the call of blood and upbringing had proven too strong and 'the damnable conjurations and conspiracies' that Henry VII so feared were now about to become a reality.

18 THE ARCHDUKE AND
THE SHOEMAKER OF AUGSBURG

Fortune favours Francis Lovell

THE ESCAPE OF JOHN, Earl of Lincoln, in March 1487 was a coup for the conspirators because notionally it brought together all the legitimate elements of the House of York into one place. In the Netherlands, under the protection of Margaret, Dowager Duchess of Burgundy, the remaining descendants of her father could now make common cause with one another against the children of Edward IV and Elizabeth Woodville, who had been bastardized by Titulus Regius and debarred from the throne. In the eyes of the conspirators, this prohibition extended to the current queen, Elizabeth of York, her sisters, Henry VII and Arthur, Prince of Wales. Henry's claim to the throne was doubly invalid. Firstly, because of the codicil to Henry IV's first parliament of 1400, which specifically barred the Beauforts from the throne, thereby negating the claim of Henry's mother Margaret Beaufort. Secondly, any claim Henry may have had in the right of his wife as the daughter and heir of Edward IV. In the spring of 1487 every scion of the House of York, with the exception of those descended from the Woodvilles, stood in opposition to the Tudor monarchy, which, from their point of view, was an illegitimate aberration hoisted on the country after the death of Richard III at Bosworth.

Francis Lovell and his cohorts, which by now would surely have far exceeded the fourteen men that he had originally brought from England, must have been pleased with developments. As he waited at one of the many ports of Flanders and Holland, Lovell could contemplate the fact that all he had planned was beginning to come to fruition: having completed his education as a 'Yorkist prince', Lambert Simnel had been safely spirited to Ireland and was now in place to play his part in the events that would unfold. In northern Lancashire and in other parts of England, 'true men' were ready and prepared to support a Yorkist invasion. Now present in the Netherlands was a true prince of the House of York: John, Earl of Lincoln, a man of untainted lineage. Coupled with this was the recognition and blessing of their enterprise by one of the most powerful women in Europe, Margaret of Burgundy, who had also underwritten the venture by hiring one of the foremost military contractors of the day in Martin Schwartz and his 2,000 *landsknechts*. By

April, Lovell and his compatriots were only waiting for the winter storms to subside in the Channel before launching their attempt to restore a legitimate Yorkist king onto the throne of England.

The addition of the Earl of Lincoln to the ranks of the conspiracy was not only symbolic, it offered further evidence of the widespread nature of latent support that existed in England for a Yorkist restoration. On 31 March,[1] the account of one James Tait was issued by Henry VII to the Earl of Northumberland and the Bishop of Exeter as evidence of Lincoln's treason. In this it would appear that Lincoln had either been especially busy in the three weeks since he had left the country on 9 March, or that he had been deeply embedded in the plot a lot earlier. Henry's report stated that on 25 March a chance meeting had taken place between one James Tait at Doncaster where the said Tait had recognized servants of John, Earl of Lincoln, disguised as merchants. Tait stated that he had won the men's confidence by recognizing a white hobby (a small riding horse) that had belonged to the Earl of Lincoln and asking after him. The earl's servants, speaking with a confident indiscretion, informed Tait that they had come from London with saddle-bags full of gold and silver,[2] and were seeking out Lincoln's friends in Yorkshire. They were to visit Hull, the original home of the de la Poles, York where they were to meet the Prior of Tynemouth, Nicholas Boston, at the 'Sign of the Boar', and they also hoped to later meet with Sir Thomas Mauleverer of Allerton and others. The servants promised that 'John Earl of Lincoln shall give them all a "breakfast" that oweth him no love or favour',[3] meaning that he would take revenge on Tudor supporters. They also informed Tait that they were, however, instructed to make no approaches to the Earl of Northumberland, stating 'he doth little for us, therefore we set little by him'. This perhaps is a reflection of Northumberland's behaviour at Bosworth and subsequent events.

Tait's report, made before the mayor and council of York and recorded in the York civic record, demonstrates that Lincoln was mobilizing support in addition to that he had already committed to the plot. Lincoln's agents were clearly looking to gain support in those areas where the de la Pole family had some influence and also amongst those men with whom Lincoln himself retained some standing as Richard III's Lord Lieutenant of the North. In this respect we see a different strand of support from that which Lovell had garnered in 1486, which was largely concentrated in Lancashire and Cumbria and among those who had long-standing connections to the affinity of Richard III, such as the Harringtons and the Broughtons. Lincoln was trying to raise support from Yorkshire and areas further north. The inclusion of Nicholas Boston from Tynemouth and Sir Thomas Mauleverer from Allerton increased the support for the conspiracy into the north east and Durham.[4] Tait's evidence of the openness with which the earl's servants were prepared to discuss their plans points to an extreme confidence or a rashness that borders on idiocy for those contemplating treason. It is probably a measure of their faith in the success of the venture and its implications for the future standing of their master that these men were able to speak so openly to someone they obviously regarded as a friendly face and were probably reflecting the confidence felt by the conspirators gathered in the Netherlands.

Henry moves against the conspiracy

This was a confidence Henry VII did not share and, recognizing that a plot was beginning to coalesce around him, Henry moved his base of operations to Kenilworth Castle in Warwickshire. Here he was accompanied by his uncle Jasper Tudor and his stepfather-in-law, the Earl of Derby. Any troops that were available were quartered at nearby Coventry. By now Henry probably had all the information he needed to discern the bones of the conspiracy and would certainly have had no doubt that Margaret of Burgundy and Francis Lovell were prominently involved. The information gleaned from the interrogation of Simonds had been useful, but for Henry and his ministers there was a great deal that Simonds either did not or could not reveal. It is probable that he was recruited by intermediaries and third parties and that the information he received was only that which was necessary for him to fulfil his role in the conspiracy. Indeed, even if he had disclosed that he had accompanied Lovell to the north where 'the boy named John' had been introduced to the die-hard Yorkists, this can hardly have been revelatory as Lovell's participation in the plot must have been obvious to Henry by this time. It is also more than likely that after the boy had passed muster amongst these northern participants that Simonds' services had been dispensed with and that his part in the plot was already over by November or December 1486 when Lambert Simnel was either in Ireland or at least preparing to travel there. What was quite clear from Henry's perspective was that Simonds had little or nothing to impart on the later aspects of the plot that were now uppermost in Henry's mind. Henry needed to know the true intentions of John, Earl of Lincoln, and, more importantly, the identity of his fellow conspirators in England who had yet to declare themselves. These were the questions that stopped Henry VII sleeping at night despite all of the security Kenilworth Castle could offer.

For Lovell, on the other hand, the future could not have been clearer: he was to return to his homeland not as a haunted fugitive or as a man bound by honour to beg support for a cause that only he felt. There would be not be a repeat of the fiascos of 1486 and no more ad hoc plots based solely on revenge. Now he would return to England at the head of a strong professional army under the leadership of the true prince of the House of York and at their head, even if only as a figurehead, an alternative to the Tudor interlude. This time he was guaranteed both a welcome and support and there would be no more skulking from house to house and hiding out on the lonely northern fells. This time when Lovell and his adherents landed they would take no pains to disguise their presence. Lovell would have also taken comfort that Henry VII had misread their intentions and was focusing his attentions on the east coast during April, and particularly in East Anglia where the de la Pole estates were concentrated.

The threat of invasion

By 4 May 1487 Henry VII had become aware that the east coast was not the rebels' destination. He wrote to the city of York that he had 'certain knowledge in sundry wise that our rebels be departed out of Flanders,'[5] but this was all Henry knew because the expected landing on the east coast had not materialized, leaving Henry now uncertain as to the whereabouts of the rebel fleet. Ironically, this information was already out of date for the conspirators had landed at Dublin on 5 May, where they were welcomed by the Earl of Kildare.[6] Kildare and his family had probably been harbouring Lambert Simnel (and, presumably, his handlers) since the previous winter and had been actively awaiting the arrival of Lincoln, Lovell and Schwartz. Lovell's fleet had set out from the mouth of the Scheldt and the Rhine sometime near St George's Day (23 April) and had to tack against the prevailing Channel winds to make the crossing to Ireland. For the sailors on board, this would have been an unremarkable voyage as many sailors from the Netherlands frequently sailed to Ireland to trade for its fish, hides and cattle; for them, a voyage up St George's Channel carried little risk. For Schwartz's mercenaries, though, landfall at Dublin must have seemed as if they had arrived at the very edge of the world, in a place of strange customs, speech and dress and somewhere completely different from the cities and towns of the Netherlands and the Rhineland with which they were familiar.

The conspirators in Dublin

There to meet with the party when they arrived was Richard Harlston, one-time Governor of Jersey and possibly the man responsible for the rumour that the Earl of Warwick had escaped to the Channel Islands. Alongside him were Sir Henry Bodrugan and John Beaumont. More significant was the presence of Garrett mor Fitzgerald, 8th Earl of Kildare: he was the reason Ireland had been chosen as a safe landfall and base and he was an integral part of the plotters' plans. Kildare, who had been voted chief governor of the Irish Council after the death of Clarence in 1478, had been supreme on the island ever since. For the conspirators, Ireland offered not only a safe haven and a chance to recoup their strength after a long sea journey, but was also a means by which that strength could be augmented by the recruiting of additional troops. These Irish soldiers came in a variety of guises; the levies from the Pale would have resembled English billmen and infantry, as would the archers. However, the gallowglasses, professional Scottish mercenaries from the western Isles, would have been strangers both to England and to English methods of fighting. There would also have been swarms of lightly armed kerns, retainers of the native clan chiefs who, armed with darts, long daggers and small personal shields, were deployed to nimbly attack the flanks of more heavily armoured formations. Irrespective of their equipment and proficiency, all of these troops would be welcome additions to the forthcoming campaign. Equally, Ireland was close to the west coast of England

and, therefore, an ideal place from which to invade England. It was, however, what the conspirators were preparing to do ahead of the invasion that was truly audacious.

An Irish coronation

On Thursday 24 May 1487, on the Feast of the Ascension, there was a gathering at the Cathedral of the Holy Trinity in Dublin. This august group of Francis Lovell, the Earl of Lincoln, the Earl of Kildare, the Archbishop of Armagh and Dr Gervais Spinelli del Palaci, the Italian Primate of all Ireland was accompanied by Walter Fitzsimmons, Archbishop of Dublin, and the bishops of Meath, Cloyne and Kildare. All were assembled for an unprecedented event, for the first time a 'king of England' was to be crowned and acclaimed outside of the kingdom with the full participation of holy mother church. The ceremony was appropriately carried out with Lambert Simnel duly transformed into 'Edward VI' by the anointing with the chrism of the cathedral priory. He was then crowned with a crown borrowed from the statue of the Virgin and enthroned on the bishop's cathedra,[7] with the Bishop of Meath, John Payne, preaching the homily recounting Edward VI's claim to the throne. This was a truly audacious act, which, even in the turbulent years since 1460, had never before been attempted. Here, truly, was the legacy of Warwick the kingmaker, fulfilled by one who had grown up in his household. It was true that the coronation did not take place in Westminster Abbey; that it was not conducted by the Archbishop of Canterbury; and 'Edward VI' had not been enthroned on St Edward's chair or crowned with the Crown Jewels. Nevertheless, the appropriate ceremony and due solemnity of a coronation had been observed. It is breathtaking that the conspirators proceeded with the liturgy knowing full well that they were not crowning the true king. However, the coronation in Dublin did legitimize Lambert Simnel as a figurehead and in essence legitimized the rebellion for those who took part in it. If the conspiracy succeeded, then the events in Dublin could be passed over as the forerunner for a much grander ceremony, which would take place in Westminster Abbey. If, on the other hand, the conspiracy failed, all these considerations would be irrelevant.

As Richard III's Chamberlain, Francis Lovell would have been crucial in providing the planning of this ceremony. It is likely that this was the very moment that Lambert Simnel had been trained and groomed for, and it is probable that Lovell provided the expertise and impetus to ensure that 'Edward VI' received as authentic a coronation as possible. We can perhaps see the difference in age and experience between Lovell and Lincoln during the service when the Archbishop of Armagh, doubtless aware of the implications (both political and divine) of crowning an imposter, refused to officiate at the ceremony. In the face of the Italian churchman's refusal to participate, the Earl of Lincoln became enraged and had to physically be restrained from launching an attack on the prelate, demonstrating a petulant pride and possibly a haughty and prickly disposition. His behaviour on such a solemn occasion would have cast doubts on his capacity to offer cool-headed leadership.

Despite the reluctance of the Archbishop of Armagh, the Archbishop of Dublin was persuaded to conduct the coronation according to the precepts of the church. After the ceremony, in order that as many spectators as possible could see the new 'king', the boy was hoisted onto the shoulders of 'Great Darcy of Platen a, man of very tall stature',[8] and carried from the cathedral to Dublin Castle where a coronation banquet was held. The image of a boy too small to be seen on his own, but carried aloft and supported by others, provides a perfect metaphor for the reality of his situation.

The coronation of Simnel as 'Edward VI' was not in itself an empty gesture, those who had crowned him now did their best to ensure that he acted as a true monarch. Nothing expressed royalty so much as the ability to mint and strike coinage, which is exactly what the Simnel regime proceeded to do. Pennies and groats were issued in his name bearing a shield with the arms of England and France quartered by a long cross on the obverse and three crowns set vertically on the reverse.[9] These three-crown groats carry the legend *Eduardas Rex, Anglie Francie* and on the obverse *at Rex Hybernie*. The act points to a remarkably high level of planning and a sure knowledge of the accoutrements necessary not just for Simnel to play the role of king but to convince the populace that he *was* king. Here Francis Lovell and John, Earl of Lincoln, used every propaganda device to legitimize their candidate's position as a monarch regnant. In comparison with their thorough preparations prior to launching their invasion, those of Henry VII and his much criticized decision to date the first day of his reign to the day before the battle of Bosworth seems positively amateurish. The use of Ireland as a base now paid dividends as 'Edward VI' could now be seen as an anointed king, appropriately consecrated by the Church and transformed by holy chrism – a true monarch-in-waiting.

Although it was important to bolster the image of royalty, it was also imperative that the momentum of the conspiracy be maintained and that the government of Henry VII be kept guessing as to the rebels' final destination. Practical considerations also played a part in determining the conspirators' next course of action. A force of 2,500 men was bound to create a burden on local food supplies and it is doubtful that any civic authority would relish the presence of so many young, restless and armed men for a long period of time. Still, it took a few days for arrangements to be made and also for the Irish recruits who wished to join the enterprise to come in. To legally sanction the recruitment of support for the newly crowned king, a parliament was called, which passed acts of attainder against the opponents of the new king. Perhaps unsurprisingly, most of those attainted carried the surname Butler, including a cerain gentleman, Thomas Butler, who had fled to England to pass on to Henry VII an account of what was occurring in Dublin.[10] The Earl of Kildare himself wisely chose not to join the invasion force, but to remain within his power base of Ireland although he did appoint his brother, Thomas Fitzgerald, to command the Irish contingent. This was no doubt a mixed force containing scions of the Anglo-Irish families of the Pale such as Edward og Plunket, the son of Lord Killeen, and men from allied clans such as the O'Connors. They were not all the 'naked Irish' as later described by the English chroniclers, but a cross-section of Irish martial society and men whose wild valour would have complemented the steely discipline of Martin Schwartz's Swabian companies.

We do not know when this heterogeneous group first set sail, but we do know that it landed on 4 June in Lancashire beyond the sands near the Furness peninsula, possibly near the anchorage now occupied by the town of Barrow-in-Furness, protected as it was by Eel Pie Island. The landing point had been carefully chosen: it was relatively remote and sufficiently secluded to ensure a safe disembarkation of the invasion force, which would necessarily have taken some time as horses, stores, arms and equipment and transport necessarily all had to be brought ashore. This was also an area dominated by friends and allies, resentful at the growth of Stanley power in the southern part of Lancashire and their closeness to Henry VII; men such as the Harringtons, the Huddlestons and others, many of them members of the Nevill and Ricardian affinities for generations. In this region, Nevill loyalties still had a relevance and a resilience that had been lost elsewhere. Here, Lovell could demonstrate the worth of his planning; these men were his friends and confidantes, with whom he had hidden for the previous eighteen months and who were ready and waiting for Lovell's return with a force behind him. The rebel army now moved inland to Furness Abbey, a large Cistercian house where the army was fed and supplied, albeit it would appear not without some reluctance, since the abbey had close relations with Henry VII's trusted servant Christopher Urswick, who was the son of a lay brother of the abbey.[11] By 5 June, the army was at Ulverston, but whilst little distance had been covered, the army was now formed up into marching array and all of the disorganization associated with disembarkation had now been left behind. From now on the army made good time, marching towards Carnforth and from there along the valley of the river Lune to Hornby Castle, the stronghold of the Harringtons. Here, no doubt, the army would have been greeted and joined by Sir James and Thomas Harrington and probably Clement Skelton and Alexander Appleby. Like Broughton and his brother these were men that Francis Lovell would have known he could rely upon, whose long struggle and detestation of the Stanleys would have made their adherence to the cause inevitable. The occupation of Hornby Castle opened up routes into Lonsdale, but more importantly the road east on to Wensleydale and the heart of Nevill country. There can be little doubt that at Hornby Lovell would have expected the presence of his brother-in-law Sir William Parr, who was married to Lovell's wife's sister, Elizabeth.[12] Lovell must have hoped that Parr would have brought the men of the barony of Kendall to join the rebel forces, especially since they had enjoyed such close relations since at least 1480. In this Lovell was to be disappointed. The failure of Sir William Parr, whose family had long associations with Warwick and Richard as Duke of Gloucester, to appear along with his men should have sounded some alarm bells. It is unlikely though that Lovell had either the time or the presence of mind to dwell on this disappointment, and morale amongst Lovell, Lincoln and Schwartz remained high. They had after all succeeded in landing in England unchallenged and with a bigger army than Henry VII had possessed when he had landed in west Wales in August 1485. Equally, those men who had committed to support the invasion for the most part had turned out with their followers. Lovell could be pleased with the way that the plan had come to fruition. Ahead lay Wensleydale, the Nevill and Ricardian heartland where Lovell had gained a following the previous year, and with territory now dominated by friendly lords, the Scropes of Bolton and Masham and another Lovell brother-in-law, Sir Richard Fitzhugh of Ravensworth.

The rebellion gathers force

Messengers from the north west had ridden south to relay to Henry VII at Kenilworth that the rebels had finally landed, albeit some four days after the event. The news probably reached Henry sometime on Friday 8 June, and he immediately sent out instructions to gather his forces. Messages went to the Duke of Bedford, the king's uncle Jasper Tudor, the Earl of Oxford, the earls of Devon and Shrewsbury, Viscount Lisle and five other barons, including Lord Hastings. The forces were to muster at Coventry and by Tuesday 12 June the royal forces were crossing the Leicestershire /Nottingham border and slowly marching north to allow other contingents from further afield to join up. The king's recruitment was hampered by 'a campaign of disinformation which has no parallel in the conflicts of the period'.[13] Lovell and Lincoln in East Anglia and other parts of the country sent agents to spread rumours and to sow dissent, stating that Henry VII had fled or was already dead 'by which subtyll meane and report many a trewe men to the king turned back'.[14] Those agents that were caught spreading these seditious rumours were immediately hung from the nearest tree as a warning to others, but the agents did their job well and there is contemporary evidence that men were reluctant to respond to the king's summons, questioning the exact nature and instruction of the summons and holding back from immediately joining the king. These rumours even affected the king's uncle by mar-riage, Lord Welles, with his forces turning 'like others in flight and [falling] back on London'.[15] Hence, it was an extremely apprehensive Henry VII who marched further and further north away from his capital, unsure both of what danger lay ahead of him and what treason lurked behind him.

Henry had good reason for apprehension because by 8 June the rebels were already in Wensleydale. While Henry had still been unaware of their presence in the country, the march of over seventy miles from Cumbria had been accomplished rela-tively easily by Schwartz's hardy professionals. On 8 June, Lovell and Lincoln were joined by Thomas Metcalfe of Nappa and Lovell's long-time associate Edward Frank, one-time Sheriff of Oxfordshire. The recruitment of these men would doubtless have heartened the rebels, but they would have been perplexed by the ambiguous attitude of the lords of the area. John, Lord Scrope of Bolton, was the most experienced of the local lords and, although his castle of Bolton had certainly offered no resistance to the rebel army entering Wensleydale from the Pennines, his enthusiasm for the cause would seem to have been less than total, and the same could be said of his relative

Thomas, Lord Scrope of Masham. Indeed, neither lord had mobilized his retinue and, therefore, was unable to join the rebellion. This lack of activity may be applied equally to Francis Lovell's brother-in-law, Richard, Lord Fitzhugh. It is possible that Fitzhugh's inactivity was caused by sickness – indeed, he died in September 1487. At any event, Henry VII took no subsequent action against the Fitzhugh family. However, there is the intriguing possibility that Lovell's wife, Anne, may have been residing nearby at Ravensworth. It is frustrating that we have no idea whether Lovell was briefly reunited with his wife at this time. Henry VII had taken back all the rich grants made by Richard III to the Scropes, so their tardiness in declaring for Henry and their general lack of enthusiasm was not from any affection for him, but rather from solid, political calculations. The Scropes must have pondered whether the dread penalties of treason were worth the risks involved. This rational calculation of risk and potential loss was to bedevil the minds of many other lords during the early weeks of June 1487.

From nearby Masham, 'Edward VI' despatched a letter to 'our trusty and well-beloved the maiour and his brethren and commanaltye of our citie of York' requesting their support and favour for 'we and such power as we have brought with us by means of travayle of the see and upon the land'.[16] Here was the first public opportunity to find out how convincing 'Edward VI' was. The issuing of a pseudo-royal summons to the largest city of the north was the real test of how the populace saw 'Edward VI' and, more importantly, of his ability to sway the political classes of the north.

John, Earl of Lincoln, had been Richard's Lieutenant of the North and was well known at York. He must have hoped that the city would remember him fondly and open its gates. Instead, the mayor and the corporation closed the gates to the rebels and threatened 'to withstand them with their bodies' if they attacked the city. No doubt the city fathers were fortified in this resolve by the fact that the royal army was moving up from the south and that the Earl of Northumberland and Lord Clifford were advancing to aid the city. It would also have been noted by the more xenophobic members of the corporation, which, in the fifteenth century, would have meant all of them, that the Earl of Lincoln and Francis Lovell were accompanied by a bewildering array of foreigners and Irish, which would have severely curbed any enthusiasm the city may have had for the rebels' cause. This represented a further blow to the rebels' morale and to the prestige of 'Edward VI', following as it did on the lack of concrete support from the supposedly strongly pro-Nevill area of Wensleydale. Amongst the knights and gentry there must have been increasing concern at the lack of solid support provided by the influential gentlemen of the north and a conspicuous failure of those gentlemen to support the conspirators or bring their retinues into the field. In some senses apathy was more corrosive to the rebellion than opposition.

If 'Edward VI's' leading men felt these concerns, they did not allow these to be shown to the rank-and-file. Equally, they did not allow the unexpected defiance of the city of York to derail the military imperatives of the campaign. On Saturday 9 June, they left York behind them and moved south along the Great North Road to

Boroughbridge and from there to Bramham Moor by Trinity Sunday, 10 June. Here the rebels had to confront an assault on the rebel encampment by Lord Clifford riding out from Tadcaster. Clifford was a diehard Lancastrian who had smarted under the rule of Edward IV, during which he had been deprived of his title and his lands. Clifford was now determined to strike a blow against what he would have viewed as a Yorkist insurrection. It must have been particularly galling for him since Richard III, both as Duke of Gloucester and as king, had enjoyed possession of his ancestral home of the castle and lordship of Skipton-in-Craven. Having been condemned to two decades of impotence in the face of Yorkist aggrandisement, Clifford was now impulsively determined to attack the much larger force of rebels. The attack was a disaster for him: outnumbered, he not only sustained heavy losses, but also lost his baggage train and had to fall back to the safety of the walls of York. It was probably Clifford's defeat that finally persuaded the Scropes to follow up the rebels' victory and lead an attack on the city's gates, proclaiming 'King Edward' at Bootham Bar. The Scropes' belated declaration for the rebels could either be viewed as poor co-ordination on their part or a deliberate attempt to tie down the forces of the Earl of Northumberland and Lord Clifford at York, both of whom were marching south. However, it is more likely to have been pure opportunism, with the Scropes looking to gain any local advantages on offer.

The bypassing of York did not, however, change the strategic imperative of the rebels, who now surged southward towards the Midlands and closer to the recruiting grounds where Lovell and de la Pole influence was strongest – the Thames Valley and East Anglia. Probably both men understood that many influential lords would be unable to show their hand until the rebel host was considerably closer. They also knew that the key to the success of the rebellion and, indeed, to the kingdom was the capture of London, where they would hope to acquire the person of the real Earl of Warwick, still ensconced in the Tower. It is tempting at this point to speculate on Lincoln's plans and the potential fitness to rule of the real Edward, Earl of Warwick. It was later asserted that Edward of Warwick was in some ways slow-witted, but this is to misread contemporary sources. Contemporaries speak of a rather sad and trusting figure who never had the opportunity to build up normal human relations, spending all of his life from the age of two as a prisoner. There is little evidence to suggest that Warwick would not have been a thoroughly acceptable monarch once he had been liberated from the mental and physical confines that had scarred his youth and childhood.

Keen to maintain momentum, the rebel host moved south at an alarming pace, precluding more distant contingents being able to either keep up or join with it. There is also evidence of dissension between Martin Schwartz and the Earl of Lincoln. Schwartz was known throughout the Netherlands and the Rhineland as a man of insufferable arrogance, whilst Lincoln had been described as being prickly under strain, although most chronicles appear to regard him as intelligent and capable. The evidence from Dublin during the coronation would seem to indicate that Lincoln could be petulant and quick to anger and so the underlying tension between the two men simmered on the road south. Schwartz, with commendable military discipline, kept the rebels marching south, bypassing such well-defended points on the road as Pontefract and continuing through Castleford and Doncaster. Schwartz and the other commanders recognized that as long as they maintained their momentum, they retained the military initiative.

Henry's response

By this time, Henry VII was moving precariously northward, still unsure of the rebels' actual location, numbers or dispositions. He would have been heartened by the fact that his forces were joined by experienced soldiers, such as Sir John Cheney, Sir John Savage and Sir Rhys ap Thomas, and their retinues, together with young peers such as Lords Strange, Hastings and Grey of Powys – the latter being the man that Lovell had despatched to Brittany from Southampton only three years earlier. Henry, buoyed by these additions to his forces, now moved on to Nottingham, where he was joined by additional bowmen from Cheshire and Derby under the command of Henry Vernon and Lord Strange. Henry's confidence in the political nation must have risen as each of these contingents joined his forces, and he could begin to have greater faith in his subjects. As more and more of these captains brought their men to the king, Henry would have sat down with his most experienced commanders – John, Earl of Oxford, and Jasper Tudor, now Duke of Bedford – and tried to assess the rebels' likely route. Acting on their advice, Henry moved his forces up to Ratcliffe-on-Trent, close to Nottingham and the Fosse Way and directly opposite Lovell's own manor of Stoke Bardolph. Here, Henry was greeted by an unwelcome sight as Sir Edward Woodville's outriders returned to camp having been bested by Lincoln and Lovell's men, who had chased them out of Doncaster and pursued them through Sherwood Forest for a further three days, forcing them back on the main royal army, to Henry's dismay.

Despite this setback, as the two armies drew closer, the rebels had to recognize an uncomfortable political reality: that the numbers joining the cause had been disappointingly small. By the standards of the day, the insurrection of 1487 had been remarkably sophisticated. Lovell and, latterly, the Earl of Lincoln had pulled off a masterpiece of coordination, bringing their invasion force to Ireland and thence to England, where they had initially been met by the support they were expecting. They had taken great pains to create a figure of equal standing to the king by crowning 'Edward VI' and issuing coinage and proclamations on his behalf. They had also undermined men's natural loyalty to the king by sowing rumour and sedition on an unprecedented scale. Yet for all these measures, they had not attracted enough men to join their cause and numbers had been slow to join once they had left the Nevill heartlands. As the rebels approached the royal forces south of the Trent, this unpalatable truth became even more evident, causing Martin Schwartz to remark bitterly to John Earl of Lincoln:

Sir, now I see well that you have dyssayvyd [deceived] yourself and also me,
But that notwithstanding, all such promise I made unto my lady the Duchess
I shall perform. Exortyng the erl to doo the same. And upon this sped hym
towards the field wt as good a courage as he had XXM [20,000] men more
than he had.[17]

Unfortunately, facing the assembled might of the king of England, Lovell, Lincoln
and Schwartz did not have 20,000 more men. They would have to decide the fate of
the kingdom with what they had.

19 STOKE FIELD

Preparing for battle

ON THE EVENING OF 15 June 1487, the rebel host crossed the river Trent, probably at Fiskerton, and entered into southern England. While there had been acrimonious exchanges between the Earl of Lincoln and Martin Schwartz over recruitment, this was also a problem shared by Henry VII. He was admirably supported by the Earl of Oxford and the Duke of Bedford, yet other nobles had remained inactive or lukewarm in their support, with only a handful of key nobles turning out for the king: the Earl of Devon and the Earl of Shrewsbury, Viscount Lisle (an illegitimate son of Edward IV), and six barons. The Earl of Arundel and his son Lord Maltravers, brother-in-law of the Earl of Lincoln, the Earl of Westmorland, the Earl of Huntingdon and the Duke of Suffolk all found reasons to either absent themselves or were slow to respond to the king's summons. This reticence on behalf of members of the higher nobility pointed to a reluctance by some of its members to actively endorse Henry VII's kingship. It also indicated the potential support the rebels may have achieved as they pushed southward.

Crossing the Trent, though, Lovell and Lincoln knew that they would have to overcome a royal army coming up through the Midlands. They may have felt an element of confidence after managing to force Sir Edward Woodville's cavalry out of Sherwood Forest and to clear the path for advance. It is more likely, however, given the discussion between the Earl of Lincoln and Schwartz that both Lovell and Lincoln began to feel a stomach-churning nausea as they contemplated giving battle to a reigning monarch whose forces substantially outnumbered their own. Despite Lovell's experience of border warfare against the Scots with Richard III in the early 1480s, his and Lincoln's only experience of a pitched battle had been Bosworth. The memories of Bosworth would have been a salutary reminder for both men of the chaos and confusion of battle and the difficulty of retaining clear lines of command amid the clash of steel on steel and the incessant cries of war and the wounded. On the other hand, they must have felt reassured by the easy discipline of Schwartz's veterans, who were no strangers to fighting against larger forces and who trusted in their own skill and discipline to carry the day. Lovell and Lincoln would have looked to Schwartz for direction as he had fought many more engagements than they had and possessed experience in the most up-to- date forms of European warfare.

Joining with this council of war would have been Richard Harleston, a great advocate of the English longbow, with martial experience going back to 1468 when he had directed the siege of Mont Orgueil castle, in the Channel Islands, and had also led a company in the Franco-Breton war of 1472.[1] Other rebels, such as Thomas Broughton, Robert Percy and Edward Frank, had as much experience as Lovell in border warfare, but they too had little or no experience of command. It was for this very reason that Martin Schwartz had been recruited (and for which he no doubt expected to be handsomely rewarded). The proximity of Lovell's manor of Stoke Bardolph would have given him some local knowledge as it is likely that Lovell would have stopped here on his many journeys from Oxfordshire to the north. After fording the Trent at Fiskerton, Lovell, Lincoln and their commanders had spent the night in the vicinity of the church at the village of East Stoke. From here, no doubt outriders would have been despatched to scout the whereabouts of the royal army and to ascertain the number and deployment of the royal forces. From the best information available, it would appear that the royal army comprised three divisions: the forward under the Earl of Oxford: the centre with Henry VII; and behind, the rearward. These divisions took different routes towards Stoke, where they planned to converge on the Fosse Way at Stoke itself.[2] This implies that Henry VII did not know the precise location of the rebel forces and that he was converging on a convenient crossing-point of the Trent in the proximity of the rebel forces. What is clear is that the rebels had already spotted the approach of the royal army early on the morning of 16 June, and had begun to deploy accordingly.

Making their dispositions

Lovell, Lincoln and Schwartz took the decision – presumably jointly – to deploy on high ground, on an escarpment running down south-west from Burnham Furlong towards the village of Elston. The command of this high ground dominated the Fosse Way from the south and blocked the road from Stoke to Newark. The rise presented a good defensive position, giving the rebels control of the high ground, thus forcing the royal forces to march to them. The nearest part of the royal army at this time was the forward under the Earl of Oxford, now advancing along the Fosse Way from Ratcliffe six miles to the south. As the rebel army took up its position, Lovell and Lincoln would have recognized not only their lack of numbers, but also the lack of uniformity of their forces. Their army was the most exotic to take part in what is now known as the Wars of the Roses. Foreign participation in English battles was not a new phenomenon, of course: in 1461, Warwick 'the Kingmaker' deployed Burgundian handgunners at the Second Battle of St Albans. At Stoke, however, the bulk of the rebel forces was foreign. Thomas Geraldine's Irish and Martin Schwartz's Germans, alongside the more traditional English forces, now created problems of deployment. The forces that Lincoln and Lovell commanded amounted to probably no more than 8,000[3] comprising 2,000 men under Martin Schwartz, approximately

3,500 to 4,000 Irishmen under Thomas Fitzgerald, and roughly 2,000 to 2,500 English recruits, either those who had arrived with Lovell and Lincoln or those recruited during their march through northern England. The level of equipment and the weapons used would have varied considerably amongst these various contingents, with the German mercenaries by far being the best equipped. The Germans would have been resplendent in their flamboyant and extravagant costumes, but would have also been well-equipped with pikes, arquebusiers (an early firearm), crossbows and short swords. On the other extreme would have been the Irish (or the 'naked Irish', according to Polydore Vergil), who, unless they were professional gallowglasses, would have had little in the way of personal protection and so would have been relatively lightly armed with short bows, darts and long knives – weapons that depended upon speed and mobility, features of the clan warfare in which they had been raised. The Englishmen who had joined the rebels would have been traditionally armed with bows and pole weapons such as halberds, pikes and pole-axes in which the English were famously proficient. The level of personal protection would have varied from man to man depending on wealth and social position. It is unlikely that any man, apart from the nobility and the gentry, would have been fully equipped since they were not part of any noble's retinue or town's company. However, most men in fifteenth-century England had an array of some armour and weapons they could call upon, including some that had been handed down from father to son, and were in themselves veterans of earlier campaigns. Thus, while is it unlikely that many Englishmen were fully kitted out in personal armour, they would certainly have been far better protected than their Irish comrades.

Tactics

Another problem confronting the rebel commanders was deciding on the tactics to adopt to exact the best use out of their diverse and very dissimilar forces. The Germans under Schwartz would have been used to operating en masse with a relatively sophisticated command system and highly synchronized movements. For this reason, it is likely that they fought as a single unit; to disperse them would have both diluted their effectiveness and exacerbated the problems of communication and language. Throughout the campaign so far Lovell and Lincoln had retained a commendable level of control over their forces and ensured that discipline had been tight, with no reports of ill-discipline and pillage; they would have wanted to ensure that this remained so. It is probable that the English soldiers were intermingled with the Irish where their better personal protection allowed them to effectively act as a form of stiffening amongst the Irish ranks. With these deployments, it would have become even more obvious to the rebel commanders that they were deficient in two key areas: those of bowmen and cavalry. Reputedly, the best archers in England came from Cheshire and these were with the king at the command of the Earl of Derby's son, Lord Strange. The rebels' lack of recruits in England meant they had far fewer of this quintessentially English force than they would have liked. This dearth of English recruits and particularly men of quality also meant that the rebels lacked cavalry. That the rebels had some cavalry was proven by the defeat of Sir Edward Woodville in Sherwood Forest. However, faced with the need for real numbers in the forthcoming battle, it was soon apparent how few the rebels actually possessed. It has been speculated that Lovell was the commander of the rebel cavalry, holding them back as a form of tactical reserve during the battle, but there is no contemporary evidence to support this.

Before the fighting began

Sometime between dawn and 9am, the priests who accompanied the rebel army would have said mass. We know from the herald's account and later testimony that a priest, Richard Simonds, was present at the battle of Stoke Field with Lambert Simnel. This causes some confusion since (as we already know) another priest with a similar name, William Simonds, was arrested and interrogated by Henry VII's agents in February that year. This raises the question as to whether there were in fact two priests named Simonds and whether they were related, since it is highly unlikely that a herald, whose role was to recognize and precisely remember names, would have made such a mistake. Simonds was not the only priest present since we know that four heads of northern religious houses were subsequently fined by Henry VII for their participation in the revolt.[4] Representatives of these houses would have ensured that the men went into battle properly shriven and ready, if necessary, to meet their Maker. Forming up on the higher ground would have given Lincoln, Lovell and Schwartz a good view of the advancing royal forces, and they may have been able to see that Oxford's forward, numbering some 6,000 men, was advancing unsupported. Sometime before 9am, the rebel force, occupying half a mile along Burham Hill, stood ready in battle array steeling themselves as they awaited the approach of Oxford's forces. As the king's army was divided into three divisions, Oxford and his men found themselves exposed in sight of the rebels and as yet without the support of the king's division. Oxford probably had with him 400 men-at-arms, 2,800 archers and 2,800 billmen (or infantry armed with pole weapons). Arriving in the vicinity of the rebel forces, it is unlikely that Oxford considered retreating onto the approaching king's division; rather, he trusted to the professionalism of his troops and their more homogeneous composition, and determined to engage and hold the rebel forces as he waited for the king to arrive.

An opportunity for an early victory

For Lovell and Lincoln, no doubt supported by the professional opinion of Schwartz, Oxford's decision presented them with an opportunity to capitalize on their superior numbers and to eliminate the forward element of the royal forces before the king could concentrate all his men. If they could defeat Oxford's division, this would have a demoralizing effect on the rest of the royal forces and allow the rebels to retain the initiative as they pressed south. They may also have made the larger calculation that a significant defeat of Henry's forces would bring about a collapse of Henry VII's regime and inevitably bring about greater recruitment and support for their own cause.

The royal forces began the battle by launching fusillade after fusillade of arrows at the rebel forces at the top of the rise. Molinet says that the effects of this were that the men were 'shot through and full of arrows like hedgehogs'.[5] The Irish kerns, under Sir Thomas Geraldine, scantily protected by European standards, suffered disproportionately as approximately 84,000 arrows fell on the rebel ranks in some three minutes.[6] The Irish lower orders in the rebel army would also have suffered grievously as the descending arrows penetrated their unprotected lower body, legs and feet. It is probable, however, that the damage done was less than that reported by Molinet, for whilst the arrow storm released by Oxford's bowmen was fearsome, it was far from decisive and was probably endured only for a short period of time before the bowmen retreated behind the supporting billmen and infantry.

It is at this point that Martin Schwartz probably took field command of the rebel forces. Trained in the modern methods of warfare prevalent on the continent, Schwartz would have wanted to use this experience and his disciplined regiments in the most effective way. Having occupied the rising ground to observe the disposition of Oxford's forces, Schwartz now used that ground to enable his forces to have the advantage of advancing downhill against Oxford. Forming up his men into a column, he could now deploy them in the new 'Swiss' method that had proved so effective for the Swiss at Grandson and Morat. In both of those battles, the Swiss pikemen had formed independent columns and marched towards and then over the enemy, with their dense and disciplined formations overwhelming the opposition. An example of this form of modern warfare was used at the battle of Flodden in 1513, where, with a similar amount of men armed in the same fashion under James IV king of Scotland, 9,000 soldiers had been formed into twenty ranks deep, with each rank comprising 450 men.[7]

Schwartz would have placed at the front his *dopplesöldner*, with their fearsome two-handed swords, and the better armoured English men-at-arms; in the centre, his disciplined pikemen would have formed the steely core of the formation; the lightly armed but nimble Irish would have taken up the flanks, where their darts and savage knives would have been able to inflict as many casualties as possible. Martin Schwartz, appraising the situation with an experienced and professional eye, would have recognized that the best and quickest means of obtaining victory was to advance forward down the hill in the Allemagne manner and roll over Oxford's outnumbered forward before Henry VII could bring his superior numbers to bear.

As a plan it had a number of advantages over standing on the defensive on Burham Hill and awaiting the king's greater numbers to firm up. Firstly, it would reduce the casualties incurred by his men as they steadily reduced the range and effectiveness of Oxford's archers. Secondly, those archers and their large numbers would place Oxford's division at a disadvantage as Schwartz's experienced pikemen closed in on them. Lightly armoured and lightly armed, they were not equipped for the close-quarter fighting that was the specialism of European infantry and which would dominate the battlefield until the later part of the seventeenth century. With his flamboyant *landsknechts* in the vanguard, Schwartz gave the order to advance, with the Earl of Lincoln probably near the front ranks to both coordinate and command the forces he had raised. The earliest account of the battle, the *Herald's Memoir*, offers no information as to where Lovell was at this point or whether he engaged with the rebels in the first assault. The supposition, based on later deduction – that he commanded the cavalry reserve with the young king 'Edward VI' (Lambert Simnel) – may well be accurate. Even if the rebels did not possess many cavalry, they would still have retained their place on the battlefield awaiting the breakthrough that the infantry would provide when it could turn defeat into a rout by riding down the men of the broken infantry formations. Lovell could well have remained on the rise waiting for this moment.

The fighting becomes harder

Doubtless Oxford's men, professional, well-equipped and trained as they were, would have felt some pangs of consternation and fear as Schwartz and Lincoln led their men forward. They would have been chilled by the unfamiliar and savage battle cries rising from the different nationalities of the rebel host. Oxford's men could only ready themselves for the impact as the rebel division smashed into them and pike and halberd came into play. Oxford's line recoiled under pressure and, as sheer force of numbers began to tell, they took a step backward. As they retreated, though their line held firm, the greater professionalism and proficiency of the royal forces did terrible execution. Even so, Oxford's men began to suffer significant casualties as they retreated, barely containing the rebels' onslaught. By now Henry VII had arrived on the battlefield and the men of his division began to bolster Oxford's ranks. The arrival of Henry's troops must have been a blow to the rebel leaders and even more so with the early death of the Earl of Lincoln, which contemporary accounts record as being either in the general melee or possibly by an arrow strike. Unlike at Bosworth, however, the death of a key leader did not lead to the disintegration of the rebel forces, which whilst probably periodically retiring from direct combat to re-form and re-group, kept the pressure up in a battle that plumbed all the depths of savagery that a medieval battle could generate.

Henry's forces with the advantage

The rebel onslaught continued for possibly one and a half to two hours when Oxford's forces, refreshed by the men brought up by the king, were manoeuvred into the wedge-shaped formation that Henry had used at Bosworth. It was now or possibly a little earlier that the deaths of Martin Schwartz and Thomas Geraldine occurred. As Oxford's men advanced, so rebel resistance, which up until now had been ferocious, began to slacken. As the pressure of the resurgent royal forces began to tell, men began to break ranks and flee and defeat now became a rout. Immediately, a savage pursuit, led by Sir Edward Woodville's horsemen, took place. Broken, the rebels fled, and it became each man for himself as many made for a gulley down to the Trent along the escarpment to Fiskerton where the rebels had forded the river the day before, whilst others headed north for safety along the Fosse Way.[8] The disintegration and then destruction of the rebel army after over three hours of brutal fighting had resulted in what the servant of the master recorder of York described as 'five thousand slain and murdered'.[9] Modern estimates place the casualties to around 4,000 on the rebel side and approximately 3,000 on the royal side, the vast majority of which were members of the Earl of Oxford's division, although no one of any prominence seems to have been killed on the king's side. The casualty rates at Stoke as a percentage of the numbers engaged make the battle of one of the most lethal of the Wars of the Roses. On top of those killed in the field and in the pursuit, those members of the Calais Garrison or other English and Irish who had survived the battle were taken by Henry's men to Newark for interrogation and then summary execution by hanging. Henry, desperate to get to the bottom of the conspiracy, had given strict orders for the Earl of Lincoln to be taken alive, and was disappointed to find that he had died early in the battle. What remained of Schwartz's mercenary companies was allowed to return to the continent or offered employment with Henry's own forces.

Defeat for the rebels

Among the rebels, Sir Thomas Broughton died that day – although an alternative legend claims that he returned to his Lancashire fells and lived out his days as a humble shepherd. Irrespective of this, there were many on the rebels' side who did die, including Sir Henry Bodrugan, John Beaumont, Thomas Harrington, Thomas Batell, and Richard Middleton. Edward Frank was captured and imprisoned in the Tower of London. Sharing Frank's fate were Robert Percy, John Broughton, Robert Hilton and John Mallory, who were all imprisoned at the king's pleasure. One who managed to avoid the slaughter and escaped to Burgundy was Richard Harleston, who became a pensioner of Duchess Margaret and who was buried at her expense in 1501. Meekly captured were the priest Richard Simonds and the imposter Lambert Simnel, who had been abandoned in flight by those who only one month earlier had acclaimed him as king. The cause of York had been smashed on the field and its most committed protagonists now lay bloodied and lifeless, buried in the rich soil of the English Midlands. The death of John, Earl of Lincoln, had deprived the Yorkist party of one of its most capable and charismatic leaders. Like many of those he had led, Lincoln had paid the ultimate price. Unable to question one of the principal architects of the conspiracy, despite his specific instructions, Henry VII must have hoped that his most incorrigible and tenacious opponent, Francis Lovell, was amongst the captured or the slain. However, despite an abortive rumour that Lovell had drowned trying to swim his horse across the Trent, Henry's most elusive opponent had once more evaded him.

20 THE END?

A hunted man

By noon on 16 January 1487, Francis Lovell had ridden away from this, his second, defeat at the hands of Henry VII, from the debacle of Stoke and from historical record, leaving behind 'the lade that his rebels called King Edward',[1] now of no further use to Lovell or the cause. Lovell was once again a fugitive with the forces of a triumphant Henry VII now scouring the countryside for him. Some people believed him to be dead: either one of the anonymous desecrated corpses so disfigured by injury as to be unrecognizable, or drowned when fording the river. However, for Lovell's true fate we can perhaps take the word of the herald present at the battle, for soon after it was recorded that 'viscount lorde Lovell was put to flight'.[2] Most contemporaries recognized that, unlike Lincoln, Lovell was still alive and that he remained a threat for Henry VII, albeit one much weakened, and so the search for Lovell went on.

Henry VII's actions against the rebels following Stoke Field

Lovell's circumstances after Stoke, however, made his predicament after Bosworth seem almost benign. After Bosworth, Henry VII had passed an act of attainder against twenty-nine persons, the vast majority of whom were members of the late king Richard's household and were dead or in royal custody. After Stoke, a further twenty-eight persons were attainted (not including the already attainted Lovell), and a further eighty-one now sued for pardon; this was in addition to others such as Sir Thomas Pilkington and Sir James Harrington who were still attainted from the aftermath of Bosworth. At the same time, two churchmen were immediately fined for their sympathies with the rebel cause. These reprisals effectively destroyed the network of Yorkist support that had sustained Lovell since he had left Colchester in the autumn of 1486. More significantly, the death of 4,000 men at the battle of Stoke Field had destroyed the basis of support that Lovell had enjoyed previously. As Henry's men began fanning out across the countryside searching for Lovell and as the ports were closed to him, Lovell must have realised how dire his predicament was. His usual bolt-holes and hiding- places in the northern fastness of Lancashire were now permanently closed to him as Stanley men moved to occupy the Broughton, Harrington and Molineux lands. In Richmondshire, the local gentry, led by John, Lord Scrope of Bolton, sought to make peace with Henry VII. In response to a royal summons, Scrope rode south and, on 26 August 1487,[3] was imprisoned at Windsor. Scrope was probably lucky to retain his head and at Windsor agreed to pay a massive bond of £3,000 for his future good behaviour: six months later, upon his release, he was restricted to travelling less than twenty-two miles from Windsor. Similar punishments were meted out to his cousin, Thomas, Lord Scrope of Masham, and their retainer Sir Edmund Hastings.

What next for Lovell?

On a practical level, more problematic for Lovell was not so much the incarceration of such prominent peers but the rush to seek pardon by the more obscure participants in his previous conspiracies. These were men who had been able to offer refuge and security because they were under the radar of Henry VII's vigilance system. Of those who applied for pardon, thirty-six were from Lancashire, Yorkshire, Cumberland, Westmorland, Durham and Northumberland, representing a cross-section of northern society below the rank of baron. These men included gentleman John Pullayn of Burghwaleys, in Yorkshire, Ralph Bothe, Archdeacon of York, Thomas Roos esquire, and merchant William Hammond of Kingston-upon-Hull, who all now sought to make their peace and turn their back on past adventures and misdemeanours. With Lord Clifford now riding high and the Earl of Northumberland filling the vacuum left by the death and demise of the old Nevill affinity, the north was no longer a safe haven for Francis Lovell. The reticence prior to Stoke shown by his brother-in-law Richard Fitzhugh, brought on perhaps by ill health, further eroded his standing and support in the region. For Lovell, and indeed for others, Stoke Field was a watershed moment. The old Nevill affinity, nurtured since the reign of Henry IV in 1399 and reaching it apogee under Warwick 'the kingmaker' and his son-in-law Richard III, had been smashed beyond repair. A new hand now ruled the north and for Lovell it was not a welcoming one.

With the north closed to him, Lovell would then have taken the only course of action open to him after Stoke Field – to put his head into the lion's mouth and head south to those areas in which he had been born and where Lambert Simnel had been created, groomed and educated. It has been suggested that it is unlikely that Lovell would have returned to the vicinity of the Lovell homelands in Oxfordshire and the Thames Valley because, after the parliament of November 1485, Lovell's lands and estates had been given to Henry VII's uncle, Jasper Tudor. The granting of the Lovell estates were, however, only part of a torrent of rewards that fell around Jasper Tudor's shoulders during 1485 and 1486. Justifiably, Henry Tudor recognized the enormous debt of gratitude that he owed to his uncle's tenacity and unbending loyalty. Jasper's continued opposition on political and familial grounds to Edward IV maintained the Lancastrian cause long after almost everyone else had come to terms with Edward IV after the battle of Tewkesbury in 1471. The debt that Henry owed his uncle was enormous and, therefore, so too were the rewards. Jasper was restored to the lands he had held as Earl of Pembroke, added to which he gained the wealthy Welsh lordships of Glamorgan and Abergavenny; he was also restored to the lands he had held jointly with his brother during the 1450s. To these were added, on his marriage to Catherine Woodville (Elizabeth Woodville's younger sister and the widow of Henry, Duke of Buckingham), the Stafford lordships of Brecon, Hay and Newport. In addition, Jasper was also rewarded with the Lovell estates of Minster Lovell, Brize Norton, Cogges, Hardwick, Rotherfield Grey, Somerton, Banbury, Woodford and Little Rissington in Oxfordshire.[4] He was also made Lord Lieutenant of Ireland and Justiciar of South Wales. Jasper was to later spend an appreciable amount of time at Minster Lovell, entertaining the king there in 1494 with 'ginger, oranges, conserva lymonis and mermelade',[5] followed by a performance by Jasper's tumblers, who the king rewarded with 13s 4d. He did not, however, spend a great deal of time there in the later 1480s as he adjusted to his new responsibilities both regionally and nationally and also supported his nephew in council and on campaign.

Another form of sanctuary

After Stoke Field, Francis Lovell would have needed somewhere to recuperate physically and mentally after spending almost two years planning, campaigning and fighting. Of far greater concern to him probably would have been the complete collapse of those efforts, his inability to reverse the verdict of fate for his friend and king, and his inability to exact any form of revenge on the usurper who had effectively twice encompassed his ruin. Hence, it would have been an emotionally crushed Lovell who had to resolve how to proceed now that he was bereft of friends once again. During this period of extreme mental turmoil, it would not be surprising that Lovell sought to retire to that area he called home, perhaps the only fixed point in a life that had now become disastrously precarious and probably the one area where he would be welcomed by loyal, friendly and well-known faces. So, after the battle of Stoke Field, as Henry VII headed to Newark, it is likely that Lovell headed to Oxfordshire

Riding towards the familiar landscape of the Thames Valley made sense in a practical as well as on an emotional level for Lovell: the Thames Valley contained the one element of the Lambert Simnel plot that had not yet been uncovered. Crucially, the involvement in the conspiracy of John Sante, Abbot of Abingdon, and his network had not been discovered by Henry VII's government. The arrest of Bishop Stillington in February 1487 and his subsequent interrogation at Windsor had diverted all attention from the activities of Sante. Since Stillington revealed little or nothing about the plot, it would appear he was arrested on his past reputation rather than his most recent activities. Stillington's arrest deflected attention from Sante who was far more involved in Lovell's plot than either the government or subsequent historians have recognized. We know that Sante, himself an Oxford man, had provided financial aid to the plot, as his emissary had been arrested taking cash to Burgundy in January 1487; also, that Sante had offered sanctuary to the Stafford brothers. John Sante had had diplomatic dealings with Margaret of Burgundy as far back as the mid-1470s. Like Lovell, Sante was a committed Ricardian whose defence of the Stafford brothers would have recommended him and his abbey to Lovell as a safe place of refuge. The government's failure to fully investigate Sante's activities had left his participation in this conspiracy free from suspicion and, therefore, able to sustain Lovell in this period of crisis.

Lovell and his family

From here, possibly Lovell got news to his wife, Anne, that he was still alive. Certainly, his family was aware that he was not among the dead at Stoke Field. We know this from the survival of a letter from London written by Anne's mother Alice, Lady Fitzhugh, to Sir John Paston (the same man who had searched for Lovell a year earlier):

> ... my doghtyr Lovell [Lady Anne] makith great sute and labour for my sone hir husbande. Sir Edward Frank hath been in the north to inquire for hym; he is comyn agayne, and cane nogth understand where he is. Wherefore her benevolers willith hir to continue her sute and labour; and so I can not departe nor leve hir as ye know well.[6]

The letter has been credibly dated to 24 February 1488 and clearly reveals the anguish felt by Lovell's wife, who seems to believe Lovell is alive and is desperately seeking any news of her husband's whereabouts. It also reveals the closeness of their family connections with Anne's mother unable to leave her daughter in her current state of distress. Also apparent is Lady Alice Fitzhugh's affection for Lovell in calling him her son and offering no censure for his actions, which had brought such ruin on her daughter.

However, objectively, the letter reveals that in February 1488 both women felt that Lovell was still alive, his whereabouts unknown. They had engaged Edward Frank ('Sir' seems to have been a courtesy that Lady Alice bestowed on Frank) to search for Lovell presumably because, not only was he one of Lovell's closest friends, but also because they were aware that Frank, being present at Stoke Field would have been one of the last people to see him alive. After the battle, Edward Frank was captured and imprisoned in the Tower; no doubt he was interrogated by Henry VII's intelligence officers desperate to find out who Lambert Simnel's secret supporters may have been. That Frank was available to have undertaken this mission on behalf of Lovell's wife and mother-in-law means he must have been released sometime in the autumn 1487. It is likely that Lady Fitzhugh and Lady Lovell had been at Ravensworth during the summer of 1487 as Lady Lovell's brother was ill at this time and died fairly soon after. If Lady Fitzhugh and Lady Lovell believed that Francis Lovell was in the north or in Scotland at this point, then they would have been able to get word to him or have received word from him. They engaged Frank at this point probably only because their own enquiries had drawn a blank and revealed nothing of Lovell's whereabouts. The very fact that they went ahead and asked Frank to continue these enquiries suggests that they may well have had some compelling reason to believe that Lovell was still alive. By the end of February one can discern a sense of foreboding in the line 'he is comyn agane, and can nought understand where he is'.[7] Both ladies, with the resources of the Fitzhughes of Ravensworth could not find a trace of him in the north and neither could one of his closest confidantes; Francis Lovell had vanished and seems to have not made contact with his family for a considerable amount of time.

Some fifty years after Lovell's disappearance, an inquisition post-mortem was undertaken in Henry VIII's reign on behalf of Lovell's nephew, Henry Norris, to address his claim to a part of the Lovell and Beaumont baronies. In refuting his claim in 1534/5, Henry VIII's judges recorded 'they say that the same said Francis was overseas ... and moreover died after the predicted attainder, but on what day and in what year the said Francis died the appointed judges do not know.'[8] This would appear to be a legal catch-all clause written fifty years after the fact and again reveals no contemporary information regarding in what county or in what year he died. It has however given rise to speculation that Lovell had escaped abroad in 1487, but to date there is no evidence to support this. On the contrary, those who knew him best searched for him in England and not abroad.

The Scottish connection

Another tantalizing clue to Lovell's location is a letter of safe conduct by James IV of Scotland issued on 19 June 1488 to Francis Lovell, Oliver Frank, Thomas Broughton and Roger Hartlington to enter Scotland for one year and then at pleasure.[9] This would suggest that, at some point between February and July 1488, Lovell was not only alive, but able to communicate with European governments at the highest level and actively plan for the future. The document, issued under the great Seal of Scotland, also reveals something extremely personal about the character of the man. The safe conduct speaks of offering entry into Scotland for Lovell and others and their servants and in this instance we can perhaps deduce that Lovell must have been a man of quite exceptional personal qualities because, even at this time of extreme adversity, when he was not only destitute but undoubtedly the most hunted man in the kingdom, there does not seem to have been any attempt by friends, attendants or servants at betrayal or disclosure. The fact the Lovell still retained the support of three other men plus their servants indicates that he had little trouble in retaining the loyalties of his men and that he still possessed a sizeable following. Unlike the vast majority of dissidents, Lovell's plans, whereabouts and actions remained undetected by Henry VII's agents and intelligencers. At no time was Francis Lovell's security cordon penetrated and it is this personal devotion that is crucial to the final mystery of his fate.

The safe conduct offered by James IV also reveals that Lovell was still seen as a significant figure in the politics of north-western Europe and one who still had a role to play. James IV reached out to Lovell because he saw him as both politically valuable and an intransigent enemy of Henry VII. In addition, he was a man who retained connections with many important people in England – the very thing, of course, that Henry VII feared most. The safe conduct indicates that Lovell must have been in communication with Scotland, at least, if not other foreign governments, and that there were channels of communication open to him at least until July 1488. There is no record that the safe conduct that was offered to Lovell was ever acted upon or taken up. True, in July 1491, Sir Richard Tunstall, the Lord Mayor of York, recorded the testimony of a 'sympill and pure person',[10] who had apparently spoken with 'Lord' Lovell in Scotland. However, that statement was subsequently withdrawn and denied. More objectively, if Lovell had escaped to Scotland under James IV's safe conduct, Henry VII would soon have known about it because James would have been sure to let Henry know that he possessed such a trump card. It would also have been a matter of profound interest in Burgundy and France, who were beginning to ready themselves for another bout of political conflict (this time over Brittany). Francis Lovell, holding the affections of Margaret of Burgundy for his robust and continual loyalty to the Yorkist cause, would no doubt have been offered a prominent position within her domains, ready to participate in the next turn of fortune's wheel. Perhaps most telling of all is that if Lovell had arrived in Scotland, it would have been easy for his wife and mother-in-law to have obtained word of his safety, which would have relieved them of the anguish they felt in their fruitless searches during the winter of 1487.

The Sante plot

That Francis Lovell met his end sometime between February and July 1488 is reinforced by the lack of any record of his involvement in events that took place in the winter of 1489. On 1 December 1489, John Mayne, a lay-brother of Abingdon Abbey, who had previously been involved in transferring money to Burgundy at the command of Abbot Sante, 'met' a London priest, Thomas Rothwell, otherwise known as Thomas Even (one wonders why a priest would need an alias?). Together they concocted a plot to release the Earl of Warwick and to overthrow Henry VII. As the plot developed, they drew in other ex-Ricardians, such as Thomas Davey, in whose house they met. Davey had been Richard III's Sergeant Tailor, a Lovell associate and one of Lovell's port deputies. Later evidence from their confessions stated that 'just by chance',

Lovell's old friend and familiar, Edward Frank, happened to be there and that Davey, Mayne and Rothwell then brought Frank into the plot. Frank had been attainted and imprisoned in the Tower after Stoke Field, but had subsequently been released. The plotters stated that only then did they approach Abbot Sante to participate in the plot. This seems disingenuous since Mayne was obviously Sante's man who more realistically had been sent to London to seek out Frank and Davey. It would appear from the later indictment that the plotters produced a rather cack-handed plot to set fire to a part of the Tower of London and, in the ensuing confusion, to rescue Warwick. The plotters wrote a letter to Warwick, suggesting that he escape to Colchester (which carried echoes of Lovell's sojourn there in the autumn of 1485), to throw the authorities off the scent. By mid-December Sante, an intelligent man, was beginning to have serious doubts about the plot and began to think that Rothwell was either light-witted or mentally disturbed when they met later in December 1489.

The plotters met again on 20 December in Abingdon when Mayne and Rothwell met with Christopher Swanne, Bailiff of Abingdon. If Sante had not been initially involved in the plot, certainly by 20 December we can see him desperately trying to take control of it. Sante's increasing control becomes clearer when a monk of Abingdon, Miles Sally, brought money to Frank, who had remained in London. The involvement of Mayne, Swanne and Sally demonstrates Sante's controlling influence over the plot, both organizationally and financially. All were brothers or lay-brothers of the abbey and acted on the abbot's instructions. The plot had, however, been compromised sometime earlier by Henry VII's intelligence service and was over before it got off the ground. Mayne was quickly arrested and, after a few days, so too were Frank and Davey. Four men, including Frank, Davy, Mayne and one other were executed for treason on Tower Hill. Swanne and Miles Sally were eventually pardoned, leading one to assume that one or the other was a traitor and, in fact, one of Henry VII's agents. John Sante was also found guilty: he could not be executed because of 'benefit of clergy' so was fined the enormous sum of £1,000, payable in instalments, plus he had all his goods, lands and possessions confiscated. Later released, a chastened Sante remained Abbot of Abingdon until his death in 1496.[11]

What *did* happen to Lovell?

The Sante plot is a codicil to the events of 1487, demonstrating clearly that by the end of 1488 Francis Lovell was no longer alive. Had he still been alive, it is inconceivable that the main participants would have acted as they did. The plot reveals a group of disparate men, now leaderless, yet pursuing the same goals, albeit with no proper direction. The poor planning of the low-level participants, the immediate breaches of security and the lack of foresight point to men following a script but without real focus. Their attempt to free the Earl of Warwick represents the death rattle of Ricardian loyalism and the last faint spasm of Lovell's legacy – one he was no longer around to see.

It is quite clear that Lovell did not participate in Sante's plot and there is no evidence that he ever took advantage of his safe conduct to Scotland or that he was ever present there. The suppositions made by Henry VIII's inquisition post-mortem of 1534/35 that he died at some point abroad are just that. So, ultimately what did happen to Francis Lovell? It is quite likely that his were the remains found by workmen in 1708 at Minster Lovell: 'the entire skeleton of a man as having been sitting at a table, which was before him with a book, paper, pen etc etc'.[12] Minster Lovell is only nineteen miles from Abingdon where the Sante plot reveals that Sante and his officials were free from suspicion and able to operate freely. Sante and his associates demonstrated that Oxfordshire remained a safe haven for Lovell and was, in fact, one of the few areas involved in the Lambert Simnel conspiracy that had not suffered severe proscription and attainders. It is perfectly feasible that, while hidden in a large vault or room underground at his childhood home in Oxfordshire, Francis, Viscount Lovell, was overtaken quietly by death whilst least expecting it. The image relayed in the letter written by William Cowper, Clerk of Parliament, is that of a man of affairs, still in contact with the world, writing at his desk and still engaging with the cause that continued to sustain him. The presence of paper and pen leads one to speculate that it was from here that the safe conduct to Scotland was requested and the reply awaited. The vault or underground room was a temporary refuge, a safe place to hide until the hue and cry had died down. We can have no way of knowing in what guise death finally took Lovell, but the fact that the skeleton was seated at a desk suggests that when the end came it was unexpected and probably non-violent. It is quite conceivable that Lovell could have been recuperating from wounds sustained at Stoke Field. Equally, it is possible that the stress and exertions of the previous three years had finally caught up with him. The loyalty that he inspired in those who knew him in life extended beyond his death when presumably it was his servants who converted his final resting place into his mausoleum, not to be discovered for over 200 years.

The mystery of Lovell's whereabouts puzzled his family and what remained of his loved ones for years afterwards. As late as 1495, neither his wife nor his sisters could offer any information regarding either his whereabouts or his actual demise. By this time, there had been no word on Lovell or his whereabouts for seven years. The boy, Lambert Simnel, had been reduced from a pretender to the throne to a spit-boy in the royal kitchens. Despite this, Henry VII's suspicions fixated on a man who all evidence suggested no longer existed. In 1495, faced with another pretender to his throne under the guise of 'Perkin Warbeck', Henry VII's agents questioned Anne Lovell for the most recent information about her husband. At this point it is clear that Henry still could not shake off the ghostly presence of Lovell. Even so, when Perkin Warbeck emerged as the latest Yorkist pretender in the autumn of 1491, he was not accompanied by Henry's most incorrigible opponent Francis, Viscount Lovell, the last champion of York.

EPILOGUE

Déjà vu: the Perkin Warbeck conspiracy

By 1491 HENRY VII faced another pretender to his throne: this time by the name of Perkin Warbeck, who, it was claimed, was the resurrected younger of the Princes in the Tower (Richard, Duke of York), and whose banners fittingly showed a child emerging from a tomb. Like Lambert Simnel, Warbeck had a Burgundian genesis and followed a road that led to Ireland. In the autumn of 1491, a youth appeared at Cork in Ireland and was 'recognised' as the young prince. Warbeck claimed to remember that, as a child, he had been delivered to a 'certain lord' to be killed; however, divine clemency had preserved his life and he was simply made to swear on the sacrament not to disclose his name, origin or family until a certain number of years had passed. Eventually, the two people who had been enlisted to look after him had died and he then travelled as a young man to Portugal and eventually to Ireland where he was recognized by the earls of Desmond and Kildare.

From Perkin Warbeck's later confession we learn that he had been encouraged to play the role of pretender by two men: John Taylor and John Atwater. John Taylor had been a yeoman in the king's chamber of Edward IV and had been a surveyor of the customs for the western ports of Poole, Exeter, Dartmouth and Plymouth. As a loyal servant of Richard III, he lost all these positions in 1485, being later pardoned in 1489; by 1491 he was living in France. John Atwater was Mayor of Cork in Ireland. Between them, Taylor and Atwater (probably at the behest of France), turned the Flemish boy, Perkin Warbeck, into the younger of the Princes in the Tower. As such, Warbeck was proclaimed king in Ireland in 1491, in emulation of Lambert Simnel's success in 1487 and in hope of gaining support once more of the Geraldine earls of Kildare and Desmond. After attracting only desultory support from either, and failing to capture the port of Waterford, Warbeck retired to France where, for purely French political reasons, Charles VIII recognised him as 'Richard IV'. When Charles signed the Treaty of Etaples with Henry VII, however, Perkin Warbeck was expelled from France, his services no longer required. From France he returned to his homeland – he was originally from Tournai in Burgundy – and arrived at the court of his 'aunt' Margaret of Burgundy, who pronounced herself overjoyed at the blessings of 'divine clemency', which had miraculously restored her nephew to her. At Margaret's court, Warbeck's imposture reached its apogee when her step son-in-law and previous supporter of Lambert Simnel, Archduke Maximillian, took him under his wing. In many ways, Maximillian, a quixotic character, whose plans and schemes always exceeded both his abilities and his resources, was an attractive and romantic figure, and this side of his nature came to the fore in his dealings with Warbeck. The notion of a lost youth returning to claim his rightful inheritance, which had been usurped by another, appealed to the high romantic in him as the rules of chivalry required that he aid the weak and friendless. Also, for the perennially impecunious Maximillian, Warbeck's presence offered a convenient means by which he could extract money from the notoriously rich, though parsimonious, Henry VII. All of these strands came together in 1493 when Warbeck attended the funeral of Emperor Frederick III, Maximillian's father, in Vienna. Not only was Warbeck present at the funeral, but he was recognized as 'Richard the IV, king of England and Duke of York'. He was even present at the Emperor's internment in the Habsburg family vault in the crypt of St Stephen's cathedral.

This European recognition garnered some support in England, most notably in Henry VII's Chamberlain, Sir William Stanley, and Lord Fitzwater, who, along with other conspirators,[1] were soon rounded up, arrested and executed. To galvanize support, in January 1495 Perkin Warbeck landed at Deal on the Kent coast, hoping to be met with a demonstration of pro-Yorkist sentiment and a popular uprising. Instead, Warbeck's small force was met by royal troops and the local militia who saw Warbeck's men as a foreign invasion. Over 150 of Warbeck's force were killed on the beach without Warbeck even disembarking. From here, Perkin Warbeck sailed to his old stomping ground of Ireland where he gained some measure of support from the eternally dissident Maurice Fitzgerald, Earl of Desmond, prompting Henry VII to famously remark 'my Lords of Ireland will crown apes next'.[2] After failing to capture Waterford, which was strongly held against both the earl and Warbeck, Warbeck sailed away to Scotland, where he was welcomed by James IV. James hoped to use the *auld alliance* with France to give him increased international standing and to enable him to wring concessions out of Henry VII, who was negotiating a marriage alliance between his young son, Arthur, Prince of Wales, and Catherine of Aragon, daughter of the Spanish sovereigns Ferdinand and Isabella. Inevitably, James sought to gain what he could at this crucial time and the presence of a pretender to the English throne at his court was a powerful diplomatic weapon. James IV primed that weapon and publicly demonstrated his faith in Perkin Warbeck's legitimacy by marrying him to the Earl of Huntley's third daughter, Lady Catherine Gordon. Lady Catherine brought the prestige of being related to the Scottish royal family, at least by marriage, and the act of allowing such a marriage was a declaration of Warbeck's royal status. James even went so far as to provide Warbeck with the clothing for his wedding and a suit of very expensive tournament armour covered in purple silk. There does seem to have been some genuine affection between James and Warbeck at this time, so much so that James was prepared to support him by invading northern England. Appropriately kitted out, Warbeck accompanied James in launching an attack on Northumberland in September 1486. Their combined forces crossed the river Tweed on 21 September and moved to attack the castle of Heaton on 24 September, having advanced all of four miles. This was the first time Warbeck had set foot on the English soil of which he claimed to be king. Support for him conspicuously failed to materialize, particularly in the north, where the invasion was seen as yet another Scottish incursion. Despite Warbeck's splendid titles and armour, no one in England believed the lie that he was the true king. On 25 September, the Scottish army, running low on supplies, retreated back across the border having achieved very little.

James' confidence in Perkin Warbeck was severely dented by his failure to garner any support in England, and he now wanted to be rid of his one-time protégé, so he hired a ship, appropriately named *The Cuckoo*, to take him and his wife to Ireland. Warbeck, now with two ships and very few supporters, arrived once more at Waterford in July 1497, which again closed its gates to him. Failing to gain any support in Ireland and accompanied by only approximately 120 men, Warbeck now made one final throw of the dice. On 7 September he landed at Whitesand Bay, two miles from Land's End, hoping to capitalize on the still seething unrest of the Cornishmen, who three months earlier had risen in rebellion under Lord Audley to protest against Henry VII's heavy taxation to pay for the defence of the Scottish border. Ironically, it had been Warbeck's presence in Scotland that had required these defensive measures. Whilst Cornwall seethed with discontent, its men had learnt their lesson at Blackheath, where the king's forces had dispersed the rebels, and there was no longer any stomach for any large rising against the king. Nevertheless, promising to end both extortionate taxation and the war against Scotland, Warbeck managed to gather a motley force of 6,000 malcontents from the West Country. Crucially, the knights, gentry and nobility of the Western shires stood aloof from his schemes, leaving only the commonality or those with little to lose, to follow him. Failing to take the city of Exeter, the rebels left it and its garrison behind them and moved on to the unfortified town of Taunton, where the rebels heard that marching towards them was Henry VII's best general, Giles, Baron D'Aubeny. Faced with this news, rebel morale and faith in 'Richard IV' plummeted and men began to desert in droves. Warbeck's nerve broke and, leaving what remained of his men in the dead of night, he headed for the sanctuary of Beaulieu Abbey in Hampshire. Here, with the building surrounded, Warbeck was arrested on 5 October and his English adventure and imposture came to an end after little less than a month. Initially, Warbeck was imprisoned in Taunton at the bishop's prison, then moved to the Tower of London from where he was 'paraded through the streets on horseback amid much hooting and derision of the Citizens'. Interestingly, Warbeck, in the Tower, seems to have formed a friendship with Edward, Earl of Warwick. Initially spared by Henry VII, Warbeck and Warwick were either deceived by Henry's agents into trying to escape or naively trusted those who proposed escape to them. Tragically, in 1499 both young men, neither of whom had ever been fully in control of their own destinies, were executed.

The Warbeck conspiracy provides an instructive comparison with Francis Lovell's later career and allows us to judge him by contemporary standards. It is a sad reflection on fifteenth-century historiography that Lambert Simnel and Perkin Warbeck are viewed together almost as a singular phenomenon. Whilst there is a perceived similarity in the names, both sharing a Burgundian origin, which would have sounded strange to English ears, there are very few real similarities between these two failed Tudor pretenders. Important differences exist that demonstrate how much more effective and far more dangerous to Henry VII the Simnel revolt was. Perkin Warbeck was the creation of two disaffected Yorkist functionaries; it was adopted by the government of France for its own ends and was to achieve its greatest success among the courts of Europe rather than in England itself. Perkin Warbeck was a parasite on international politics during the 1490s where he thrived as an illusion, a chimera. Whilst espoused and recognized by foreign monarchs, it was only for as long as expediency allowed. During his whole career as an imposter, Perkin Warbeck spent a total of only thirty-three days on English soil: he was a foreign creation that crumbled ignominiously when he came into contact with the realities of English politics.

The revolt of Lambert Simnel and the whole episode of his invasion, on the other hand, had been born out of the realities of English politics rather than being created from beyond the realm. Lambert Simnel was a product of the post-Bosworth world, a world of misplaced men that, for many, had been turned upside-down, just as it had been for Francis Lovell. The supporters of Richard III and those who later supported Simnel were, in the main, Ricardians, not Yorkists. They saw Henry VII's victory and claim to kingship as aberrations they were determined to reverse. Initially unable to raise popular revolts based on deposing or killing Henry VII (although they came remarkably close), they recognized the need to give men a figurehead to rally around. In this, Lovell and his supporters, by creating Lambert Simnel as 'Edward, Earl of Warwick', were the true inheritors of the legacy of Warwick 'the Kingmaker', taking a lesson from the Yorkist policy of 1460 when Warwick determined to raise Edward IV up in competition with the Lancastrian king, Henry VI. In this they were remarkably successful, for they had not only tapped into a broad stream of English disaffection with the first Tudor, but also into the latent loyalty that the House of York and the Nevills still retained. Initially, it was Francis Lovell's personality and credibility that secured two extremely important things: firstly, the adherence and recognition of foreign backers at the highest level prepared to invest in both him and his proposal; secondly, the use of personality and friendship to embroil a genuine Yorkist prince in John, Earl of Lincoln, in the plot. For both of these elements Lovell's previous standing had been crucial.

Equally impressive was the soaring ambition of the man. As befitted someone who had grown up in Warwick's household, Lovell was nothing if not supremely audacious, as witnessed by the unique act of crowning the pretender in Dublin cathedral with a full rights of the Church. Such an act would ensure that when they invaded England, they did so with a duly consecrated king whose very presence was meant to confuse men's consciences and loyalties. Lovell and Lincoln, despite Schwartz's subsequent complaint, were able to mobilize effective support throughout their marching route. It is true that not as many joined them as they would have liked, but their march was never impeded and cities such as York found it expedient to deal with the rebels. They were able to continually wrong-foot royal forces and to cause genuine concern in the minds of Henry VII and his councillors and commanders. Such was Henry's unease that even before the revolt had materialized, he had decamped to Kenilworth and was so preoccupied with the plot that all other concerns were driven from his mind. So preoccupied was he that when he was forced to cancel the garter ceremony on 23 April 1487, Henry embarrassingly failed to notify the Duke of Suffolk and Lord Maltravers, who only became aware of this when they arrived at St George's chapel in Windsor to be informed that the celebrations had been postponed. Henry VII was genuinely fearful of the rebel juggernaut as it thundered down from the north since no one seemed able to (or, indeed, wished to) stop it. Henry also knew that the further south the rebels came and the closer they came to their own recruiting grounds, the more imperative it was militarily and politically for him to give battle; to trust again, as he did at Bosworth, to the force of arms.

At Stoke Field the rebels and their experienced commanders seized the initiative and held it for over two hours, despite losing one of their most prominent leaders with the early death of the Earl of Lincoln. Indeed, it is worth emphasizing the difference in commitment shown by the Ricardian forces engaged at Bosworth and those at Stoke Field. Despite Lincoln's death during the battle, the fight continued as men traded blows for three to four hours – almost three times longer than the battle of Bosworth. It was a long and blood-soaked morning until the king's division arrived and the rebel force finally buckled, broke and fled. At Stoke Field men fought until defeat was inevitable and showed none of the indifference and duplicity that had characterized Richard III's army. The rebel army also demonstrated a confidence in their commanders that was absent from Richard III's army in August 1485. Never again was Henry VII's throne to be so seriously threatened, nor would Henry have to face a rebellion from amongst his own subjects. The battle of Stoke Field was the culmination of a political crisis that had begun in 1483 and did not end until 1487. Stoke Field marked the end of an organized Ricardian opposition within England. No rebellion on anything approaching the same scale would ever occur again, and never again would dynastic change appear so close. The Ricardian *revanche* died at Stoke Field, and with it the chance to recover what had been lost at Bosworth.

Those who had been committed to challenging Henry VII's rule and who had questioned his legitimacy were the previous supporters of Richard III; they were not necessarily Yorkists whose natural allegiances had brought them to the House of York; they did not automatically accept Henry VII's marriage to Elizabeth of York, or recognize Prince Arthur as Edward IV's grandson. It was those who recognized the claim of Titulus Regius who rose with Francis Lovell and the Earl of Lincoln. Stoke Field was a devastating defeat, and it marked the true end of Ricardian England. This differentiates Lambert Simnel from Perkin Warbeck for when Perkin, the 'dreadful dead man',[3] landed in England to seek support, all that was left were the ghosts of those who had died and been proscribed or attainted ten years earlier.

Having been born into a time of turbulence and increasingly deadly feuds and aristocratic violence, Francis Lovell had absorbed its lessons. From childhood, he was brought up in the bosom of the wider Yorkist family, which had given him an attachment he never lost. Through that family he came to meet and to share the ambition and confidence of the man who would be his lifelong friend – a man whom he would stand by for the rest of his life. We cannot know what Lovell thought of the actions that brought Richard III to the throne or whether he had any moral qualms about that king's apparent lack of scruples. What we can recognize is that once the decision had been made, he stood by it and its consequences through thick and thin, demonstrating an exemplary loyalty and tenacity.

After Richard's death, Lovell exhibited a remarkable resourcefulness as he strove to restore what he believed to be a true sovereign and to exact revenge on the man he regarded as a regicide. In his plans and their execution he showed himself to be an adept politician, able to hold and to inspire men's loyalties and devotions. He also stood out as a man with organizational and political abilities that few had suspected previously. He was able, not just to forge a coalition among the disaffected and malcontents, but to mould a number of different components into a highly effective international conspiracy, embracing elements from England, Ireland and Burgundy, and to forge these elements into a cohesive and dangerous opposition to Tudor rule while it was in its infancy. For his loyalty, devotion and resource, Lovell deserves to be better remembered. By being dazzled by the outsized personalities of the great Tudor sovereigns, we are in danger of being blinded to the causes and achievements of their opponents.

It is of Francis Lovell, rather than Richard III, that we can truly say 'loyaltee me lie' – loyalty binds me.

APPENDIX I

The estates of Francis, Viscount Lovell, in 1485

Berkshire
Ufton Pole
Buckland
Denford

Buckinghamshire
Broughton Lovell
Woburn

Cheshire
Longdale
Twintwistle
Nottram
Nantwich (1/6)
St Lawrence Chapel
Monkescropenhall
Aldford
Eccles
Alderly

Derbyshire
Elmston
Holmesfield Dronfield

Essex
Boreham
Walkfare
Power
Sheepcote

Leicestershire
Shepshed
Laughton
Whitwick
Kirby Bellair

Lincolnshire
Blankney
Braunceston
Potter Hanworth

Northamptonshire
Titchmarsh, incl.:
• Polebrook
• Alderwyncle
• Ashton
• Warmington
Tannesover
Halse and Brackley
Duston
Chelveston cum Caldicott
Thorpe Achurch
Thorpe Waterville
Walgrave
Duddington
Sutton
Pitsford

Nottinghamshire
Granby
Sutton
St Leonard's Hospital

Oxfordshire
Ducklington
Brize Norton
Cogges
Minster Lovell
Rotherfield Grey
Somerton
Kincott
Fringford
Stonor
Lillingstone Lovel
Rutland
Ridington

Shropshire
Acton Burnell
Holegate
Longden
Woolstasten
Smethcott
Abdon
Millichope
Uppington
Acton Reynard
Sutton
Hope Bowdler
Wotton
Coreston
Eudon Burnell
Cantlop
Golding
Frodesley

Ramshurt
Rushbury
East Wall
West Wall
Wall sub Haywood
Coates
Wilderhope
Condover
Ambaston
Chatwall

Staffordshire
Yoxall

Suffolk
Donnington
Brundish
Cretingham
Clopton Hall
Ilkytteshall

Warwickshire
Arley Church
Emescot
Seckington
Wolvey
Halford
Broome

Wiltshire
Elcombe
Ufcote
Mannington
Wanborough

Worcestershire
Upton Snodsbury
Wick Burnell
Brighthampton
Boughton
Pepulton
Pershore

Yorkshire
Stillingfleet
Dringhame
Upton
Brain Askham
Killerby
Wold Newton
Bainton
Bedale
Ascove
Leaming
Moreby
Naburn
Carlton
Bradley
Utley
Lodiesdane
Linton Church

APPENDIX II

The Lovell Family Tree

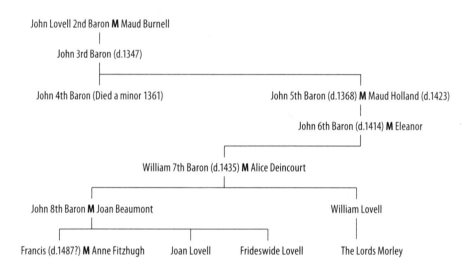

John Lovell 2nd Baron **M** Maud Burnell

John 3rd Baron (d.1347)

John 4th Baron (Died a minor 1361)

John 5th Baron (d.1368) **M** Maud Holland (d.1423)

John 6th Baron (d.1414) **M** Eleanor

William 7th Baron (d.1435) **M** Alice Deincourt

John 8th Baron **M** Joan Beaumont

William Lovell

Francis (d.1487?) **M** Anne Fitzhugh   Joan Lovell   Frideswide Lovell

The Lords Morley

The Fitzhugh Family Tree

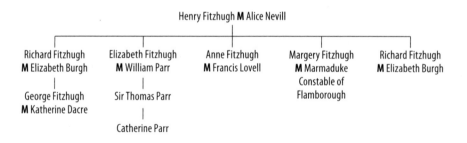

Henry Fitzhugh **M** Alice Nevill

Richard Fitzhugh **M** Elizabeth Burgh

George Fitzhugh **M** Katherine Dacre

Elizabeth Fitzhugh **M** William Parr

Sir Thomas Parr

Catherine Parr

Anne Fitzhugh **M** Francis Lovell

Margery Fitzhugh **M** Marmaduke Constable of Flamborough

Richard Fitzhugh **M** Elizabeth Burgh

The Yorkist Royal Family

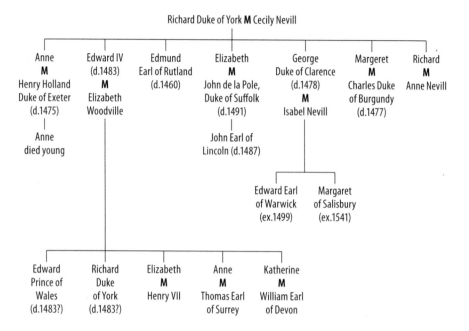

NOTES

Chapter 1 – The Ghost

1. Ross, C., *Richard III* (Yale University Press, 1992), p.50.
2. Lander, J. R., *The Wars of the Roses* (Sutton, 1992), p.188. Quoted from the Great Chronicle of London 1484.
3. Baldwin, D., *The Kingmaker's Sisters: Six Powerful Women in the Wars of the Roses* (The History Press, 2009), p.119
4. Ross, *Richard III*, p.50.

Chapter 2 – Family, Youth and Wardship

1. His full title was the 8th Baron Lovell of Titchmarsh and Baron Holland, Deincourt and Grey of Rotherfield. In his time, he was the richest baron in England below the rank of earl, with an income of over £1,000 per annum and substantial estates in Oxfordshire, Northamptonshire, Berkshire and Shropshire.
2. Pollard, A.J., *Warwick the Kingmaker: Politics, Power and Fame* (Hambledon, 2007), p.167. See also Hicks, M., *Warwick the Kingmaker* (Boydell, 1998), Ch. 3.
3. Pollard, *Warwick the Kingmaker*, p.168.
4. Baldwin, D., *The Kingmaker's Sisters: Six Powerful Women in the Wars of the Roses* (The History Press, 2009), p.63.
5. Pollard, *Warwick the Kingmaker*, p.11.
6. Hicks, *Warwick the Kingmaker*, p.34.

Chapter 3 – The Bosom of York: The de la Pole Connection

1. Ross, C., *Edward IV* (Yale University Press, 1991), p.221.
2. Pierrepont-Barnard, F. (ed.), *Edward IV's French Expedition of 1475: The Leaders and their Badges, being MS2.M16* (Clarendon Press, 1952; re-issued Gloucester Reprints, 1991), Folio IV.
3. Ross, *Edward IV*, p.221.
4. *CPR*, p.468.
5. Ross, *Edward IV*, p.232, quoting from Commynes, P., *The Memoirs for the Reign of Louis XI, 1461–1483*, Jones, M. (trans.) (Penguin, 1972).
6. Between February 1474 and February 1477, five grants were made by the king concerning Lovell property and benefices, all of them on the periphery of the estates. Three of the grants were benefices or exchange of benefices and covered properties in Nottinghamshire and Worcester, principally concerning the hospital of St Leonard Stoke. Other grants suggest a maintenance of existing arrangements such as that governing the stewardship of the key Lovell lordship of Titchmarsh, in Northamptonshire, where Ralph Hastings, knight of the body, remained as steward even after the death of Alesia, Lady Lovell. The intact nature of the inheritance must have become an increasing point of interest for Francis Lovell as he neared his maturity.
7. On 8 November 1477 at Westminster. 'License for Francis Lovell, son and heir of John Lovell knight and Joan his wife and kinsman and Alesia, late the wife of Ralph Boteller, knight and sometime wife of William Lovell to enter freely into all castles, lordships, manors, lands ...'
8. Ross, *Edward IV*, p.197.
9. *Ibid*, pp.336–337.
10. *The Calendar of Patent Rolls, Edward IV–Richard III*, p. 463.

Chapter 4 – 'The Whirling Times'

1. Hicks, M., *False, Fleeting, Perjur'd Clarence* (Headstart History, 1992), p.133.
2. Dockray, K., *Richard* III: *A Sourcebook* (Sutton, 1997), p.26, quoting from Dominic Mancini.
3. *Ibid*, p.27.
4. Hicks, M., *False, Fleeting, Perjur'd Clarence*, pp.122–6
5. *Ibid*, p.154.
6. Dockray, *Richard III*, p.28, quoting from the Great Chronicle of London. A similar story can be found in Commynes, P., *The Memoirs for the Reign of Louis XI, 1461–1483*, Jones, M. (trans.) (Penguin, 1972). An interesting aspect to this famous story is that the only surviving portrait of Clarence's daughter, Margaret Pole, Countess of Salisbury, shows her with a barrel motif clearly hanging from her bracelet.
7. *Ibid*, p.28, quoting Polydore Vergil.
8. William Herbert II had enjoyed his father's estates and offices in Wales and his title of Earl of Pembroke since 1471. In 1466, he had been married to the queen's youngest sister, Mary. Upon her death in 1478, Herbert was forced to exchange both his title and his family estates for the earldom of Huntingdon and assorted lands in Somerset and Suffolk, and his previous estates, including the lordship of Pembroke, were merged with the Principality of Wales.
9. Ross, C., *Edward IV* (Yale University Press, 1991), Ch. 10. These manipulations affected Edward's relationship with the nobility between 1478 and 1481 and demonstrated Edward's extremely narrow understanding of the role of royal patronage in supporting his kingship.

Chapter 5 – A Man and His Estate

1. Ross, C., *Edward IV* (Yale University Press, 1991), p.278.
2. Louis XI was engaged in a long campaign in the Low Countries against Mary of Burgundy and her husband, Archduke Maximillian, to wrest from them as much Burgundian territory as possible. The Burgundian inheritance had fallen to Mary after the death of her father, Charles the Bold, at the battle of Nancy in January 1477. Ever since, Louis had been trying to win for France as much territory as possible, especially in Flanders and the Duchy of Burgundy. Faced with continual French assaults, Mary had appealed to Edward for assistance.
3. Ross, *Edward IV*, p.280. In addition, Edward purchased 80 butts of sweet malmsey wine for use of the king and his army against the Scots.
4. Ross, *Edward IV*, p.282.
5. Ross, C., *Richard III* (Yale University Press, 1992), p.45. Richard appointed 20 knights bannerets and the Earl of Northumberland, 18. Most were northerners apart from Sir Edward Woodville, Sir Walter Herbert, Sir John Ebrington and Richard's senior henchman, Sir James Tyrrell.
6. Dockray, K., *Richard III: A Sourcebook* (Sutton, 1997), p.37. This is based on a royal proclamation issued on 12 June 1482: 'We therefore trusting with full powers our illustrious brother Duke of Gloucester, in whom, not only for his nearness and fidelity of relationship, but for his proved skill in military matters and his other virtues, we name depute and ordain him our lieutenant General.'
7. *Ibid*, pp.37–8.
8. *Ibid*, p.39, quoting the Crowland Chronicle.
9. A palatine was an area in which the royal writ of the king did not run. The Lord Palatine exercised all civil and judicial functions on behalf of the king. The creation of a palatine was an extremely rare occurrence, the last being the Palatine of Lancaster created by Edward III for his son, John of Gaunt.

Chapter 6 – The Turning Point

1. Ross, C., *Edward IV* (Yale University Press, 1991), p.414.
2. Ross, C., *Richard III* (Yale University Press, 1992), p.68, quoting Mancini.
3. Pontefract Castle was a grim northern fortress belonging to the duchy of Lancaster. The castle had enjoyed a baleful reputation since 1399, when it had been the prison in which Richard II had been starved to death.
4. Ross, *Richard III*, p.72, quoting Mancini.
5. Hicks, M., *Richard III* (Sutton, 2000), p.109, quoting from the Crowland Chronicle.

6.   *Ibid,* p.109, quoting Mancini.
7.   *Ibid,* p.112.
8.   *Ibid,* p.125.
9.   Dockray, K., *Richard III: A Sourcebook* (Sutton, 1997), p.53, quoting the great Chronicle of London.
10. Edward IV himself had removed the Lancastrian Earl of Devon, the brother of the Lancastrian Duke of Somerset and others he regarded as traitors and had had them beheaded outside the abbey regardless of the protestations of the abbot.
11. Dockray, *Richard III*, p.57.
12. *Ibid,* p.64, quoting Polydore Vergil.
13. *Ibid,* p.63, quoting from the Great Chronicle of London.

Chapter 7 – The Massacre of the Innocents#
1.   Dockray, K., *Richard III: A Sourcebook* (Sutton, 1997), p.77, quoting Dominic Mancini.
2.   *Ibid,* p.80. For Dockray quoting Polydore Vergil, see pp.187–90.
3.   *Ibid,* p.80.

Chapter 8 – Ricardus Rex
1.   Crosland, M., *The Mysterious Mistress: The Life and Legend of Jane Shore,* (Sutton, 2006). Sir Thomas More wrote of how Shore overcame public shame by walking '… in countenance and pace so womanly, and albeit she were out of all array save her kirtle only yet when she so fair and lovely … that her great shame won her much praise amongst those that were more amorous of her body than curious of her soul.'
2.   See Ross, *Edward IV*. Ross takes an ambivalent attitude towards John de la Pole in his chapter on Edward's second reign: Ross is of the opinion that Edward IV did not think highly of his brother-in-law's abilities, based on the king's failure to include him in the privy council; yet Ross also makes the point in a later chapter that complaints from the East Anglian gentry regarding the conduct of Suffolk's officers could not be addressed since Suffolk was too powerful to offend.
3.   *CPR* Edward IV /Richard III, p.365.
4.   Hicks, M., *Richard III* (Sutton, 2000), p.149, quoting John Kendall.
5.   *Ibid,* pp.114–15, quoting a letter of 12 October 1483 to his Chancellor, John Russell, Bishop of Lincoln, regarding the rebellion of Henry Stafford, Duke of Buckingham.

Chapter 9 – 'And the Weald is up'
1.   Hicks, M., *Richard III* (Sutton, 2000), p.157.
2.   Gill, L., *Richard III and Buckingham's Rebellion* (Sutton, 1999), p.75.
3.   *Ibid,* pp.75–8.
4.   *Ibid,* p.72.
5.   Hicks, *Richard III*, p.160
6.   *CPR,* Edward IV, p.371.
7.   Hicks, *Richard III*, p.153.

Chapter 10 – 'Great about the king'
1.   Gill, L., *Richard III and Buckingham's Rebellion* (Sutton, 1999), p.95.
2.   *Ibid,* p.96.
3.   *Ibid.*
4.   Dockray, K., *Richard III: A Sourcebook* (Sutton, 1997).
5.   *CPR,* Edward IV .
6.   *Ibid.*
7.   *Ibid.*
8.   *Titulus Regis, Rotulli Parliamentorum,* Volume VI.
9.   Crowland writes in retrospect and its opinion of the Parliament of 1484 is influenced by the fact that Titulus Regis was repealed by Henry VII and copies of the Act were hunted down and destroyed. We are lucky that the one remaining copy was discovered and preserved by the historian George Buck in the seventeenth century.

10. Higginbottom, S., *The Woodvilles: The Wars of the Roses and England's Most Infamous Family* (History Press, 2015), p.146.
11. Ross, C., *Richard III* (Yale University Press, 1992), pp.158–161.
12. Dockray, K., *Richard III: A Sourcebook* (Sutton, 1997), p.113, quoting Polydore Vergil.
13. *Ibid.*

Chapter 11 – 'Twice bastardized Richmond'

1. Hicks, M., *Richard III* (Sutton, 2000), p.38.
2. Dockray, K., *Richard III: A Sourcebook* (Sutton, 1997), p.98, quoting the Crowland Chronicle.
3. Weightman, C., *Margaret of York, Duchess of Burgundy 1446–1503* (Sutton, 1993), p.145.
4. Hicks, *Richard III*, p.173.
5. *Ibid*, p.175.
6. *Ibid*, p.175.
7. Hicks, *Richard III*, p.39.
8. Ross, C., *Richard III* (Yale University Press, 1992), p.139.
9. *Ibid*, p.141.
10. *Ibid*, p.142.
11. Skidmore, C., *Bosworth* (Weidenfield and Nicholson, 2015), p.179.
12. *CPR*, p.547.
13. Skidmore, *Bosworth*, p.181. Skidmore offers evidence of Tyrrell as Richard's Master of the Horse making offerings at Vannes Cathedral as 'le Grande escuire d'Engleterre'.
14. *Ibid*, p.182.
15. *Ibid*, p.181.
16. Ibid, p.182.
17. *Ibid*, p.191.
18. It would appear that they were married in secret sometime between 1429 and 1431 at Westminster. No contemporary source alludes to any irregularity in the marriage other than incredulity that it took place at all.
19. Skidmore, *Bosworth*, p.191. These were Peter Courtenay, Bishop of Exeter, John, Earl of Oxford, Sir Edward Woodville and Jasper Tudor.
20. *Ibid*, p.191.

Chapter 12 – The Road to Bosworth

1. Dockray, K., *Richard III: A Sourcebook* (Sutton, 1997), p.81, quoting Polydore Vergil.
2. *Ibid.*
3. *CPR*, 13 December 1483, p.374. Geoffrey Frank was the brother of Edward Frank of Knighton, Yorkshire, who served with Lovell as Sheriff of Oxfordshire and who was one of Lovell's closest associates.
4. *Ibid.* An agent of both Lovell and the king, Richard Rugge received an annuity of £10 from the manor of Walsall and a further 20 marks from the earldom of Warwick.
5. *CPR*, p.379.
6. *Ibid.* Morgan had already been substantially rewarded with estates in Dorset and this would have reinforced his area of local control.
7. Skidmore, C., *Bosworth* (Weidenfield and Nicholson, 2015), p.175.
8. *Ibid.*
9. *Ibid.*
10. Skidmore, *Bosworth*, p.175, quoting from the great Chronicle of London.
11. *CPR*, 29 November 1484, p.519.
12. The principal centre of the de Vere family was Hedingham Castle in the far north of Essex.
13. *CPR*, p.478. 'Grant to ther kings councillor Francis lord Lovell the following annuities from Michaelmass last from the issues of Cokingham and Bray, co. Berks £10 for seven years, £40 during the life of Margaret Harcourt, late wife of Robert Harcourt knight and £24 during the life of Anne, sometime the wife of John Stonor Esquire.'
14. *CPR, p.478*, 13 August 1384, Westminster.
15. Dockray, *Richard III*, p.108.

16. *Ibid*, p.116, quoting from Pollard. For the north of England in the reign of Richard III, see p.131. Pollard places this decision to 18 February 1484.

17. *Ibid.*

18. Skidmore, *Bosworth*, p.188. Charles VII referred to Henry Tudor as 'Fils de Jeu, Roi Henri d'Engleterre'.

19. *Ibid*, p.189.

20. *CPR*, pp.489–91.

21. Skidmore, *Bosworth*, p.193.

22. Hicks, M., *Richard III* (Sutton, 2000), p.179. The similarity in dress between a queen and anyone was shocking in an age where hierarchy was advertised by appearance. That a queen and an illegitimate girl should even appear to be closely dressed was an affront to a society in which rank defined all.

23. *Ibid.*

24. Skidmore, *Bosworth*, p.199.

25. *Ibid*, p.200.

26. Dockray, *Richard III*, p.99, quoting the Crowland Chronicle.

27. *Ibid*, p.99.

28. *Ibid.*

29. Skidmore, *Bosworth*, pp.201–2.

30. Sir Edward Brampton had already had a remarkable career in England up until 1483. He was to have an even more remarkable career after Bosworth, a battle he missed: in the period 1490–96 when he was one of the main originators and supporters of Perkin Warbeck and his conspiracy.

31. Skidmore, *Bosworth*, p.203.

Chapter 13 – Bosworth

1. Philip de Crevcouer (1418–94) was the Seignouer de Esquerdes. He had a distinguished military career, initially under Charles the Bold and later under Louis XI and Charles VIII. He was governor of Trois and Picardy from 1486 capturing Artois and Arras for France. He negotiated the Treaty of Etaples in 1492 with Henry VII.

2. Ross, C., *Richard III* (Yale University Press, 1992), p.201.

3. Skidmore, C., *Bosworth* (Weidenfield and Nicholson, 2015), p.227. This would appear to be a case of culpable denial by the French government. If Henry's enterprise succeeded, then the enterprise would be deemed a success. If, on the other hand, it failed, it could be attributed to an English adventurer, backed by foreign soldiers or those who were the lowest in society, led by a Savoyard who was not a subject of the king of France. Philibert de Chaundee would remain in Henry's service and after Bosworth was created Earl of Bath.

4. Harleian manuscript. Volume 3 p128

5. *Ibid*, p.129. It would appear that the government transferred responsibility for both assessment and collection onto the shoulders of the local commissioners who, it was felt, best knew the amount that could be most advantageously prised from local landholders and notables.

6. *Ibid*, p.136.

7. The Vaughans had been present at the execution of Jasper's father, Owain Tudor, after the battle of Mortimer's Cross in February 1461. In revenge, Jasper had beheaded Sir Roger Vaughan at Chepstow during his retreat to West Wales after the Lancastrian defeat at Tewkesbury in 1471.

8. Ross, *Richard III*, p.205.

9. Christchurch, Poole and Weymouth all had long associations with the Beauforts and the Lancastrians. It was at Weymouth that Margaret of Anjou had landed in 1471 and Margaret Beaufort's father, John, Duke of Somerset, was buried with his wife at nearby Wimborne Minster.

10. CPR, 25 May 1484 at Westminster, p.544.

11. Dockray, K., *Richard III: A Sourcebook* (Sutton, 1997), p.120.

12. *Ibid.*

13. Skidmore, *Bosworth*, p.231.

14. *Ibid.*

15. Bennett, M., *The Battle of Bosworth* (Palgrave Macmillan, 1985), p. 88. Richard Williams assumed that Henry's fleet was heading for landfall at Angle, on the south side of the estuary, and so stayed put.

16. Bennett, *The Battle of Bosworth*, p.89.

17. *Ibid*, p.171. See Appendix B for the poem (anon.), commissioned by the Stanley family, which is one of the earliest contemporary pieces of work to record events at Bosworth. It clearly and accurately identifies Richard's household knights as: Ralph Harbottle, Henry Horsey, Henry Percy, Thomas Mackenfield, John Grey, Thomas Montgomery, Robert Brackenbury, Richard Charlton, Christopher Ward, Robert Plumpton, William Gasgoyne, Marmaduke Constable, Martin of the Sea, John Melton, Gervais Clifton, and a further nineteen others.

18. Skidmore, *Bosworth*, p.259, detailing Mitton's rewards from Richard.

19. Bennett, *The Battle of Bosworth*, p. 156, quoting *Rotuli Parliamentorum*. All are named in the Act of Attainder of Autumn 1485.

20. *Ibid*, p.112.

21. Dockray, *Richard III*, p.122.

22. Skidmore, *Bosworth*, p.278.

23. *Ibid*.

24. Skidmore, *Bosworth*, p.285.

25. *Ibid*, p.301, quoting Polydore Vergil.

26. Bennett, *The Battle of Bosworth*, p.114.

27. From The Ballad of the Lady Bessie (anon.), quoted in Bennett, *The Battle of Bosworth*.

28. Skidmore, *Bosworth*, p.305, quoting a contemporary French archer.

29. Knocked to the ground, Cheyney was lucky not to be trampled on in the ensuing melee. However, despite being severely wounded, he managed to survive the battle.

30. Skidmore, *Bosworth*, p.309.

31. *Ibid*; see also Bennett, *The Battle of Bosworth*, p.117, and Griffiths, R.S. and Thomas, R.S., *The Making of the Tudor Dynasty* (Sutton, 1993), p.165.

32. Skidmore, *Bosworth*, p.310.

Chapter 14 – 'Loyaltee me Lie'

1. Vergil, P., *Three Books of Polydore Vergil's English History: Comprising the Reigns of Henry VI, Edward IV and Richard III*, (ed.) Ellis, H. (Camden Society, 1844), p225

2. Baldwin, D., *The Battle of Stoke Field: The Last Battle of the Wars of the Roses* (Pen & Sword, 2006), p.15.

3. *Ibid*, p.15

4. Baldwin, *The Battle of Stoke Field*, p.48.

5. *Transactions of the Leicestershire Archaeological and Historical Society*, 1975–6, p.48. 'And my Lord Lovell shall come to grace greater than ye show to him that he may pray for me'.

6. Jasper Tudor married Catherine Woodville, the widow of Henry Stafford, Duke of Buckingham. Catherine brought with her a dowry of the Buckingham lordships of Brecon and Hay. This award ended the ability of William Herbert, Earl of Huntingdon, to obtain an annuity of £400 from these estates, which he had been granted by Richard III in 1483 when he had married Richard's illegitimate daughter, Lady Katherine.

7. Bennett, M.J., *Lambert Simnel and the Battle of Stoke* (Palgrave Macmillan, 1987), p.35.

Chapter 15 – The Assassin

1. The creation of Jasper as Duke of Bedford was a pointed return to previous Lancastrian policy, invoking a title whose last adult holder had been Henry V's brother, John, who had died in 1435. The resurrection of this title for Jasper ensured a continuity of Lancastrian legitimacy.

2. Bennett, M.J., *Lambert Simnel and the Battle of Stoke* (Palgrave Macmillan, 1987), pp.29–41.

3. *Ibid*, p.36.

4. *Ibid*. These knights were Sir Thomas Maleverer, Sir Thomas Plumpton, Sir William Gasgoyne, Sir Robert Uchtred and Martin of the Sea.

5. Baldwin, D., *The Battle of Stoke Field: The Last Battle of the Wars of the Roses* (Pen & Sword, 2006), p.15.

6. Bennett, *Lambert Simnel and the Battle of Stoke*, p.37.

7. *Ibid*, p.38.

8. Lord Clifford's father, John, Lord Clifford (known to Shakespeare as 'Butcher' Clifford – *3 Henry*

VI) had been killed in a skirmish with Warwick on the eve of the battle of Towton and subsequently had been attainted. His northern Yorkist rivals such as the Scropes and Lord Fitzhugh, along with Warwick and Richard III, had enjoyed his estates while one local legend claimed that he had been forced to live as a lowly shepherd on the Cumbrian Fells since 1475.

9. Seward, D., *The Last White Rose: The Secret Wars of the Tudors*, (Constable, 2010), quoting *The Annals of the House of Percy*, p.16. There was some suspicion regarding the motivation of Henry Percy, Earl of Northumberland. It has been suggested that Percy wished to marry his daughter to Edward, Earl of Warwick, with whom he had become familiar when Warwick resided at Sheriff Hutton, and make his daughter queen. This seems part of the generally ambivalent behaviour of Northumberland from the battle of Bosworth until his death in 1489.
10. *Ibid*, p.16, quoting Francis Bacon.
11. Griffiths, R.A., *Sir Rhys ap Thomas and his Family* (University of Wales Press, 2014), p.47. The wages of the garrison for this period were £48, with ten shillings being spent on gunpowder to defend the castle.
12. Sir Humphrey had been attainted with Lovell in Henry VII's first parliament in December 1485. At Worcester, however, he flourished a forged royal commission in which he stated that he had been pardoned and was raising troops on the king's behalf. When sufficient men had been raised, he revealed his true intent – a ruse he had probably learned from Warwick in his revolt of 1469.
13. Pierce, H., *Margaret Pole, Countess of Salisbury* (Dinefwr Press, 2009), p.9. In a letter to the Mayor of York, on 13 May 1485 the name of Edward, Earl of Warwick, takes precedence over that of John, Earl of Lincoln.
14. Seward, *The Last White Rose*, p.20. Sir Richard Burdett, a neighbour, was later charged with aiding and abetting their escape.
15. *Ibid*, p.22. Lovell is not named since he had already been attainted in Henry VII's first parliament in October 1485 and further punishment was legally unnecessary.
16. Baldwin, *The Battle of Stoke Field*, p.17, quoting the *Paston Letters*.

Chapter 16 – A Lad named John
1. *The Herald's Memoir, 1486–1490*, (ed.) Cavell, E. (Richard III and the Yorkist History Trust, 2009), p.117
2. The author of *Lambert Simnel and the Battle of Stoke* (Palgrave Macmillan, 1987).
3. *Ibid*, p.47.
4. *Ibid*, p.43.
5. *Ibid*, p.42.
6. *Ibid*, p.50.
7. Seward, D., *The Last White Rose: The Secret Wars of the Tudors*, (Constable, 2010), p.23.
8. Bennett, M.J., *Lambert Simnel and the Battle of Stoke* (Palgrave Macmillan, 1987), p.43.
9. Baldwin, D., *The Battle of Stoke Field: The Last Battle of the Wars of the Roses* (Pen & Sword, 2006), p.17.

Chapter 17 – The Diabolical Duchess
1. Louis XI in 1477 exercised his right as overlord of France to re-occupy the county of Artois and the duchy of Burgundy. Since both provinces had originally been awarded as appanages to French princes of the blood, they were governed by Salic law, which meant that they could be inherited only along the male line. Charles, leaving a female heir, gave Louis the excuse he needed and the opportunity to launch his armies into both territories.
2. Weightman, C., *Margaret of York, Duchess of Burgundy 1446–1503* (Sutton 1993), p.148.
3. For the Perkin Warbeck Conspiracy (1491–97), see Epilogue.
4. Weightman, *Margaret of York*, p.158.
5. Weightman, *Margaret of York*, p.159.
6. Sir Edward Brampton would figure prominently in the Perkin Warbeck conspiracies of the following decade, being instrumental in transforming Warbeck into the imprisoned Richard, Duke of York.
7. Bennett, M.J., *Lambert Simnel and the Battle of Stoke* (Palgrave Macmillan, 1987), p.61.
8. Seward, D., *The Last White Rose: The Secret Wars of the Tudors*, (Constable, 2010), p.28.

9. *Ibid*, p.28.
10. Bennett, *Lambert Simnel and the Battle of Stoke*, p.54.
11. *Ibid*, p.53.

Chapter 18 – The Archduke and the Shoemaker of Augsburg

1. Baldwin, D., *The Battle of Stoke Field: The Last Battle of the Wars of the Roses* (Pen & Sword, 2006), p.114.
2. There are similarities here with Sante's agent departing with gold and silver to the continent on 1 Jan 1487, indicating that the conspirators were able to finance their supporters and move large sums of money around the country without being intercepted by Henry VII's intelligencers.
3. Bennett, M.J., *Lambert Simnel and the Battle of Stoke* (Palgrave Macmillan, 1987), p.55.
4. Allerton at that time was part of the palatine bishopric of Durham and under the jurisdiction of its bishop, not the county administration of Yorkshire.
5. Bennett, *Lambert Simnel and the Battle of Stoke*, p.61.
6. Ashton-Hill, J., *The Dublin King: The True Story of Edward, Earl of Warwick* (History Press, 2015), p.134.
7. *Ibid*, p.134.
8. *Ibid*, p.135. A cathedra was the throne of a bishop.
9. *Ibid*, p.135.
10. Baldwin, *The Battle of Stoke Field*, p.131. For a detailed account of Simnel's coinage and a fuller explanation, see Ashton-Hill, *The Dublin King*, pp.136–43.
11. Bennett, *Lambert Simnel and the Battle of Stoke*, p.67.
12. Elizabeth Parr was the grandmother of Henry VIII's last wife, Catherine Parr.
13. Baldwin, *The Battle of Stoke Field*, p.47, quoting extensively from Professor Mackie's study of the Paston Letters.
14. *Ibid*.
15. *Ibid*.
16. *Ibid*, p.42.
17. Weightman, C., *Margaret of York, Duchess of Burgundy 1446–1503* (Sutton, 1993), p.160, quoting from the Great Chronicle of London.

Chapter 19 – Stoke Field

1. Bennett, M.J., *Lambert Simnel and the Battle of Stoke* (Palgrave Macmillan, 1987), p.91.
2. Baldwin, D., *The Battle of Stoke Field: The Last Battle of the Wars of the Roses* (Pen & Sword, 2006), p.61.
3. Bennett, *Lambert Simnel and the Battle of Stoke*, p.92. Philip Haigh estimates the rebel forces being as high as 10,000. In the light of the heated discussions prior to the battle between Schwartz and Lincoln, such a high figure would seem to be unlikely. See Haigh, P.A., *The Military Campaigns of the Wars of the Rose*, (Sutton, 1995), p.176.
4. Baldwin, *The Battle of Stoke Field*, p.73. These were: Nicholas Boston-Prior of Tynemouth; Abbot William Sever of St Mary's, York; Abbot John Darenton of Fountains Abbey; and William Hesleyngton of Jervaux. Prior John Auckland of Durham along with Richard Redman were also regarded as being sympathetic towards the rebels.
5. Baldwin, *The Battle of Stoke Field*, p.64.
6. There are a large number of computations on the volume of arrows likely to have been loosed by Oxford's men; the most detailed of these computations can be found in Baldwin, *The Battle of Stoke Field*, pp.53–69.
7. Barr, N., *The Battle of Flodden 1513* (Tempus, 2001), p.99.
8. Baldwin, *The Battle of Stoke Field*, p.68. These routes are evidenced by the mass graves that archaeologists have uncovered at both of these locations.
9. Barr, *The Battle of Flodden 1513*, p.69.

Chapter 20 – The End?

1. *The Herald's Memoir, 1486–1490*, (ed.) Cavell, E. (Richard III and the Yorkist Press, 2009).

2.   Baldwin, D., *The Battle of Stoke Field: The Last Battle of the Wars of the Roses* (Pen & Sword, 2006), p.84.
3.   *Ibid*, p.73.
4.   Bayani, D., *Jasper Tudor*, p220, quoting *CPR, Henry VII* (Made Global Publishing, 2015). Jasper also obtained the Lovell manors of Acton Burnell, Holgate, Langdon, Woolstanton, Southcote, Alidon, Millichop and Uppington in Shropshire.
5.   *Ibid*, p229
6.   Baldwin, *The Battle of Stoke Field*, p.86.
7.   *Ibid*.
8.   *Ibid*. An inquisition post-mortem was a legal enquiry into the lands, estates and obligations that a tenant-in-chief held upon his death and an assessment of what was owed and what rights should return to the Crown.
9.   *Ibid*, p.85, quoting from the Register of the Great Seal of Scotland. See also O'Connor, S., 'Francis Lovell and the Rebels of the Furness Fells', *The Ricardian* (1987), pp.366–70.
10. Baldwin, *The Battle of Stoke Field*, p.85.
11. Seward, D., *The Last White Rose: The Secret Wars of the Tudors,* (Constable, 2010), pp.48–56. Interestingly, on his death John Sante bequeathed all his worldly goods to Henry VII 'in token of all the grace shown to him by the king … praying to God for a good continuation of the king's royal estate'. In death it seems that Sante finally came to terms with the Tudor dynasty.
12. Baldwin, *The Battle of Stoke Field*, p.89.

Epilogue
1.   These included Sir Simon Montford, Sir Thomas Thwaites (the ex-Chancellor of the Exchequer), William Daubenay, Thomas Cressner and Robert Radcliff. Damning evidence against all had been given by the double-agent Robert Clifford, who may have been quickly turned or may even have always been one of Henry VII's agents.
2.   Potter, G. R. (ed.) *The Cambridge Modern History Vol. I* (Cambridge 1957), p.472.
3.   Arthurson, I., *The Perkin Warbeck Conspiracy* (Alan Sutton, 1994) p.61, quoting a contemporary prophecy of John of Bridlington.

BIBLIOGRAPHY

Abbreviations
CPR Calendar of Patent Rolls

Original Sources
The Herald's Memoir, 1486–1490, (ed.) Cavell, E. (Richard III and the Yorkist Press, 2009)
CPR, *Edward IV* 1461–67 (1897–1901)
CPR, *Edward IV* 1467–77 (1897–1901)
CPR, *Edward IV* (1897–1901)
CPR, *Edward* V (1897–1901)
CPR, *Richard* III, 1476–85 (1897–1901)
Chronicles of London, (ed.) Kingsford, C.L. (London, 1905)
Croyland Chronicle, Historiae Croylandensis Continuatio, (ed.) Fulman, W., (Oxford, 1684)
Commynes, P., *The Memoirs for the Reign of Louis XI, 1461–1483,* (trans.) Jones, M., (Penguin, 1972)
The Historical Recollections of a London Citizen in the Fifteenth Century, (ed.) Gardener, J. (Camden Society, 1898)
London: The Great Chronicle, (ed.) Kingsford, C.L. (The History Press, 1977)
The Usurpation of Richard III: Mancini, Dominic (ed. and trans.) Armstrong, C.A.J. (Oxford University Press, 1969)
The Paston Letters 1422–1509, (ed.) Gardiner, J. (Alan Sutton, 1986)
Rotulli Parliamentorum, (ed.) Strachey, J., London, 1767–77
Vergil, P., *Three Books of Polydore Vergil's English History: Comprising the Reigns of Henry VI, Edward IV and Richard III,* (ed.) Ellis, H., (Camden Society, 1844)

Secondary Sources
Ashton-Hill, J., *Eleanor: The Secret Queen* (The History Press, 2010)
Ashton-Hill, J., *The Dublin King: The True Story of Edward, Earl of Warwick* (History Press, 2015)
Baldwin, D., *The Battle of Stoke Field: The Last Battle of the Wars of the Roses* (Pen & Sword, 2006)
Baldwin, D., *The Kingmaker's Sisters: Six Powerful Women in the Wars of the Roses* (The History Press, 2009)
Bennett, M., *The Battle of Bosworth* (Palgrave Macmillan, 1985)
Crosland, M., *The Mysterious Mistress: The Life and Legend of Jane Shore,* (Sutton, 2006)
Dockray, K., *Richard III: A Sourcebook* (Sutton, 1997)
Gill, L., *Richard III and Buckingham's Rebellion* (Sutton, 1999)
Griffiths, R.A., *Sir Rhys ap Thomas and his Family* (University of Wales Press, 2014)
Griffiths, R.A, and Thomas, R.S., *The Making of the Tudor Dynasty* (Sutton, 1993)
Haigh, P.A., *The Military Campaigns of the Wars of the Rose* (Sutton, 1995)
Hicks, M., *Richard III and his Rivals: Magnates and their Motives in the Wars of the Roses* (Hambledon, 1991)
Hicks, M., *False, Fleeting, Perjur'd Clarence* (Headstart History, 1992)
Hicks, M., *Warwick the Kingmaker* (Boydell, 1998)

Hicks, M., *Richard III* (Sutton, 2000)

Higginbottom, S., *The Woodvilles: The Wars of the Roses and England's Most Infamous Family* (History Press, 2015)

Lander, J.R., *The Wars of the Roses* (Sutton, 1992).

O'Connor, S., 'Francis Lovell and the Rebels of the Furness Fells', *The Ricardian* (1987)

Pierce, H., *Margaret Pole, Countess of Salisbury 1475–1541* (Dinefwr Press, 2009)

Pierrepont-Barnard, F. (ed.), *Edward IV's French Expedition of 1475: The Leaders and their Badges, being MS2.M16* (Clarendon Press, 1952; re-issued Gloucester Reprints, 1991), Folio IV

Pollard, A.J., *Warwick the Kingmaker: Politics, Power and Fame* (Hambledon, 2007)

Ross, C., *Edward IV* (Yale University Press, 1991)

Ross, C., *Richard III* (Yale University Press, 1992)

Seward, D., *The Last White Rose: The Secret Wars of the Tudors* (Constable, 2010)

Skidmore, C., *Bosworth* (Weidenfield and Nicholson, 2015)

Transactions of the Leicestershire Archaeological and Historical Society, 1975–6

Weightman, C., *Margaret of York, Duchess of Burgundy 1446–1503* (Sutton, 1993)

FURTHER READING

Calendar of Close Rolls, Edward IV, 1461-1468; *Edward IV,* 1468-1476; *Edward IV – Edward* V –
   Richard III, 1476-1485, (1949-54).
Calendar of Fine Rolls, Edward IV, 1461-1471; *Edward IV – Richard III,* 1471-1485, (1949 - 1961).
Chronicles of London; ed. Kingsford, C.L, London, 1905.
Croyland Chronicle, Historiae Croylandensis Continuatio; ed. Fulman, W, Oxford, 1684.
The Paston Letters 1422–1509, (ed.) Gardiner, J. (Alan Sutton, 1986).
Rotulli Parliamentorum, (ed.) Strachey, J., London, 1767–77
Vergil, P., *Three Books of Polydore Vergil's English History: Comprising the Reigns of Henry VI, Edward
   IV and Richard III,* (ed.) Ellis, H., (Camden Society, 1844)

Further reading

Ashton-Hill, J., *Lambert Simnel and the Princes in the Tower* (The History Press, 2015)
Ashton-Hill, J., *The Third Plantagenet* (The History Press, 2013)
Barron, C and Saul, N; *England and the Low Countries in the Late Middle Ages,* Sutton, Stroud, 1998.
Boardman, A.W; *The Battle of Towton,* Sutton, Stroud, 2000.
Clark, L; *The Fifteenth Century: English and Continental perspectives,* Boydell, London, 2010.
Clayton, D. (ed); *Trade, Devotion and Governance; Papers in Later Mediaeval History,* Sutton, Stroud,
   1994
Evans, H.T., *Wales and the Wars of the Roses* (Sutton, 1998)
Fern, S., *The Man who Killed Richard III,* (Amberley, 2015)
Fryde, E.B., *William de la Pole, Merchant and King's Banker* (Hambledon, 1998)
Givens-Wilson, C., *The English Nobility in the Late Middle Ages* (Routledge, 1996)
Griffiths, R.A., *King and Country: England and Wales in the Fifteenth Century* (Hambledon, 1991)
Grimes, S.B., *Henry VII* (Yale University Press, 1993)
Hammond, P.W. (ed.), *Richard III: Loyalty, Lordship and Law,* (Richard III Society and the Yorkist
   History Trust, 2000)
Hipshon, D., *Richard III and the Death of Chivalry* (The History Press, 2009)
Lander, J.R., *Conflict and Stability in Fifteenth Century England,* (Hutchinson University Library,
   1979)
Lewis, M., *Richard Duke of York* (Amberley Publishing, Stroud, 2016)
Lovine, M., *Tudor Dynastic Problems 1460–1570* (George Allen, 1973)
Penn, T., *The Winter King: The Dawn of Tudor England* (Allen-Lane, 2011)
Petrie, J. (ed.), *Richard III, Crown and People* (Richard III Society, 1985)
Pollard, A.J., *The North of England In the Reign of Richard* III (Sutton, 1996)
Skidmore, C., *Richard III, Brother and King* (Weidenfield and Nicholson, 2017)
Wolfe, B.P., *The Crown Lands 1461–1536,* (George Allen, 1970)
Wolfe, B.P., *Henry VI,* (Yale University Press, 2001)

INDEX